MW01489037

Business Forecasting: A Practical, Comprehensive Resource for Managers and Practitioners

By

Robert A. Krueger

Library of Congress Control Number: 2007907039
ISBN: 1-4196-7779-9
EAN13: 9781419677793

Table of Contents

Preface...i
Chapter 1..1
The Forecasting and Planning Environment.............................1
    Economic Advantages of Forecasting 2
    Forecasting Hierarchy and Strategy..............................3
    Forecasting Categories...6
    Forecasting Steps..10
Chapter 2...17
Demand Data..17
    Demand Characteristics...17
    Data Acquisition...18
    Data Requirements..20
    Data Modification...21
Chapter 3...23
Decomposition of a Time Series..23
    Decomposition Defined...24
    Components of a Time Series.......................................25
    Evaluating the Components of a Time Series.................27
    Forecasting Using the Decomposition Method..............38
    Testing for Accuracy and Reliability............................42
Chapter 4...53
Smoothing and Adaptive Methods.......................................53
    Moving Averages...53
    Forecasting with Moving Averages..............................60
    Exponential Smoothing...67
    Adaptive Filters...82
    Conclusions...88
Chapter 5...90
Forecast Evaluation and Modification..................................90
    Accuracy and Reliability...90
    Tracking Forecasts...95
    Correcting for Lag..100
Chapter 6...104

Other Time Series Techniques...............................104
    Least Squares Trend....................................104
    Percent of Sales Model.................................106
    Erratic Demand..109
    The Box-Jenkins Forecasting Method.............112
    Non-linear Trend Analysis...........................114
Chapter 7..122
Causal Models..122
    Simple Linear Regression............................123
    Correlation Analysis...................................127
    Multiple Regression....................................136
Chapter 8..155
Short Life Cycle Forecasting Models....................155
    Before Season Forecasting...........................156
    In-Season Forecasting.................................157
Chapter 9..164
Forecasting with Demographic Data....................164
    Forecasting Environment.............................164
    Usage in Industrial Forecasting.....................165
    Sources...168
    Applying Demographics to Forecasting..........169
Chapter 10...173
Econometrics and Some Related Techniques..........173
    U.S. Economic Structure.............................175
    Business Cycles...176
    Diffusion Indices and Rates of Change...........181
    Analyzing Company and Industry Sales..........193
    Forecasting the Longer Term........................196
    Forecasting GDP.......................................210
Chapter 11...237
Qualitative Techniques......................................237
    Executive Judgment...................................239
    Panel Consensus..239
    Delphi Method..240
    Market Research..241
    Probability Trees and Bayesian Revisions........242
    Technological Forecasting...........................249
    Growth Curves...250

Chapter 12..254
Strategic and Long-Range Planning and Forecasting..............254
    The strategic plan...258
Chapter 13..263
Operational Forecasting...263
Postscript..298
Selected References...301
Index...303

Preface

Business forecasting encompasses the full range of business activity, from the immediate through the long-term. It is a primary determinant in strategic planning and decision-making. It is basic input to marketing, sales, financial, operational, and purchasing planning. An understanding of forecasting, it advantages, limitations, and techniques is an essential ingredient in business planning and management.

There has been substantial progress in forecasting methodology and its use in business. Unfortunately, the opposite is also true: forecasting is sometimes akin to shaking the bones or intuition. There is a very real place for experienced judgment in forecasting when it is objective and backed by data. In fact, forecasting is not just mechanical; it may require examination and interpretation of the forecast. Quantitative forecasts can logically be modified to account for competitors' (as well as internal) changes in pricing or promotional events that cannot be anticipated by pure numbers.

This book is written for:

❖ The practitioner who is responsible for forecasting and who wants to examine the various techniques available in order to develop the best forecasting methodology for his company.

❖ The manager who frequently comes into contact with forecasts but is unfamiliar with the mysteries attendant to their formulation. By gaining an understanding of forecasting methodology, the relationship between forecasting and planning, and forecasting applications and limitations, the executive adds knowledge that he needs in his decision-making role.

❖ The managers of businesses who cannot afford to maintain a planning and forecasting staff department but who realizes the significance that planning and forecasting have upon the welfare of the business. The methods described in this book provide consistently better results than the alternative of not systematically forecasting.

❖ Executives who are dissatisfied with the forecasts they receive.

❖ Anyone who wants an in-depth knowledge of forecasting. An understanding of forecasting makes an individual more valuable to the company.

An in-depth knowledge of mathematics and statistics is unnecessary. Methods are described in a step-by-step format with examples that are real world oriented and designed to assist in understanding the applicability of the techniques discussed.

The trade off between mathematical precision and readability was resolved in favor of the latter. Although mathematicians may legitimately find fault, I ask their indulgence in the interest of understandability for those not trained in the mathematical discipline.

Chapters 1 and 2 introduce the forecasting discipline, its relationship to planning and operations, and the applicable general rules. The chapters following examine in detail a wide range of forecasting methods with step-by-step, how-to instructions. The concluding chapters provide forecasting examples set in the long-range and operational environments.

Frequently, data from the past is used in the examples because of the ready availability of historical series.

ADDENDUM
One of several statistical functions available when developing a regression formula is data analysis. See page 142 for an explanation. If you have Vista, Office 2007, installation of the program is slightly different. In Excel click office button, click Excel options, click add-ins, click analysis tool pack, then OK and install.

Chapter 1

The Forecasting and Planning Environment

No one can predict the future with certainty, but without a reasoned approach there is only reaction to the moment or a guess regarding the future. Without a plan, decision-making may result in inappropriate commitment of resources and surprise when conditions overpower the business. Customers are unhappy, profits suffer because cost is excessive, and the firm is unprepared for the longer term. Forecasting is prelude to planning.

Thorough planning at each level of the business is essential if perplexity is to be avoided. Planning ranges from the long-term to the immediate. It seems incongruous to plan when the future is uncertain, but a plan, intelligently conceived, adds order and direction to the business endeavor. A plan can be modified as conditions dictate. The first step to organized planning is forecasting.

Executives must consider the future objectively. Frequently, budgets and forecasts of sales, market share, and other business activity are determined intuitively; they are what management wishes them to be. Although judgment is a key ingredient in planning and decision-making, if management is to have reasonable control, objective forecasts of business activity and the economy, responsible interpretations of information, and a systematic approach to planning the future are essentials. But as will be seen, judgment does enter into the forecasting picture.

The future cannot be predicted absolutely but it can be forecasted in a way that facilitates planning and the orderly operation of the business. Estimates are concerned with market potential, sales of a single item or a product line, future profit potential, and direction for the future.

This book is written to be comprehensive and understandable so that companies of all sizes may take advantage of forecasting. The large number of methods described allows a company to select that methodology that best fits its particular situation, thus avoiding square pegs in round holes.

Economic Advantages of Forecasting

There are uncontrollable events that invade every aspect of the business environment. These events trigger responses throughout the system. Sales demand in the nearer term, for example, affects inventory levels, the production plan, and purchasing in manufacturing. The affects in retail and distribution operations are similar. Demand in the mid-range and in the longer term relates to future capacity: determining manpower levels, machine and facilities requirements, and financing support. The actions of competitors influence the short- and long-term future of the company. Picture a retail chain that is contemplating expansion and is also considering which products and quantities to buy for the next selling season; or manufacturing executives who must decide upon expansion and the financing to bring it about. To be able to anticipate the future reasonably helps managers decide a course of action that reduces the impact of these triggering events.

Decision-making influences profit and financial viability. Critical decisions depend upon knowledge and a fundamental part of that knowledge rests in anticipating the future. Forecasting helps to reduce the future's uncertainty.

Marketing needs reliable forecasts both in aggregate dollar volume and in the potential of each of the products its makes or sells. Marketing anticipates changes in product structure and sales levels. Forecasts are indicators that help gauge change.

Top management shares marketing's concerns, but it digs deeper because it is ultimately responsible for the success of the business enterprise. If it is to successfully allocate resources, plan future capital expenditures, and chart the strategic course of the firm, management needs to forecast the economic future, both in general and in specific terms. Price trends, market share, market growth, competitive actions, and cost are pertinent to its planning. To decide a course of action is only part of the story; timing and magnitude are the other considerations. Realistic forecasts are an integral part of the management process; but in the long-term, forecast reliability is a serious problem. The vagarious personality of the future is a forecasting fact that must be faced. As distance increases accuracy decreases, but estimating the future (or several possible futures) is essential.

In a manufacturing company a short-term marketing objective is to service customers with on-time deliveries. To do this cost effectively requires good forecasts of individual end items. Production control schedules manufacture and purchasing buys the raw materials to support manufacture. Unless everything is made to order, the forecast is a primary determinant of what will be made, when it will be scheduled, and the quantity that will be produced. Mistakes cause inventory to skyrocket (wrong items produced) while products needed for orders are unavailable. Mistakes cause an unstable manufacturing environment in which over-cost dilutes profit. Equally affected are the materials management, employment, costing, and industrial engineering functions. A reliable short-range forecasting procedure coupled with an integrated manufacturing control system is a powerful profit tool. In retail operation the factors above are equally applicable except purchasing for resale replaces manufacture and point of sales data are inputs to forecasting, if available.

Forecasting Hierarchy and Strategy

Forecasts may be ranked or classified in several ways, for example, by the time frame of the forecast (long-, mid-, or short-range), by the purpose served, and by level of complexity. In business, several (perhaps many) forecasts are needed to satisfy long- and short-term goals.

The further into the future that the forecaster looks the hazier is the landscape; the more difficult it is to see the terrain. Business is without choice, however; it must consider the future in its decision and planning process. To lessen the sting of uncertainty and inaccuracy, management should:

- ❖ Develop a strategic planning process that encompasses the total range of planning, from the immediate to the long-term. Subject the plan to periodic scrutiny, being reassured that it is valid and that the total range of budgets, programs, and plans support the strategic goal.

- ❖ In developing the strategic plan, gather as much information as possible and make as many forecasts as necessary. Because of inaccuracy, which at times may be serious, track, measure, and evaluate error, and consider error statistics as part of the forecast. This book describes the methodology of determining accuracy and forecast validity.

Strategy is the plan or the means by which stated objectives (goals) are achieved. Strategy is concerned with the future of the business. The strategic plan is time phased in the long-range plan, wherein intermediate goals or objectives are established. The strategy to a degree and the long-range plan is dependent upon a forecast. Because of the changes in economic, social, political, and technological factors over time, commitment of resources to implement a planning goal is made at the last possible moment, when the indicators, forecasts and judgment signal go and delay will not allow the time needed to achieve the goal.

As the long-range forecast changes, the timing of the intermediate objectives may be shifted.

Strategy may be divided into two categories: grand or master strategy, which states the overall mission of the company and the means by which the mission will be accomplished, and the functional strategies that support the master strategy. The latter include but are not limited to marketing, financial, diversification or growth, product structure, and research and development strategies.

In the long-term – usually the future more than one year away – forecasts are prepared to assist in the planning of new facilities and capital equipment buys, as input in determining the structure of and the firm's approach to the future marketplace, as source data for financing future operations, and to assist in setting the direction of the research and development effort.

Unfortunately, forecasts more than one year in the future are subject to gross inaccuracy. Especially prone to error are forecasts of long-term economic indicators, population estimates, and technological forecasts. The timing of business cycle turning points is difficult (some will say, nearly impossible) to predict. At times, forecasts will be reliable, but the world is subject to unforeseeable events that significantly modify the projections of leading economists. Political events, either domestic or foreign (oil embargo, terrorism), changes in trends and discontinuities muddy the waters of the future. Because of this uncertainty company estimates, which may rely upon economic or other externally generated data as input to its system, suffer accuracy problems.

To mitigate this unpredictability, adopt the strategic approach. By all means forecast, developing a procedure that historically gives the most reliable results. Incorporate error statistics to measure and evaluate the range of variation that may be expected. Or translate a quantitative forecast to general terms if this will suffice. Often, anticipating the direction of the economy and the general slope of the trend (magnitude over time) is sufficient for developing objectives. Forecasts with numbers may deceive users into believing that reliability is much higher than it really is. Conversely, forecasts without numbers are tenuous at best. It is better to err on the side of numbers, however.

Adopting a what-if approach may be the best solution to long-range planning. Develop several forecasts (with numbers), each recognizing a different scenario. Also, look at the general trend and what leading economists predict for the future. In finality, interpreting this input will lead to a judgment call.

Long-term actions should be time phased, of course, with commitment of resources delayed until the final moment and only after reviewing and redefining or verifying the strategy.

In the mid-term – the future six months to one year away – forecasts are prepared to assist in the planning of equipment purchases, manpower requirements, marketing campaigns, cash flows, and promotional and advertising programs. Forecasts are an integral and important part of the annual business planning and budgeting process. Mid-range plans are in consonance with the strategy.

In the short-term – the future to the immediate planning horizon, usually one to six months – forecasts support operations. Some of the parts in which forecasts play a leading role are: scheduling the production of individual end items and material purchases, scheduling and controlling capacity utilization, planning the finished goods inventory level and distribution plan, establishing the hiring plan, and allocating promotional and advertising dollars. Short-range forecasts are generally reliable forecasts when an appropriate quantitative method is employed. The planning horizon may actually be longer than stated above depending upon lead times.

In addition to classifying forecasts by time frame, they may also be divided by the economic level that they serve. Each of the following types is important and is most effective when integrated into a business-forecasting scenario.

❖ Forecast of the economic and business climate: provides directional information regarding both the near- and long-term. A company may be a consumer of professional services or it may prepare its own estimates. Private economists, professional associations, government, and the business press are potential sources. Chapter 10 gives a detailed rendering of how a company can forecast the long-term. In the mid-term forecasts are a basis for preparing marketing plans and the annual financial budget. Longer range, they are important in strategy formation. Included in this paragraph are demographic projections when applicable to the industry.

❖ Forecast of industry sales (market potential): serves a purpose similar to the general economic forecast except that it narrows the terrain to the industry in which the firm participates. One approach is to make an empirical analysis of the market and the market structure to include the changing volume of market segments and simultaneously prepare quantitative forecasts of industry sales by segment; then compute company share of each of these segments. Market research may also be appropriate.

Forecasts and the analyses made there-from span the full business planning time frame, serving immediate and strategic needs.

❖ Product forecasts: calculated in aggregate and for each individual end item. Disaggregation of the composite forecast is one method; summing individual item forecasts is another. Aggregated demand forecasts are input for both operational and budget planning. Individual end item forecasts are input to the operational and operational support functions

Forecasting Categories

Forecasts are usually thought of in terms of techniques that can be worked to arrive at a conclusion about the future. While this is basically correct, the forecasting system includes not only the forecast itself but also measures of accuracy, significance, and tracking of the variation over time.

Forecasts are categorized either as quantitative or qualitative methods. The former depend upon statistical and mathematical manipulation of data whereas the latter apply judgment in one form or another. Qualitative techniques, however, may employ supplementary statistical techniques. In the real world, seldom does a forecast escape management scrutiny. The danger of management review is interference in the process without adequate cause. Conversely, a forecast should not be developed without management input. If there is a business condition not known to the forecasting methodology, for example, modification is justified.

The following paragraphs briefly describe some of the more important methods. Likely candidates are tested in the demand environment to determine reliability. What is best in one company may not be best in another. Ranking the effectiveness of methods is avoided because individual experience in a specific environment is the real criterion. Detailed discussions are provided in the succeeding chapters.

Qualitative Techniques

These techniques rely upon judgment and are basically subjective, even if data are incorporated into the procedure. Although they have been used in all forecasting situations, they are most appropriate for estimating the demand for new products, directing the research and development effort (what new products will the future market demand?), determining the long-range direction of the economy, and formulating future market strategy. The latter two requirements usually combine data with judgment.

Primarily, a qualitative procedure is selected when data are unavailable or in formulating long-range estimates where gross inaccuracy in economic forecasts may be expected.

- ❖ Naïve methods (really not methods at all) include such procedures as using the last observed value, the last observed value adjusted for seasonality, or the average of the last two values as the forecast. Avoid this simplistic approach unless the product line is simple with a stable sales history. In those circumstances, it may be adequate for short term, individual end item predictions, but that is questionable.

- ❖ Executive judgment is a forecast made by an individual based upon his experience and whatever facts he wishes to consider. This is the most subjective method.

- ❖ Panel consensus is similar in nature to executive judgment except that it utilizes a group of experts to arrive at consensus. An individual may dominate discussion.

- ❖ Delphi method utilizes a panel of experts, however, they do not meet nor are they allowed to discuss the matter with each other. An interrogator prepares a series of questions. The answers to each set of questions are the basis for the next set. The method is complex, requires cooperation and understanding, and may not lead to consensus. It is the most objective of the judgmental type techniques.

- ❖ Market research is a systematic way in which to statistically study real markets. This is a powerful forecasting tool that requires the services of experts. The method is expensive and complex.

- ❖ Historical analogy refers to techniques that base the forecast of one product on its demand similarity with another product. They are especially useful in new product forecasting.

- ❖ Bayesian models incorporate the probability of structural change, frequently in the form of revisions to original probability estimates. Subjective information often has a significant role in the analysis.

Intrinsic Methods

Intrinsic techniques are quantitative in concept and depend upon historical data for the demand being forecast. The forecast is based upon factors internal to the company, or, perhaps, to an industry, and may employ one of the several averaging methods described in this book. This is time series analysis.

These techniques focus upon the historical pattern of the demand itself, with the forecast being a projection of the past into the future. Although the pattern of past demand (say, for a manufactured item) may be changing, the assumption is that the change is orderly. Time series analysis is concerned with trend and the rate at which the demand is changing, but also considers cyclical and seasonal variations.

Because the future is expected to be like the past − that is, existing patterns will continue into the future − forecasts predicated upon time series methods are most appropriate to the near- or mid-terms, but are generally not applicable to the long-term. They do not readily predict turning points (as when sales growth turns to sales decline).

Time series analysis is most useful in forecasting individual end item and aggregate product family demand in support of sales, manufacturing and distribution operations, and operational support functions and in retail product and inventory planning. They are also useful in some financial forecasting, particularly margin projections and cash balances. Inventory levels, capacity requirements, and demand for raw materials may be derived from the sales forecasts.

The following are brief descriptions of the methods explained in the succeeding chapters:

- ❖ Decomposition is a means of dividing a time series into its component parts: trend, cyclical fluctuation, seasonal variation, and randomness. A fundamental reason to employ decomposition is to gain an understanding of the demand series. It is also a short- and mid-range forecasting technique.

- ❖ Moving averages are arithmetic or weighted averages of a number of past demand observations that may adequately forecast the short term. If there are pronounced seasonal fluctuations in the demand series, the moving average must be long enough to negate their influence. Normally, a series with seasonals requires a twelve-month moving average.

- ❖ Exponential smoothing is a method similar to moving averages except that more recent demands are given more weight. The equation assigns an exponentially decreasing set of weights to past data based upon the weighting factor assigned by the forecaster. Exponential smoothing may function within a wide range of application, but it is most frequently useful in the short-term for individual end item or product group forecasting.

- ❖ Adaptive filtering is a technique with a rationale similar to exponential smoothing except that the best set of weights is determined during the process.

- ❖ A time series may be linear (approximates a straight line) or nonlinear (follows a curve). The techniques described thus far are generally linear in nature, but they are sometimes inadequate in describing time series that are identified by a curved trend. There are a number of equations that logically describe different curved trends. These techniques are also applicable to long-range forecasting.

- ❖ Box-Jenkins is as much a philosophy as it is a method. The objective is to isolate the basic pattern and construct a model that specifically represents that pattern. It is complex. Exponential smoothing is a special case of the Box-Jenkins methodology.

Extrinsic Methods

These techniques – also called causal methods – are quantitative and relate independent data (variables) to the item being forecast. The forecast is based upon the explicit relationship between the independent variable(s) and the demand being forecast.

An independent variable is any data series that moves in relation to the element being forecast. For example, the value of an economic indicator (such as a leading indicator) may be historically and statistically relational to company dollar volume. The causal model mathematically defines the relationship.

Causal models are applicable for forecasting total industry sales in a market, total company sales, sales of major company segments (product class or group), prices, and financial earnings. Sales forecasts may be made in constant or current dollars or in units. These methods may also be used to forecast the general economy or major economic segments. They are often more effective in the longer term.

Other estimates of the future may be derived from longer range sales forecasts: manufacturing, warehousing, and distribution facilities requirements, feasibility and timing of new store openings, capital expenditures, contracts for material purchases, profit expectations, and cash flows.

- ❖ Regression and correlation models relate demand to be forecast (the dependent variable) to economic, demographic, or internal indicators (the independent variable). A model may consist of one or more independent variables. The demand to be forecast may be linear or nonlinear. In either case, applicable equations are available for forecasting the demand.

❖ Econometric models in the strictest sense involve a system of interdependent regression equations designed to estimate an economy or an economic unit. The more general interpretation that is used in this book includes all regression models (a single or multiple regression equation, for instance) when designed to forecast or describe an economic unit.

❖ Leading indicators are economic factors whose movement precedes the movement of another economic factor. Individual leading indicators are erratic; therefore, only composite indices should be used. Together with their related diffusion indices (measures the breadth of a recession or recovery) and rates of change (measures degree and direction), leading indicators may be valuable forecasting tools.

Forecasting Steps

To maximize the chances of forecasting successfully, the characteristics of the forecast method are matched to the characteristics of the business situation. The forecast/decision cycle is simply forecasting to support the decision-making process with feedback after the decision is implemented. Thus, forecasting influences decision-making behavior. There are several basic steps that are applied in the forecasting process. The following paragraphs briefly discuss them.

Determine What Must be Forecast

The first two questions that managers and forecasters ask are: what critical information about the future is needed in order to make profitable decisions? and, what is the objective of each forecast?

Forecasting is not a routine that is accomplished independently of management. Management defines specifically what is needed. The objective may be to plan production and material buys for the next three months, to decide upon the need for a new factory, determine the structure of the future market, or a myriad of other requirements.

This book suggests a strategic approach because it is a definitive way in which to examine the entire organizational panoply. This procedure considers the business situation as it currently exists through the long-term projections and integrates all company planning. Strategic planning is supplemented by operational planning which is characterized by product information required to support operations.

In the strategic approach, top management conceptualizes the future in terms of the business organization. The conceptualization may be supported by forecasts, but in any event, forecasts will be made to test the feasibility of the generalized direction outlined in the concept. It is a closed loop system that results in careful consideration of facts, and forecasts may result in planning modifications until the final strategy is formulated.

Small businesses adopt the same procedure as large businesses except that the scope of the strategy will be less ambitious and fewer people will be involved. Probably more informality will exist in small organizations, but this is not an excuse for reducing the extent of the planning function.

Whereas forecasting in support of strategic planning is periodic (for example, every six months), forecasting in support of purchasing, inventory planning, and manufacturing is continual. Frequent, short-term projections for each end item are a necessity. Strategic planning looks to the future in the aggregate, taking the longer view. Operational planning looks to the near-term. The difference in orientation suggests that different forecasting techniques be employed; the exact ones selected are dependent upon the goal to be achieved.

Identify an Appropriate Family of Techniques

Once the forecasting goals have been defined, different techniques are examined with the purpose of identifying those that are compatible with the forecasting need. In the final analysis different techniques may be applicable to different management requirements. Several techniques may be combined into one methodology.

Before deciding upon the method, collect and analyze pertinent historical data. It is important to know the relationship between the business, the economy, and the market as represented in those data. A means of analyzing time series data is described in Chapter 3.

It is equally important to evaluate the influence that changing market and internal factors have upon demand, such factors as price changes, design modification, sales promotions, sales campaigns, and competitor actions. These factors may cause a temporary aberration to the level of demand or they may have a long-term influence. More detail is provided in appropriate sections of this book.

Once the nature of the demand is known, families of techniques are examined to identify those that may be applicable. If the requirement is for monthly product forecasts, revised monthly, data must be available in monthly increments. If the requirement is to forecast demand for a large number of individual end items monthly, the capability to process a vast amount of data rapidly must exist. If the requirement is to project facility needs for the next ten years, the projections may be based upon annual data. In the first two instances, time series analysis will probably be appropriate, with certain techniques more applicable than others, depending upon the exact situation. In the latter case, a method that compares demand with external factors is most likely to reveal the future market, which estimates may then be translated into company share by a combination of external and internal data components combined into a regression model, as example.

The validity of the methods selected as candidates is based upon their ability to adequately describe the business situation being studied. It may occur that a simple technique will give satisfactory results in the test or that a simple technique that really does not describe the business situation will be reasonably accurate. However, avoid the temptation of using these techniques because they may be disappointing once in use, unless they provide a high degree of historical accuracy at least the equal of more complex models. Even then, approach them with caution; gun in hand, as they may bite you when least expected.

Testing and Comparing Techniques

Each quantitative technique selected as a candidate is tested in the forecasting environment.

The forecasting base for the tests is the historical data that pertain to the demand being forecast. With several years of history available, for example, each technique can be developed employing this base data. The most recent periods of actual data are withheld from the development process and used to prepare forecasts. Comparison and evaluation of each candidate technique may then be undertaken. A caveat is that a time series that is changing from its historical pattern must be addressed on those terms.

Results are compared on the basis of accuracy. The demand deviation of forecast from actual is computed by methods explained in this book. These processes measure accuracy and indicate relevancy.

Tracking

Little in this world remains constant. This is especially true in the forecasting arena. A method that gives good results today may not do so in the future, therefore, a means of continuously monitoring the forecasting system becomes part of the process. Tracking is that activity that alerts the forecaster to change. It is a means of recognizing changes in pattern and accuracy. It may be described as an early warning system that discloses conditions to be addressed.

Because the tracking procedure signals change through an increase in forecast error or the emergence of a new pattern in the errors, the forecaster is alerted to examine the situation with the purpose of discovering the underlying causes.

Selecting a Forecasting Method

The selection of a forecasting methodology results from examining forecasting models in relation to applicable criteria. Four have been selected as supplemental to the information provided in the previous sections and as appropriate to the majority of forecasting situations: the purpose of the forecast, the time frame being forecast, the data pattern, and accuracy.

The interaction of these considerations is illustrated in the following paragraphs.

In some situations, only the long-term general direction of the economy, the potential size of the market as related to the economic projections, roughly computed, and anticipated profit margin range may be necessary to the decision. A complex approach may provide more detail than is necessary to the decision being considered. One alternative is to estimate the mid- and long-term economic future by obtaining the projections of experts (try the Internet) and from that information estimating market potential either by qualitative means or by a regression formula that relates market size to the overall economy or to designated economic indicators. However, Chapter 10 describes methodology that can be applied by the company to project the economic future. A combination approach may be applied when market growth is expected; for example: determine the rough growth pattern by regression analysis and the possible action of competitors by decision tree or Bayesian methods. Of course, other approaches may be equally effective given the specific situation. Although the decision derived from the forecast may require a major commitment of resources over time, it may be possible to time phase and peg the commitment to defined indicators, thus allowing periodic review of the decision as each phase is reached. To reiterate: Chapter 10 explains ways in which the company itself can forecast the economy.

In the shorter term, being precise is more important because commitment closely follows decision. In support of a manufacturing company's production control system, for instance, sales forecasts for each end item are generally essential. The greater the accuracy of the forecasts the less safety stock required and the more efficient the shop operation. Planning of materials buys and the scheduling of production frequently depends upon end item forecasts.

In estimating the longer term future the level of accuracy is generally not as important as it is in the short-term because in the long-term there is time in which to modify a plan. This is not to say that reliability is unimportant, rather that more tolerance is allowable. Precision is not the criterion. Knowing the direction or long-term trend and the approximate magnitude that may be expected is often sufficient. In any event, the probability of getting the same accuracy in the long- term as in the short-term is remote.

The selection of a method considers the forecasting time frame and the factors that affect the future. The longer term future of a product, for example, probably relates in substantial part to outside influences such as economic conditions, competitor actions, and technological change, whereas the short-term may be adequately expressed by examining the history of the demand being forecast (time series analysis).

In the examples above, regression plus judgment was suggested as a means of forecasting in support of management's consideration of entering a new market. Regression is also applicable in determining the longer-term direction and magnitude of sales. This is true because in the long- term, conditions are less dependent upon the past history of the product, more dependent upon outside influences. In the short-term, however, demand history is usually expressive of the need. Two methods that bridge the gap between long- and short-term are Box-Jenkins and decomposition, the latter described in detail in Chapter 3. It is likely, however, that the long-term, say, as represented by GDP may just as effectively be forecast by extrapolation (but see Chapter 10).

The data pattern enters into the selection of the method when the underlying pattern contains seasonals and trend. If this is the case, the technique selected must have the capability of considering them. This book supplies several methods for applying seasonals and trends.

It is not valid to assume that the more sophisticated the method the more accurate the forecast. Many studies indicate that this is not necessarily true. Once a category of techniques has been identified as applicable to the forecasting situation, each is tested historically to determine which one(s) is the most reliable, therefore, the degree of accuracy, per se, is not the only criterion.

Select the least complex method that gives satisfactory results but generally not a simplistic or naïve one, a model that expresses correctly the demand pattern. If a computer is available (is there a business without a computer?), more complexity is practical. In fact, it is feasible to develop a methodology that combines several forecasting techniques into one forecasting system. Combined forecasting is described in Chapter 10.

A model can be developed that consists of several or many individual techniques. In this system, the user or the computer can gauge the effectiveness of each technique within the system. Then, the system (the computer) through simulation selects the most effective model for the time periods under consideration by comparing the results of forecasting several recent historical (known) periods with each of the system's models. The model that gives the best results is used to forecast. In each subsequent forecasting period the selection process begins anew. This process is especially useful for forecasting demand from historical data. The simulation model is described more fully in Chapter 13.

Some Forecasting Facts

Forecasts will almost always be wrong to some degree because there are forces at work that cannot be defined. Reasonable accuracy coupled with error tracking is the proper approach. Measure and control inaccuracy.

Generally, aggregate forecasts are more accurate than individual end item forecasts because plus and minus random fluctuations tend to cancel each other in the aggregate. If there are large errors in individual item forecasts, it may be better to forecast the product groups then disaggregate that forecast.

Short-term forecasts are more accurate than long-term forecasts. Unforeseeable events cloud the future.

To determine the timing of customer demand use the requested delivery date as verified by Customer Service. Do not use ship dates (if you can avoid it) because orders may be shipped early or late. Bookings should also be forecast to see if sales are on track with plan and whether customers are responding as anticipated. More detail is given in the next chapter.

Quantitative methods are generally more reliable than qualitative methods because there is more objectivity. However, unusually large demands will frustrate the forecast if they are not typical. It may be appropriate to eliminate such orders from the forecasting database. After forecasting, add back this demand to the forecasted total in the period in which it appeared. This is a proper exercise of judgment.

Past sales promotions, product improvements, a non-typical spike in demand, and competitive practices are a few of the events that may disrupt a normal historical pattern. Compensate (if their influence is significant) by smoothing the history or applying judgment, but do not arbitrarily tamper with the series.

Tampering with the forecast is not uncommon. To second-guess usually means that the forecast remains unimproved. It is better to deal with inaccuracy statistically as explained in this book. If forecasts are "impossibly bad" try to find the underlying causes. Also try other methods, as the one being used may not be indicative of the demand pattern.

If a sales promotion, price change, or advertising campaign is to take place, modify the forecast to account for the special event or change. This may be accomplished quantitatively if typical, pertinent historical data are available or judgmentally if other means are not available, with the proviso that optimism may cloud judgment.

The following is a recap of some of the significant factors that affect the level of future sales (also see the Tracking Forecasts section in Chapter 5):

- ❖ Pricing decisions, either for an individual item or on an overall basis. Such action may change demand because of the competitive price relationship or the desirability of the item.

- ❖ New product introductions or deletion of current products, your products or those of a competitor.

- ❖ Promotional or special prices and allowances not normally given.

- ❖ Sales targeting to substantially increase sales in the short term.

- ❖ Stock-up by a major customer or initial stocking of new stores, distribution centers, or factories.

- ❖ Key accounts general market information. Take advantage of their market research.

- ❖ Major orders of a size that are substantially larger than the norm.

- ❖ Anticipated or real changes in key account sales levels, such as losing business to a competitor or gaining new business.

- ❖ Increase or decrease in advertising.

- ❖ Cancellation or modification of all or part of a major program.

- ❖ Technological changes, yours or a competitor's.

If one or more of the above exists, the forecaster *must* consider it.

Chapter 2

Demand Data

Data are the raw materials from which forecasts are made.

Historical data are a common source for forecasting techniques. There must be either an historical pattern that applies to the future or a relationship between the demand to be forecast and one or more independent variables. The historical consistency in the relationship or pattern may vary but only within a limited range, which is determinable statistically.

In the business environment, demand is the occurrence most frequently forecast; whether that demand is aggregate (product family) sales or individual end item sales. Earnings, capacity and inventory are other forecasting possibilities. In a causal relationship, the data used to forecast demand may be economic indicators, demographic predictions, internally generated histories other than the demand series itself, competitive relationships as in pricing, or a combination of these factors. In time series forecasting the demand history itself is the data needed.

Demand Characteristics

Within the forecasting environment consistency is essential, but the historical data pattern need not be a straight line. Sometimes the pattern or relationship is obscure, but in most instances demand is a combination of trend, seasonal and cyclical factors and unpredictable randomness or noise. To be able to discern the pattern first requires that the series be separated into its component parts.

Trend is the long-term direction in which the demand series is moving. Costs, sales, or prices, for example, that generally increase over time represent ascending (increasing) trends. Movement may also be in a downward direction or it may be horizontal. Horizontal movement is really not a trend because demand remains constant within a limited range and individual demands are as likely to exceed the average as they are to be less than the average.

The cyclical component is business or economic activity that varies from the norm in a pattern that resembles a wave. The duration of a cycle is usually more than one year.

Seasonal variations are periodic movements that repeat at the same time each year. Generally, seasonals are the result of a repetitive occurrence in the marketplace, such as consumer purchases of a product that are traditionally heavier at certain times of the year, like sales during the Christmas buying season.

The components defined above are more thoroughly explained in chapter 3.

Data Acquisition

Data sources are many.

Extrinsic (causal) techniques usually require information external to the company. The government is wealthy with data. The Departments of Commerce (including the Census Bureau) and Labor and the Federal Reserve are three main sources. The Department of Commerce not only publishes an abundance of economic data, it has offices that collect data related to many different industries. A call to a regional office will help to ascertain the types of information available including those not published on the Internet. Trade and professional associations, consultants and research companies, and the business press are other sources. Generalized publications such as *The Wall Street Journal* and specialized magazines such as *American Demographics* may provide valuable information useful in forecasting. The library is also a rich source for data. Undoubtedly, the best source is the Internet because the government and private agencies publish a wealth of economic series.

Intrinsic techniques depend upon history internal to the company.

The most serious limitations to the development of an effective forecasting system may be the unavailability of data in the company's records, historical records limited in scope, or records unavailable in usable form. Information systems are sometimes designed to serve financial requirements without regard to the needs of marketing and manufacturing. If the history does not extend into the past the length of time necessary for statistical evaluation, use the data available realizing that it will provide less than optimal results. If the history is in unusable form, it may be possible to rework the data.

Another potential problem is the accuracy of data. An off the cuff assumption of many managers is that company records are accurate. Unless there has been a concerted effort directed to data accuracy, the chances are that there are some serious problems, especially in operational, engineering, and inventory records. This is a subject that should receive managerial attention not only because it colors the forecasting scene but also because it affects all aspects of the business.

Related to the accuracy problem is the selection of a demand series. In product forecasting, the selection of shipments as representative of demand is inappropriate because they may not represent the true status of demand nor the time frame in which customers really want delivery.

Bookings occur first. At the time that the customer places his order, he specifies a delivery date. In many companies, orders are requested within a narrow time frame and in other companies, well in advance of the requested ship date. Because of the enthusiasm of the sales department and the (possible) lack of a system that can realistically assign delivery dates, orders may be promised unrealistically, thus orders are shipped late as bookings by customer requested delivery date exceed manufacturing or distribution capacity. Probably, total bookings will be larger than total shipments because of cancellations.

It should be realized that these limitations can and are being overcome by the implementation of state of the art marketing and manufacturing systems.

Further, with an understanding of the above, it is important to estimate both bookings and the amount sold by delivery date. What the forecaster estimates is:

- ❖ The total amount that will be sold within each specified bookings time bucket. This forecast is applicable in those companies in which bookings are made considerably in advance of the requested ship date. This is especially important to manufacturers of highly seasonal items. If orders are taken close to the requested delivery date, a bookings forecast may be unnecessary. Bookings history regardless of shipping experience is a key forecasting series for individual end-items as well as product groups in those companies where time separation is an important factor. These estimates serve the marketing and financial communities. It is also advisable to forecast bookings for each major customer. Whenever orders differ substantially from anticipation, Sales contacts the customer and ascertains the reason, especially if there is a decrease in the expected sales level. Now, we know that sales representatives are in close contact with key accounts, but surprises do occur. What affects bookings also affects the forecast by delivery date.

- ❖ The amount that will be sold by delivery date. This is a primary input to the production planning and scheduling system and to the material planning and purchasing activities. In total, the quantity corresponds to the bookings forecast. The customer's requested delivery date is the benchmark for forecasting demand by period once Customer Service (or the computer) assigns a promise date. If there is a conflict between customer dates and company assigned dates, this is a management concern. Statistics should be routinely collected regarding requested and promised dates. These forecasts are also input to profit planning.

❖ Although not a forecasting requirement, statistics should be collected regarding the number of orders and quantities shipped as promised. The statistics collected concerning requested, promised, and ship dates has consequential ramifications with regard to serving the customer. They impact upon capacity, systems, scheduling and inventory in basic ways. Incompatibility between the figures indicates the need for change.

Yet, another possible problem is the inability of people to be objective. This may be manifested in model design, subjective adjustments to the forecast, or selectivity of the inputs to the forecasting model. Of course, objectivity is the goal. As a first step, consider all data series that may possibly be candidates and learn as much about the demand to be forecast as possible, specifically, its characteristics. Decomposition can be useful. Test several likely methods and compare results. Once a model or method is selected, avoid tampering with the results, but see the Modification section below. Also, measure accuracy and track forecast results as described in Chapters 3 and 5.

Data Requirements

The forecasting methodology may use a single demand series, such as sales history, or it may incorporate independent variables. Any of the techniques described in this book, including combined and simulation style methodology, are appropriate forecasting candidates.

A time phased history of the demand to be forecast and of any independent variables selected for the forecasting model is a basic requirement. For best results, the historical series should have a relatively stable pattern, however, many series do not. Less than desirable series can still be used but the forecaster must understand the limitations. At the close of each forecasting period a review is made to determine if the model continues to be valid. Explanations for managing these situations are given in later chapters.

The general rules pertaining to the requirement for history are:

❖ Intrinsic (time series) techniques need a minimum of two years of the demand history being estimated to ensure an adequate base. If seasonals are not present, less than two years may suffice. Decomposition, however, needs a minimum of three years of history. It is advantageous to have more than two years of history when employing the Box-Jenkins methodology to identify a model. Generally, three years is better than two and four or five years are best if there has not been a fundamental change in the pattern of demand.

❖ Extrinsic (causal) techniques need a minimum of three years of history. Leading indicators if used as an independent variable may require a longer history – five years or more – to verify the relationship between the demand being forecast and the leading indicator series. For regression models, the three-year history applies except that it is a mathematical requisite to have two more observations than there are independent variables. More than the minimum history is beneficial.

Data Modification

Axiom one states that once the quantitative forecast is developed it should not be tampered with; but does this preclude modification? At times, modification is appropriate as discussed in the closing paragraphs of Chapter 1. If there are circumstances contrary to the historical pattern, interpolation of the data is justified. Judgment or consensus is the method of last resort. The preferable path to follow is to relate the present to a previous, similar situation and modify the numbers based upon that data series.

Forecasts are changed only when there is a compelling reason as when a radical permanent difference is anticipated. In such cases, the forecasting methodology is reviewed for it viability and to determine if another technique is now more applicable.

At times, the structure of the forecast is sound but a one or two period blip (not a permanent change) is untypical. This calls for an adjustment as described in the last section of Chapter 1.

An important attribute to incorporate into the forecasting system is a what-if capability. This allows the forecaster to hold certain variables constant while varying others to determine the impact upon the business. As an example, price could be varied to see the affect on sales while holding all other variables influencing sales constant. Or, the Sales Manager may say, "I can increase sales by 10% through increased sales effort and selective advertising. I can do this because trade and economic indicators are showing that an economic recovery in underway. I think that if we put a lot of extra effort into our sales campaigns at this time, we could do it. I anticipate that the curve upward will begin in a few months. Let's do several forecasts with different anticipations as a basis for planning." If the forecasting method is tied into an integrated business system, the influence upon inventories, capacity, customer service, and the financials can also be appraised.

Chapter 3

Decomposition of a Time Series

It seems logical to introduce the least complicated techniques first, and then climb the ladder to the more complex. This book deviates from that logic because it is important to understand what components are contained in a time series; what is hidden in the numbers.

Decomposition was developed as a method for subdividing a time series into its component parts. Knowing why a time series acts the way it does is important in understanding the nature of the demand being studied and as a means of analyzing business activity. If there is a seasonal pattern, for example, management wants to know what part of the total demand results from the seasonal nature of the product. Decomposition allows executives to dissect and examine a time series' basic structure.

This chapter defines each of the components found in a time series, explains the method for dividing a series into its subparts, describes how decomposition can be used as a forecasting technique, and together with Chapter 5 explains how to ascertain the goodness of forecasts.

Much of the research into this method has been done in relation to long range planning, but decomposition, as a predictor technique, is usually most effective when the forecast is applied to the period three months to one year in the future. It may be used to forecast individual end items, but more often, it is a method for forecasting aggregate demand, like sales for a grouping of related products. Analysis of the time series provides a basis for predicting turning points, thus it can help managers determine the timing of planning events. Other techniques such as exponential smoothing are generally best for individual end item forecasting in the short-term. Long-range forecasting of aggregates responds more accurately to causal methods. Decomposition's real power lies in its ability to divide a data series into its component parts for analysis.

Decomposition explains the movements in the historical data thus allowing management to predict changes in each of the sub-patterns. Its major limitation is that it does not consider relationships that may exist between the demand being forecast and independent variables.

Although decomposition is not the simplest method, it is the first presented because it will help the reader understand the nature of a data series.

Decomposition Defined

Decomposing a time series means dividing the measurement of an economic activity, such as product demand, into its component parts. The components that may be present are trend, cyclical fluctuation, seasonal variation, and randomness (noise).

If the measurement being analyzed is sales history of a product group, as example, decomposition will explain why sales behave as they do. Questions that marketing and operations managers' need answered are:

- ❖ Precisely what part of sales each month results from the seasonal nature of the product (if seasonality exists)? By knowing how much of the demand is attributable to seasonality, managers have information upon which to plan short-term capacity and manning needs and finished goods inventory levels. Sales strategy and timing are dependent in part upon when to expect sales and the magnitude that may be anticipated. In sales, the total is significant, but so is knowing the seasonal nature of the product.

- ❖ To what extent are sales being affected by business cycles? If there is a relationship between the business cycle and the demand being studied, the level of that demand will depend upon the cycle, either in part or in whole. Historical data and the trend may indicate that product demand will be at certain levels in future periods, but this may be misleading if the future affect of a business cycle is not considered.

- ❖ Are sales increasing (or decreasing) in a predictable way? Trend is the long-term direction in which demand is moving. Trend may be disguised because demand is also being influenced by other factors, other components of the time series. By computing trend, direction becomes known and this assists managers in making decisions about such activities as capital expenditures for equipment and facilities, the direction of research and development, future sales strategy, the size of the sales force, and the number of branch warehouses.

- ❖ To what extent are sales unpredictable? Knowing what part of sales results from randomness provides a basis for setting fluctuation (safety) stock levels, making other decisions pertaining to the level of production, and in evaluating risk.

One or more of the above factors may influence an historical data series.

Once the nature of historical demand is known, future demand may be forecast by the method described in this chapter or by one or more of the other forecasting methods discussed in this book.

Components of a Time Series

The trend component is a measurement of the long-term direction in which demand is moving and the magnitude of the movement. A trend may be increasing, decreasing, or non-existent. Figure 3-1 illustrates a typical trend pattern. A straight line called the trend line often represents trend. It is derived by statistical methods that are explained later. Trends may also be nonlinear. In business forecasting a linear (straight line) representation is often adequate. Later chapters illustrate the methods for developing nonlinear trends and forecasts.

Defining long-term is a key consideration in deciding the number of periods to use in calculating the trend. For example, in a five-year historical time series of sales, would it be appropriate to use all of the five years? the last four years? the last three years? or some other period? What is most likely to represent the future? Trend lines drawn for various lengths of time will often differ. Guidance in selecting the proper length is given later in this chapter.

Trend Pattern

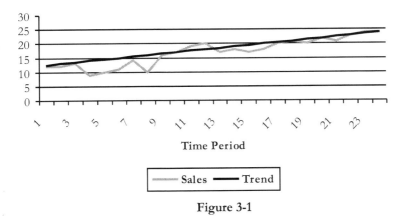

Time Period

Figure 3-1

The cyclical component is frequently referred to as the business cycle. It represents economic or business activity that varies from the norm in a pattern that roughly resembles a wave. The time span from peak to peak is more than one year and may be multiple years for a single cycle. Its duration is measured between peaks or troughs. A cyclical pattern experienced by a company may reflect the national economy or be related to a specific business activity such as housing starts, disposable income, consumer price index, interest rates, etc. or it may be related to a non-economic phenomenon. It may lag or lead the company's cyclical pattern or be coincident to it. Figure 3-2 illustrates a cyclical component.

Cyclical Pattern

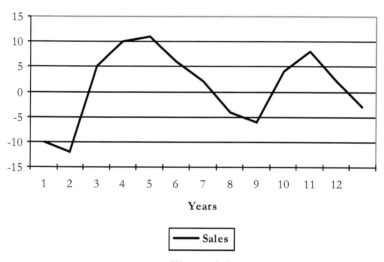

Years

Sales

Figure 3-2

It is not possible to predict with certainty the length or magnitude of a business cycle nor when a turning point will occur. But it may be estimated if the company's cycle can be related to independent indicators. The relationship, if one exists, may correlate with the movement of one economic indicator, for example, or with several. The relationship may be linear or non-linear. Chapters 7 and 10 further discuss the subject and develop a rationale.

Seasonal variations are repeated periodic movements that occur within a single year. There may be multiple seasonal variations within a twelve-month period. They result from a repetitive occurrence in the marketplace such as back-to-school sales of children's clothing, spring and fall seasonal consumer products, holiday specific items, and manufacturers who supply goods to other businesses who have seasonal fluctuations in their sales. Many businesses experience some seasonal variations. Figure 3-3 illustrates a seasonal pattern. Note that there are two peaks. The one of major magnitude takes place in the period July-August, the lesser in April.

Seasonal Pattern

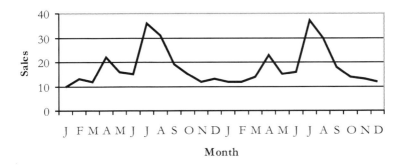

Figure 3-3

Random fluctuations are a part of every time series. They are the result of nonrecurring events that affect the level of demand in a specific period. Typical causes are weather, the actions of competitors, and the whim of customers.

Mathematically, a multiplicative model expresses the relationship between the components:

$$F = T \times S \times C \times R$$

T represents trend, S represents seasonal variation, C represents cyclical fluctuation, R represents randomness, and F equals total demand.

Evaluating the Components of a Time Series

Three years of history is the minimum needed to provide a reasonable evaluation of a monthly time series. If a lesser number of years is all that is available, however, the forecaster should not be dissuaded, just more cautious when interpreting the results.

Figure 3-4 is a chart of a product group's demand history (in units) that is used as an example in this chapter. Small numbers are used for simplicity's sake. Examination of the monthly totals for each of the years seems to indicate a seasonal pattern that peaks in June and reaches its low point in December. A review of total demand for each of the years suggests the presence of an upward trend. A cyclical pattern may also be present but is not evident from the raw demand data. If it is found that the cyclical component is insignificant or nonexistent, that portion of the equation can be eliminated.

Demand History

	J	F	M	A	M	J	J	A	S	O	N	D	Ttl
1998	120	180	175	270	420	600	390	240	180	150	170	105	3000
1999	180	275	270	410	645	920	350	600	280	230	265	175	4600
2000	225	175	260	380	590	880	530	350	265	210	250	85	4200
2001	240	320	350	500	770	1115	730	455	330	280	335	175	5600
2002	240	340	345	525	815	1130	760	465	340	290	345	205	5800
2003	240	355	365	540	840	1190							

Figure 3-4

Seasonal Variation

Because of the repetitive nature of seasonal variations, an index can be developed that will indicate to the forecaster the percentage of total yearly demand expected each month. In figure 3-4 for the year 1998 sales for June are 20% of the sales for the year (600 ÷ 3000) whereas sales for December are only 3.5%. If such a consistent relationship exists in the other years, it becomes historically significant and must be considered when forecasting demand. By constructing a seasonal index these relationships may be estimated.

The first step of the analysis is subjective and requires the examination of the data to see if there are any unusual variations in the demand pattern. Two are indicated in Figure 3-4.

In comparing the months of July and August 1999 with the same months of the other years, it appears that demand is reversed. In checking customer service records, it was found that two large customers had placed their orders later than usual. Consequently, the promised delivery date carried into the next month. The forecaster switched these demands, which, in this case, simply reversed the demand for each month.

January and February 2000 appear to be reversed also. In checking the order file, however, a specific reason for this occurrence could not be determined. The data were not rearranged.

In the first instance, the unusual demand pattern could be attributed to a circumstance not likely to recur. In the three succeeding years, orders were placed as expected; therefore, the forecaster concluded that making the change would better reveal the normal demand pattern. In the latter instance, he could have reasoned similarly. Because he could not pinpoint a reason he chose not to make a change. This procedure must be used with caution and a great reluctance to change raw data. The point is that such subjective analysis and adjustment of data can avoid serious forecast errors at times.

Constructing a Seasonal Index

The seasonal index is based upon the use of twelve month moving averages (MA) to reduce the influence of trends, cyclical variations, and random fluctuations on the precision of the estimates.

The demand data in Figure 3-4 have been rearranged to facilitate calculation. These rearranged data appear in the Demand column of Figure 3-5.

Seasonal Index Computations

Month	Demand	12 Month MA	Centered MA	Ratio	Month	Demand	12 Month MA	Centered MA	Ratio
Jan 98	120				Jan 01	240	432.1	423.8	56.6
Feb	180				Feb	320	440.8	436.5	73.3
Mar	175				Mar	350	446.3	443.5	78.9
Apr	270				Apr	500	452.1	449.2	111.3
May	420				May	770	459.2	455.6	169.0
Jun	600	250.0			Jun	1115	466.7	462.9	240.9
Jly	390	255.0	252.5	154.5	Jly	730	466.7	466.7	156.4
Aug	240	262.9	259.0	92.7	Aug	455	468.3	467.5	97.3
Sep	180	270.8	266.9	67.4	Sep	330	467.9	468.1	70.5
Oct	150	282.5	276.7	54.2	Oct	280	470.0	469.0	59.7
Nov	170	301.3	291.9	58.2	Nov	335	473.8	471.9	71.0
Dec	105	327.9	314.6	33.4	Dec	175	475.0	474.4	36.9
Jan 99	180	345.4	336.7	53.5	Jan 02	240	477.5	476.3	50.4
Feb	275	354.6	350.0	78.6	Feb	340	478.3	477.9	71.1
Mar	270	362.9	358.8	75.3	Mar	345	479.2	478.8	72.1
Apr	410	369.6	366.3	111.9	Apr	525	480.0	479.6	109.5
May	645	377.5	373.5	172.7	May	815	480.8	480.4	169.7
Jun	920	383.3	380.4	241.8	Jun	1130	483.3	482.1	234.4
Jly	600	387.1	385.2	155.8	Jly	760			
Aug	350	378.8	382.9	91.4	Aug	465			
Sep	280	377.9	378.3	74.0	Sep	340			
Oct	230	375.4	376.7	61.1	Oct	290			
Nov	265	370.8	373.1	71.0	Nov	345			
Dec	175	367.5	369.2	47.4	Dec	205			
Jan 00	225	361.7	364.6	61.7					
Feb	175	361.7	361.7	48.4					
Mar	260	360.4	361.0	72.0					
Apr	380	358.8	359.6	105.7					
May	590	357.5	358.1	164.7					
Jun	880	350.0	353.8	248.8					
Jly	530	351.2	350.6	151.2					
Aug	350	363.3	357.3	98.0					
Sep	265	370.8	367.1	72.2					
Oct	210	380.8	375.8	55.9					
Nov	250	395.8	388.3	64.4					
Dec	85	415.4	405.6	21.0					

Figure 3-5

Calculating the seasonal variations is the first procedure in decomposition. Once seasonal fluctuations are removed from the data series, the trend component can be determined from the deseasonalized data.

In our example, demand is a measurement of unit sales (end items in a product family). If demand is expressed in dollars, sales must first be converted to constant dollars to avoid the affect of inflation or deflation. Use of current dollars could falsify the trend.

There are several techniques for figuring a seasonal index, the results of which are equivalent and valid. One such method follows. The steps for calculating seasonal indices are:

Step 1: Calculate a twelve-month moving average by adding demand for January through December 1998 and dividing by twelve months. This moving average will be centered at the month of June 1998. Each succeeding value is the following twelve month average. The total demand for January through December 1998 equals 3000. Dividing 3000 by 12 equals 250.0. This figure appears in the twelve month moving average column at June. Demand for February 1998 through January 1999 equals 3060. Dividing 3060 by 12 equals 255.0. This number is entered at July 1998.

The arithmetic can be simplified in calculating the twelve-month totals. Rather than adding twelve numbers together to get the total for February 1998 through January 1999 (which is 3060), the total can be obtained by subtracting the first old value (in this case 120, January 1998) and adding the new value (which is 180, January 1999 as illustrated below). Each succeeding calculation is handled in the same manner: $3000 - 120 + 180 = 3060$. In Excel, the average function can be used, which eliminates the need for calculation.

Step 2: Calculate the centered moving average by adding together two moving averages and dividing by 2, as $(250 + 255) \div 2 = 252.5$ for July 1998, and $(255 + 262.9)/2 = 259$ for August. Note that the first value in the sum is the last value in the preceding sum.

Step 3: Determine the estimates that will be used in constructing the seasonal index by dividing actual demand by the centered moving average and moving the decimal point two places to the right (the equivalent to multiplying by 100), as $(390 \div 252.5) \times 100 = 154.5$. Enter on the July line. And $(240 \div 259.0) \times 100 = 92.7$. Enter on the August line.

Step 4: Construct a seasonal index from the percentages (ratios) calculated in Step 3. Figure 3-6 arranges the ratios in columns. There are various ways in which data may be averaged to obtain the index. The one suggested is the modified (medial) mean in which the largest and smallest values are discarded to arrive at an average. This procedure reduces the effect of random variability. If fewer than five years of history are available, simple averaging of all data may be appropriate. However, more than five years of history is better when using the modified mean, assuming there is not a significant pattern change. The ratios for each of the Januaries 1999 through 2002 are: 53.5, 61.7, 56.6, and 50.4. These ratios were taken from Figure 3-5 and entered into Figure 3-6, as were all other ratios in Figure 3-5. By eliminating the largest and smallest numbers and averaging, the modified mean is obtained: $(53.5 + 56.6) \div 2 = 55.1$. The modified mean for February is: $(73.3 + 71.1) \div 2 = 72.2$.

Index of Seasonal Demand

	1998	1999	2000	2001	2002		Modified Mean	Index
Jan		53.5	61.7	56.6	50.4		55.1	54.9
Feb		78.6	48.4	73.3	71.1		72.2	71.9
Mar		75.3	72.0	78.9	72.1		73.7	73.4
Apr		111.9	105.7	111.3	109.5		110.4	110.0
May		172.7	164.7	169.0	169.7		169.4	168.8
Jun		241.8	248.8	240.9	234.4		241.4	240.5
Jly	154.5	155.8	151.2	156.4			155.2	154.6
Aug	92.7	91.4	98.0	97.3			95.0	94.6
Sep	67.4	74.0	72.2	70.5			71.4	71.1
Oct	54.2	61.1	55.9	59.7			57.8	57.6
Nov	58.2	71.0	64.4	71.0			67.7	67.4
Dev	33.4	47.4	21.0	36.9			35.2	35.1
Ttl							1204.5	1200.0

Figure 3-6

Step 5: Adjust the total of the modified means to equal 1200. Divide 1200 by the sum of the modified means to calculate a multiplier: $1200 \div 1204.5 = .9963$. The quotient becomes the multiplier for calculating adjusted monthly seasonal indices. The adjusted January index is: $55.1 \times .9963 = 54.9$. The adjusted February index is: $72.2 \times . 9963 = 71.9$. The figure 1200 is used because this is a monthly index. A quarterly index uses 400.

The index defines the relationship between demand in each of the months and the average deseasonalized monthly demand. Because each of the ratios is expressed as a percentage, 100 is the average, and the index indicates the distance that the demand for that month is from the average.

Example: The January index is 54.9, which indicates that January's expected demand is 45.1% below the average deceasonalized demand $(54.9 - 100 = -45.1)$. The June index is 240.5, which indicates that June's demand is 140.5% above the average $(240.5 - 100 = 140.5)$.

The seasonal pattern is readily discernible and can be plotted on a graph, if desired, to visually display the pattern. The low sales month is December. Sales gradually increase with the peak occurring in June. A sales decline begins thereafter. The pattern is important for planning production and procurement of materials in manufacturing and stocking in distribution and resale operations. Because the other data components have not yet been determined, the analysis is incomplete.

Trend

Once the seasonal indices have been calculated, the trend component is developed. The trend pattern can be observed in the twelve month moving average column of Figure 3-5. There is an upward trend until July 1999 at which time a declining trend begins. In July-August 2000, the trend again changes direction.

The demand being studied totals five full years of history. The first year's moving average is computed from January through December 1998 and is centered at June 1998. The last of the five-year history is the year 2002 and its twelve-month moving average is centered (all the entries are centered) at June 2002. Centering results in forty-nine entries.

One way in which to view trend is discussed above. A better method is to employ simple linear regression, which will result in a straight-line estimate of trend. This method is also known as the system of rectangular coordinates or least squares.

Calculating the Trend

Mathematically, the relationship of two variables can be expressed as: $Y = a + bx$.

The independent (known) variable in this example is time, designated by the symbol x. The values for the parameters a and b are calculated by other equations, with a the constant number, b the slope of the line, and x the coded time period. Their values are substituted in the regression equation.

There are several methods of fitting a trend line when the independent variable is time.

Step 1: Here is one way: prepare a table in the following format:

First: Transfer the values in the twelve-month moving average column of Figure 3-5 to the Y column of the table. In this case, there are 49 numbers that would be recorded sequentially. The table above provides representative samples of the entries, not a complete table.

Second: Complete the X column. Because there are an odd number of months (49 in this example) find the middle period in the Y column, which is the twenty-fifth period and enter a zero in the X column at that point. There are twenty-four periods remaining on each side of zero. Number these sequentially: -1, -2, -3, etc. for the earlier periods and +1, +2, +3, etc. for the later periods. These codes represent the months. If there are an even number of periods, say 48, the two middle numbers are designated –1 and +1 and numbering will be by two's: -3, -5, -7, etc. and +3, +5, +7, etc. An example is given in Chapter 7.

Third: Calculate the XY values. The first XY value in the table is −6000.0 which results from multiplying −24 by 250.0.

Fourth: Calculate the X squared values. The first is 576, which is the product of −24 x −24.

Fifth: Sum the columns.

X	Y	XY	Xsquared
-24	250.0	-6000.0	576
-23	255.0	-5865.0	529
-22	262.9	-5783.8	484
		Other values	
-2	358.8	-717.6	4
-1	357.7	-357.5	1
0	350.0	0	0
1	351.3	351.3	1
		Other values	
22	480.0	10560.0	484
23	480.8	11058.4	529
24	483.3	11599.2	576
Sum (Σ)	19226.7	42665.5	9800 (rounded)

Step 2: Find the parameter $\underline{a}$ by solving the equation: $a = \Sigma Y \div n$. This is the sum of the Y values in the table divided by the number of periods, in this case 49: $19226.7 \div 49 = 392.4$ (the intercept).

Step 3: Find the parameter $\underline{b}$ by solving the equation: $b = \Sigma XY \div \Sigma X^2$: $42665.5 \div 9800 = 4.354$.

Once the values for $\underline{a}$ and $\underline{b}$ have been calculated, the regression equation is employed to determine trend. Trend in our example is linear. It may be graphically displayed by finding two values for Y, for instance the first and last, and connecting the two points by a straight line.

In forecasting, however, the trend factor for each month in the historical time series is calculated. These trend factors are also used to calculate the cyclical index. The results are shown in Figure 3-7. For example, the trend factor for December 1998 is:

$$Y = a + bx$$
$$Y = 392.4 + 4.354(-18)$$
$$Y = 392.4 + (-78.4)$$
$$Y = 314.0$$

The symbol x is representative of time. The origin is June 2000 (the mid point in the series). Its moving average is 350.0 and the x column code for the origin is zero. June 1998 is therefore -24 (counting from the origin) as was illustrated above; thus December 1998 is –18. June 1998 is $Y = 392.4 + 4.354(-24) = 287.9$. The results of these computations may be seen in the trend factor column of Figure 3-7.

The twelve-month moving averages from figure 3-5 were used to calculate the parameters for the linear regression equation (entered in the Y column). Because each twelve-month moving average includes a full year of demand, the seasonal factors are dampened, thus they may be considered nullified for this purpose.

An alternate method of determining the parameters is to divide the actual demand by its seasonal value. This procedure results in deseasonalized demand, which is used as the Y factor in calculating the regression equation parameters. The centered moving average may be used is lieu of the moving average (preferred by many). Although the values calculated for the parameters vary slightly, method-to-method, forecast results will be close. If the trends are graphed, the lines will be parallel.

There are three important considerations associated with the estimation of trend:

❖ Frequently, trend can be adequately expressed as a straight line as illustrated, but not always. Non-linear trends are explained in Chapter 6.

❖ The long-term trend in our example is obvious, but this may not always be the case. Trend, however, should always be calculated.

❖ When using monthly data, normally, five or more years of history are included in the calculations; however, a trend may change over time. Business conditions change, products mature and sales slow or products become obsolescent, and changing economic conditions may affect sales. If management recognizes a change in the pattern of sales, it may be advisable to project trend using different lengths of history, perhaps four years or three years, perhaps less, to determine which most nearly approximates the emerging pattern. This is a judgment call. The pattern change must be one that management expects to continue, not a temporary aberration. The length selected must be longer than the length of the cyclical fluctuation, because cycles also influence forecast values. Generally, the longer the time period the better the results unless a period of radical change is expected.

Deseasonalized demand can be the basis for projecting annual sales (the next twelve months). Here is an example for January 1999: actual sales of 180 ÷ 54.9 (seasonal index) x 100 x 12 months = 3934. Actual sales are 4600 (January through December 1999 sales). Because sales are computed monthly, 12 is the multiplier. If quarterly data are used, multiply by 4. Economists often annualize data to get an annual projection, for example in statements such as, "GDP grew at an annual rate of 4% last quarter", that is 1% growth x 4. What this means is that if GDP continues to grow at the same rate each quarter, GDP will be 4% higher than it was at the end of last quarter. Projecting annual growth from a one period base may have the forecaster sliding down a slippery slope. Note the "if" factor above. Better to employ one of the forecasting methodologies described in this book.

Cyclical Variation

Once the seasonal and trend values are established, the cyclical component can be separated from the time series. Cyclical variations estimated by this procedure also contain randomness, which is discussed in the next section. Identifying the causes for cyclical behavior is not possible with this technique. Identifying the trend and magnitude of economic cycle activity is a complicated matter, but by research the forecaster can relate the business cycle or pertinent parts thereof to company activity (see Chapter 10). The business cycle as it pertains to the company may or may not be directly related to economic factors.

Calculating the Cyclical Indices

The last column of Figure 3-7 contains the cyclical indices. The values were calculated from the equation: Cyclical Value = Moving Average ÷ Trend x 100.

The cyclical index for December 1998 is: C = 327.9 ÷ 314.0 x 100 = 104.4.

The twelve-month moving average for 1998 is 327.9. It was obtained from Figure 3-5 and recorded in Figure 3-7. The trend component of 314.0 was calculated in accordance with the procedure in the previous section.

Had the calculations been based upon annual data (years instead of months), actual demand rather than a moving average would have been used in the equation because actual demand is the sum of twelve months, thus the seasonal variation, if any, would not be a factor.

Trend and Cycle

Month		12 Mon MA	Trend	Cycl Index	Month		12 Mon MA	Trend	Cycl Index
98	Jun	250.0	287.9	86.8		Jly	351.3	396.8	88.5
	Jly	255.0	292.3	87.3		Aug	363.3	401.1	90.6
	Aug	262.9	296.6	88.6		Sep	370.8	405.5	91.5
	Sep	270.8	301.0	90.0		Oct	380.8	409.8	92.9
	Oct	282.5	305.3	92.5		Nov	395.8	414.2	95.6
	Nov	301.3	309.7	97.3		Dec	415.4	418.5	99.3
	Dec	327.9	314.0	104.4	01	Jan	432.1	422.9	102.2
99	Jan	345.4	318.4	108.5		Feb	440.8	427.2	103.2
	Feb	354.6	322.7	109.9		Mar	446.3	431.6	103.4
	Mar	362.9	327.1	110.9		Apr	452.1	435.9	103.7
	Apr	369.6	331.4	115.5		May	459.2	440.3	104.3
	May	377.5	335.8	112.4		Jun	466.7	444.6	105.0
	Jun	383.3	340.2	112.7		Jly	466.7	449.0	103.9
	Jly	387.1	344.5	112.4		Aug	468.3	453.4	103.5
	Aug	378.8	348.9	108.6		Sep	467.9	457.7	102.2
	Sep	377.9	353.2	107.0		Oct	470.0	462.1	101.7
	Oct	375.4	357.6	105.0		Nov	473.8	466.4	101.6
	Nov	370.8	361.9	102.5		Dec	475.0	470.8	100.9
	Dec	367.5	366.3	100.3	02	Jan	477.5	475.1	100.5
00	Jan	361.7	370.6	97.6		Feb	478.3	479.5	99.8
	Feb	361.7	375.0	96.5		Mar	479.2	483.8	99.0
	Mar	360.4	379.3	95.1		Apr	480.0	488.2	98.3
	Apr	358.8	383.7	93.5		May	480.8	492.5	97.6
	May	357.5	388.0	92.1		Jun	483.3	496.9	97.2
	Jun	350.0	392.4	89.2					

Figure 3-7

Cyclical Fluctuation

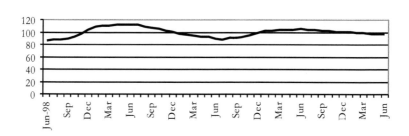

Figure 3-8

An examination of the cyclical indices reveals a cyclical pattern roughly resembling a wave that changes direction every twelve to thirteen months. In this instance, the cycle's duration is approximately two years. In the future, the timing and duration of the cycle could and probably would change to some degree. The cycle is shown graphically in Figure 3-8.

Random Fluctuation

All of the components of the time series have been discussed except irregular movement. Randomness results from a number of causes which are unpredictable, and many of which are unidentifiable. Sometimes, however, identification is possible, as when there is an unusual occurrence such as an extended strike or war. Because random fluctuations are generally unpredictable, there is not an assured method for isolating this component, but an approximation of its influence upon the time series can be made.

Figure 3-9 illustrates the results obtained when the irregular movement (randomness) is removed from the cyclical factors.

Computation of Irregular Movement

Partial Series

Year	Month	Cyclical Index	3 Month Moving Total	3 Month Moving Average	Random Factor
2001	May	104.3			
	June	105.0	313.2	104.4	100.6
	July	103.9	312.2	104.1	99.8
	August	103.3	309.4	103.1	100.2
	September	102.2	307.2	102.4	99.8
	October	101.7	305.5	101.8	99.9
	November	101.6	304.2	101.4	100.2
	December	100.9	303.0	101.0	99.9
2002	January	100.5	301.2	100.4	100.1
	February	99.8	299.3	99.8	100.0
	March	99.0	297.1	99.0	100.0
	April	98.3	294.9	98.3	100.0
	May	97.6	293.2	97.7	99.9
	June	97.3			

Figure 3-9

Step 1: Calculate a three-month moving average from the cyclical index as in Figure 3-9. June 2001 moving average is 104.4, which is obtained by adding May, June and July and dividing by 3. The result is entered opposite June, the middle month, as $(104.3 + 105.0 + 103.9) \div 3 = 104.4$. July 2001 moving average is calculated from the months of June, July and August: $(105.0 + 103.9 + 103.3) \div 3 = 104.1$.

Step 2: Divide the cyclical index by the three-month moving average and multiply by 100 to move the decimal point; June 2001: $105.0 \div 104.4 \times 100 = 100.6$

The effects of randomness are represented by a percentage greater than or less than 100 (which is 100%). In this example, there is virtually no random behavior.

Had the random factor been 96, the effect would have been 4% (100 − 96). If the sales of a product were 120 units and the irregularity was removed, 115 units would remain, that is: 120 x 96%.

Separating the random fluctuation from the cyclical variation will not change the forecast. The result obtained by using the cyclical index with randomness included gives the same result as using the three-month cyclical moving average and the separated random factor. The important point that is learned from the exercise of isolating randomness is the extent to which demand is influenced by chance.

Forecasting Using the Decomposition Method

A primary purpose in applying decomposition to a time series is to gain an understanding of the composition of the specific demand being studied. Had the example given above been the sales demand for a product group, for instance, the marketing and production executives would have a detailed knowledge of the characteristics of that product group's behavior. That knowledge is invaluable in plotting marketing strategy and planning production.

The data collected during the analysis may be used as the basis for forecasting. Component values for the appropriate period are substituted into an equation, which is solved to arrive at a forecast. If one of the components does not exist, the equation is rewritten to exclude it (ignore that component). If at least two of the elements of trend, seasonal, and cyclical are not present, one of the other methods of forecasting described in this book will give better results. For the purposes of forecasting by this method, however, a trend may be horizontal; that is, it may be a constant number that is used in each month being forecast.

In the preceding example, the period January 1998 through December 2002 is the base time series that was used to calculate trend and the cyclical and seasonal indices (see Figure 3-5). Because the twelve-month moving averages were centered at June, the June 2002 entries in Figure 3-5 represent calculations through December 2002. The forecaster also knows the actual demands for the months January through June 2003 (the time is now July 2003). This six-month period will be employed to test the reliability that may be expected of forecasts made by the decomposition method.

The forecasting model described earlier is: $F = T \times S \times C \times R$. Because the cyclical and random factors are combined in the cyclical component, the model is simplified to read:

$$F = T \times S \times C$$

Forecasting is a straightforward procedure. The results are shown in Figure 3-10.

Forecast Results

	Trend	Seasonal	Cyclical	Forecast	Actual Demand
January 2003	501.3	.549	.96	264	240
February	505.6	.719	.97	353	355
March	510.0	.734	.97	363	365
April	514.3	1.104	.97	549	540
May	518.7	1.688	.97	849	840
June	523.0	2.405	.97	1220	1190

Figure 3-10

The trend component is calculated from the equation: $Y = a + bx$. The parameters as previously defined are: $a = 392.4$ and $b = 4.354$.

Time is represented by the symbol x. There are 49 moving average values in Figure 3-5 from which the parameters a and b are calculated. The origin (zero) is June 2000 with twenty-four values on each side of the origin. The code number +24 is centered at June 2002. Because twelve month moving averages were centered in the middle of the twelve-month periods, June 2002 (code 24) includes data (sales) through December 2002; therefore, January 2003 is period 25, February 26, etc.

The trend value for January is: $392.4 + 4.354(25) = 501.3$.

The seasonal factor is taken directly from Figure 3-6. January is 54.9, which transforms to 0.549.

The cyclical factor is not clearly defined; that is, it is not possible to mathematically determine the next value with certainty. In many cases, however, an approximation is possible. If there is no other way in which to estimate the cyclical index for the coming time periods, judgment is applied. Examining the cyclical pattern in Figure 3-7 indicates that the cycle has been declining for the last twelve months. The forecaster has, therefore, estimated the near term future in a way that resembles the cyclical column in Figure 3-7.

Reviewing the past indicates that a turning point for the cyclical component applicable to this company can be expected approximately every twelve months. Of course, this is speculation. Most frequently turning points are not well defined and they are not a constant. The forecaster, however, has decided to eyeball the series and assign values as he believes are appropriate, for example, .96 and then .97 (see Figure 3-10).

Comparing forecast with actual demand in Figure 3-10 reveals excellent forecasting results except for January, which, as previously stated, was a departure from the regular historical pattern. The percentage differences are 2.5% or less, very close results.

Because demands are known, the correct cyclical indicators can be calculated, with the assumption that the seasonal and trend components are valid. The trend for February 2003 is: $392.4 + 4.354(26) = 505.6$, thus $T \times S \times C = 355$ (known February demand), which is $505.6 \times .719 \times C = 355$ or $363.5C = 355 = .977$. March $= .975$; April $= .955$; May $= .959$; June $= .946$.

The forecaster's assumption that a turning point is imminent is incorrect, but the guess is not without logic. In fact, the decline has continued and a dilemma of sorts has arisen. Will the decline continue? Has a turning point been reached? What is the importance of a one, two, or three point change in an index? At .97 the June forecast is 1220, at .96 it is 1207, and at .95 it is 1195. How shall the forecaster proceed with regard to estimating the future cycle?

The monthly rate of change is usually not significant one month to the next, but over a period of four or more months it may be influential.

For the immediate forecast horizon a judgment call is appropriate because the average percentage difference between cyclical reality and projection will not materially affect the forecast result. The forecaster may choose to modify opinion by a simple procedure such as averaging the previous three or four month's indices: $(.955 + .959 + .946) \div 3 = .953$; $(.975 + .955 + .959 + .946) \div 4 = .959$, then adding or subtracting the average rate of change to each succeeding month.

The logic of the above discussion is based on the minor rates of change in cyclical values. Should there be a more dramatic percentage change a more complex approach is required.

There is a temptation to use 1.00 when the cyclical indicators hover in a range very close to one. Before being temped, however, test to see that the difference is inconsequential. In our example, an indicator of one results in an average forecast error for the six month series of about five percent whereas the forecaster's error is less than two percent.

If the cyclical movement for our sample company is economic in nature, a short-term possibility is to tie the cyclical future to leading economic indicators. If so, the prediction of cyclical values becomes more objective and may be estimated employing a regression model, with the leading indicator used as the independent variable. Projections of professional economists in the case of lagging or concurrent indicators lend more credibility and objectivity, but use caution as the prediction may not be as predictable as advertised.

Leading indicators are time series that reach their turning points before the measures of total economic activity. If these leading economic indicators also lead the cyclical indicators in the demand series being studied, and movement is in at least an approximate relationship, that relationship may be mathematically defined. If the cyclical movement cannot be related or if a more sophisticated procedure does not work, judgment is applied and the prediction is based upon a study of the history of the cyclical time series as was done to arrive at the conclusions described above Leading indicators, other economic series, and other methods of estimating cyclical behavior are described more completely in Chapter 10.

Before sailing into predicting business cycles and turning points, a thorough review of Chapter 10 is in order. It may be necessary to take business cycles into account regardless of the forecasting model and especially when estimating the mid-term to long-term future. Chances are that in the short-term the impact of the business cycle will not be greatly felt because the forecasting model will account for the "business trend." Of course with that said, a situation could arise to contradict that statement.

This discussion clearly indicates that forecasting is not merely the massaging of numbers but also the application of knowledge and experience.

Predicting a future cyclical pattern is difficult, especially in the mid- and long-terms. In contemplating the cyclical future, there are several relevant points to remember:

- ❖ Cyclical fluctuations as they apply to a company or an industry may result from general economic conditions or from only one or a limited number of the components of, say, the gross domestic product, or the cause may be some measure peculiar to a particular industry or to some portion of an industry.

- ❖ Economic cycles fluctuate unevenly. A cycle may last two years or many years, measured from peak to peak (or trough to trough). Additionally, the natural flow of an economic (business) cycle is interrupted by many factors, for example, the intervention of the Federal Reserve, war, international trade balances or treaties.

- ❖ The economy is generally unpredictable, probably notoriously so when trying to fix the general timing of turning points or forecasting (assigning numbers) to an economic time series. Economists disagree even in their broad evaluations.

- ❖ As little as a few percentage points of difference in the beginning period of the cyclical index can make a substantial difference in a longer term forecast since the individual errors accumulate.

❖ Decomposition is one of many forecasting methods described in this book. It is most applicable to the short-term and to product groups and probably should be avoided in estimating the long-range future.

Testing for Accuracy and Reliability

Because there is always uncertainty, there will always be forecast error. Measuring and evaluating the deviation allows management to determine the degree of accuracy that may be expected in the future. The relationship between actual demand and forecasted demand is depicted in Figure 3-11.

Forecasting is only part of the job. Determining the level of accuracy that may be expected is a vital function in the forecasting process. If it can be determined that the deviation from actual will generally fall within predictable limits, managers can estimate with a degree of confidence the range within which actual values will occur; that is, they may estimate the range of forecast error. The measures explained below are useful with intrinsic forecasting methods. Statistical measures of accuracy and significance of a more complex nature are applied to causal methods, as described in Chapter 7.

❖ If the percentage difference is calculated for each of the months a simple measure of accuracy is obtained; for example, January is $24 \div 240 = 10.0\%$ (Figure 3-11). Looking at the other months reveals low percentages and that translates to accurate forecasts. Why is January's high percentage out of line with the low percentages of the other months? As pointed out earlier, January is not typical of the time series pattern. For three years in a row the actual demand has been 240 whereas all succeeding months in these years show an upward trend (see Figure 3-4).

❖ Techniques such as standard deviation, mean absolute deviation (MAD), mean absolute percent error (MAPE), and mean squared error (MSE) add a degree of sophistication to the process of measuring forecast accuracy. Each of these is briefly explained in the following paragraphs. Chapter 5 provides a further discussion of forecast error measurement, range forecasting, and tracking. Applying measurements of deviation to the forecasting process can help the forecaster select the best method, that which results in the smallest error over time. It also allows tracking, which is an early warning devise that alerts the forecaster to changes in the demand pattern. The measures to be described below prepare the reader to comprehend the relationship between forecasting and forecast reliability. They are predicated upon an understanding of the normal distribution. The normal distribution assumes that data are distributed equally on each side of a mid-point. The mid-point is the mean (average) value, and the standard deviation measures the dispersion around the mean. The distribution of the population is relatively symmetrical. This means that a value is just as likely to occur on one side of the average value as on the other side. To relate this concept to demand, it is equally probable to have a forecast that is, say, 50 units less than the demand as one 50 units more than the demand. Normal distribution is reflected in the bell shaped curve. The mid-point, the highest point on the curve (the peak) is the mean (average) in the illustration. The plus and minus numbers 1 through 3 represent the standard deviations. They are sometimes referred to as sigma. Distributions may also be skewed, but in most forecasting applications, the normal distribution adequately describes the situation.

❖ Mean absolute deviation is a simple way in which to measure forecast error. To find the MAD, sum the absolute error column in Figure 3-11 and divide by the number of occurrences (periods): $76/6 = 12.7$. The absolute error is the difference between actual demand and forecast disregarding the plus and minus signs. If the forecasting technique is unbiased, the sum of the errors in the Difference column will be close to zero, but it will seldom equal zero. If the sum of the errors is either a large positive or negative number, the indication is that the forecasts are constantly biased; however, the six month forecast in our example may not be typical because of the size and nature of the January and June deviations, thus the forecaster will assume symmetry until more evidence is available. Bias can occur, for instance, when the results of the forecasts regularly lag actual demand. The MAD may be used to estimate the average level of accuracy that may be expected from future forecasts, but does not provide a range within which forecasts may vary. As an average, some values will be higher and some lower. MAD and the other error measures described herein are useful in comparing the relative goodness of competing forecasts techniques; that forecast with the lowest MAD (measured over time) is the most accurate. Remember, conditions change and that may change the results in subsequent computations. Another important measurement is to estimate the likely range of the deviations from actual. One way to estimate a range within which errors may be expected is through standard deviation.

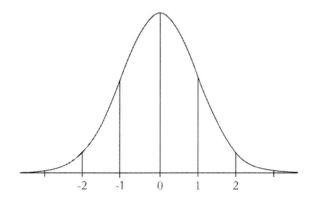

❖ In a normal distribution it is expected that roughly 68% of the errors will be contained within one standard deviation (one-sigma) and roughly 95% to 96% will be within two standard deviations with the distribution of the errors approximately equal on each side of the average; that is 34% on each side of the average in a one-sigma distribution. As computed below the standard deviation is 10.7. Relating this to the example, it may be expected that the forecast error will be plus or minus 11 (as rounded) or less 68% of the time and 22 or less 95% of the time (11 x 2). Now, let us calculate standard deviation mathematically, dividing the procedure into steps (see Figures 3-11 and 3-12):

Step 1: subtract forecast from demand for each period (ignore the sign). These are the numbers in the absolute error column. January is 240 - 264 = 24.

Step 2: compute the average (mean) error by summing the absolute errors and dividing by the number of months: 76 ÷ 6 = 12.7. The mean error is also the MAD.

Step 3: subtract each deviation from the mean ignoring the signs. The result for January is 24 – 12.7 = 11.3; February is 2 – 12.7 = 10.7.

Step 4: square each of the differences calculated in step 3. January's result is 11.3 x 11.3 = 127.7.

Step 5: sum the squares, which totals 683.4.

Step 6: divide the sum of the squares by the number of observations (months in this case) which is 683.4 ÷ 6 = 113.9.

Step 7: find the square root of 113.9, it is 10.7.

❖ Once the standard deviation has been calculated the probable range of error can be estimated. First, multiply the standard deviation by the probability factor; subtract the product from the average error, this gives the lower end of the range; now, to find the upper end of the range, add the product to the average error. Note the magnitude of the spread between the upper and lower limits. The forecaster will ponder this situation and may try different approaches (models) to see if the upper end can be reduced. However, the upper end will always be significantly larger than the lower end. The following example is based upon the standard deviation of 10.7:

For a one-sigma probability, which is 68%:

10.7 x 1 =10.7; 12.7 – 10.7 = 2 (lower end)
10.7 x 1 = 10.7; 12.7 + 10.7 = 23.4 (upper end)

For a two-sigma probability, which is 95%:

10.7 x 2 = 21.4; 12.7 – 21.4 = -8.7 (lower end)
10.7 x 2 = 21.4; 12.7 + 21.4 = 34.1 (upper end)

If the lower limit of the range is a negative number it becomes zero since an error cannot be less than zero; therefore, at 95% the low end of the range is zero.

❖ The mean squared error is found by squaring each error, summing and dividing by the number of periods. Because the errors are squared, MSE assigns greater weight to large errors than it does to small errors; thus, it is harder to interpret the results than it is with other measures. If the objective is to minimize large errors, this measure may be appropriate. In Figure 3-11 the MSE is 274.3 (1646 ÷ 6). The standard deviation as calculated above does not change; MSE cannot be used in its calculation.

❖ Mean absolute percent error (MAPE) is the average percent of error. It is calculated by dividing the absolute error for each period by the demand and multiplying by 100 to give the result as a percentage, thus, January is 24 ÷ 240 = 10%. The Percent Difference column in Figure 3-11 gives the percentages. Next, sum the column and divide by the number of periods: 16.4 ÷ 6 = 2.7%. This indicates that the forecast will be wrong by about plus or minus 2.7% on average. To calculate the standard deviation as a percentage, begin with the MAPE, which is 2.7% (it is also termed the mean or average error; see Figure 3-13).

Step 1: subtract each percentage error (percent difference) from the MAPE: January is 10 − 2.7 = 7.3, ignore the signs. This is the deviation from the mean.

Step 2: square the deviation for each month: 7.3 x 7.3 = 53.3.

Step 3: sum the squared deviations: 66.1.

Step 4: divide the sum by the number of observations (months): 66.1 ÷ 6 = 11.02; now find the square root, which is 3.3 (rounded). The standard deviation is 3.3%.

❖ The range of error is calculated as described above. The results follow, negatives are zero:

For a one-sigma probability, which is 68%:
      3.3% x 1 = 3.3%; 2.7% - 3.3%= -0.6
      3.3% x 1 = 3.3%; 2.7% + 3.3% = 6.0%

For a two-sigma probability, which is 95%:
      3.3% x 2 = 6.6%; 2.7% - 6.6% = -3.9%
      3.3% x 2 = 6.6%; 2.7% + 6.6% = 9.3%

Evaluation

The six-month forecast is a test against known demand. The procedures explained above measures the degree of accuracy that may be expected in the future; however, there are limitations that need to be addressed before describing the ways in which error statistics can be used:

❖ A six-period window does not afford an adequate time horizon in which to get a reading of future forecast goodness, but it can be an important indicator. Because only six months of demand *not* already used in formulating the forecast technique were available, the forecaster did not have a choice. It is inappropriate to employ the same data used in forecast development to test for accuracy, as that would bias the results. The forecaster will keep a close eye on each succeeding forecast to see if the level of accuracy continues.

Forecast Error

Month	Actual Demand	Forecasted Demand	Difference	Percent Difference*	Absolute Error	Squared Error
03 Jan	240	264	-24	10.0	24	576
Feb	355	353	2	0.6	2	4
Mar	365	363	2	0.5	2	4
Apr	540	549	-9	1.7	9	81
May	840	849	-9	1.1	9	81
Jun	1190	1220	-30	2.5	30	900
Totals			-68	16.4	76	1646

Figure 3-11 *Signs ignored

Standard Deviation Factors

Month	Difference	Deviation	Deviation Squared
January	24	11.3	127.7
February	2	10.7	114.5
March	2	10.7	114.5
April	9	3.7	13.7
May	9	3.7	13.7
June	30	17.3	299.3
	76		683.4

Figure 3-12

Standard Deviation Factors (MAPE)

Month	Percent Difference	Deviation	Deviation Squared
January	10.0	7.3	53.3
February	0.6	2.1	4.4
March	0.5	2.2	4.8
April	1.7	1.0	1.0
May	1.1	1.6	2.6
June	2.5	0.2	0.04
	16.4		66.1

Figure 3-13

❖ A look at the difference column in Figure 3-11 shows that four of the six months are negative deviations. In a normal distribution it is equally probable that a deviation from the mean will be a plus or a minus. The six-month period, however, is not sufficient to conclude that the series is not normally distributed. Also, the total of the column must be considered cautiously. In the normal distribution the total will be close to zero because of the equal probability of plus and minus deviations. In this series the large difference is due to January and the misrepresentation of the June cyclical index, but the June percent difference indicates a reasonable forecast.

❖ About one-third of the error for the six months is a result of the January deviation (Absolute Error column, Figure 3-11).

Even more startling is the percent difference: more than 60% of the difference is attributable to January. January is an anomaly, inconsistent with the rest of the demand series. It is logical to discount it, but not without caution, and probably by comparing future forecast error statistics with and without January. As the months progress, the influence of January will recede, at least until next January.

❖ Measuring accuracy is an essential part of the forecasting process. Selecting the best forecasting method cannot necessarily be accomplished on the first try, particularly if the forecasted series is as short as that in our example. Forecast error is evaluated on a continuing basis. At the conclusion of each demand period the deviation is recalculated to determine if the forecasts are drifting further from actual. This may signal a pattern change. Additionally, reevaluation, probably at three period intervals, helps to insure the best methodology for the long run. The longer the forecasted series the more likely the best technique will be found. This statement assumes that there is not a significant pattern change in the series.

Interpretation of Error Measures

Here is a comparison of error statistics:

	January Included	January Excluded
MAD	12.7	10.4
MSE	274.3	214.0
MAPE	%2.7	%1.2
Standard Deviation, percent	%3.3	%0.8
Standard Deviation, units	10.7	10.3

The question begging for an answer is: which measure should the company use?Perhaps the determining factor is the use to which the forecast will be put, for example, as input to profit planning, to ascertain the number of end items to manufacture or buy, the size of safety stock levels as in a distribution facility, and/or to determine the number and size of contracts to write for raw materials or end items. There is not a simple answer. Often a forecast serves multiple purposes. Companies will approach the question differently. As the results from more forecasting periods become known, the forecaster will have a better understanding of how the company's demand series works and how management uses the estimates.

The example in this chapter assumes that the sample company has not previously had a formal system of estimating the future. Of course, this is not true of many (probably most) companies. The principles and discussion herein apply equally to companies that are investigating different or more formal forecasting methodologies. The four significant features of forecasting are: know the composition of your demand (decomposition), select a methodology that gives the most accurate results, measure and track accuracy, and periodically review and evaluate that which you are doing.

In our example, there are three factors that contribute to the demand pattern: seasonal variation, trend, and the cyclical component. The following is an abbreviated discussion of the importance of knowing the relationship between the individual parts of a time series.

Knowing the seasonal pattern is important in planning production, resale buys, stocking distribution centers, and purchasing. It is also vital to Marketing to discover what drives the customers' levels of buys; what can be expected during the next seasonal peak periods. Are they year around customers who buy more heavily during certain months? If so, month-by-month buys can be plotted and a forecast made for each key customer. These forecasts when compared with actual demand are used to anticipate peak season sales and to formulate marketing approaches, by major customer. Are sales increasing, decreasing, or holding steady? If the peak occurs because some customers only buy during certain months, discovery of why may allow a sales endeavor that will increase sales to those customers. Of course, there is much other useful information that may be gleamed from the study of individual accounts, not only as pertains to the seasonal component but also to trend and cycle.

In a predictable way, sales may be increasing (up-trend), decreasing (down-trend), or horizontal (little movement from the average). What are the reasons? Is there a general upturn (or downturn) in business? Is the customer base growing, perhaps at the expense of business from key customers? Are certain important customers steadily increasing (or decreasing) their level of buys? The essential ingredient is to determine what is happening so that the why can be addressed and sales plans developed.

The cyclical component is the most difficult to ascertain because it is not as predictable as the trend and seasonal components. Yet, it is material to know the affect that the business cycle has upon sales, especially in relation to each of the company's major customers. Knowing, derived from a historical study, allows assumptions to be made about future business, thus prelude (as with the other components) to developing sales plans and tactics.

If the company's sales are materially affected by the business cycle, parts thereof, or some other cyclical type element, a study to determine the relationship is necessary and justified. Such a study includes the means of predicting the cycle's future, a difficult if not impossible task, but not hopeless (see Chapter 10).

It may be advisable to subject each major customer's sales history to the decomposition process, including forecasting, to gain understanding of what may be logically expected, and as an early warning to possible changes.

The measurement of deviation from actual discussed above is an essential part of the forecast process.

The MAD, MSE, MAPE, and standard deviation are useful measures for determining which of several forecasting methods being tested is the most reliable. That forecasting technique which produces the smallest forecast error is the most accurate and possibly the most reliable; however, consistency and frequency are also considerations. They are discussed below. Accuracy as an only criterion can lead one down the garden path. And remember that the outcome applies only to that moment in time for the historical series tested. Understand that the demand pattern is subject to change as time rolls along. Changes in economic conditions, trends, and customer purchase levels affect the demand pattern. A one time calculation and comparison of error statistics is not enough; periodic review of the forecasting procedures is necessary.

The MAPE has the advantage of expressing its error measurement as a percentage, which is an easily understandable way to communicate forecast accuracy and reliability. The MAPE is a best means for setting a standard (goal or target). A company, for instance, can establish a limit on the deviation from actual that is tolerable, such as ± 4%, or some other percentage as may be appropriate to its profit or operational picture. Many firms would be joyous if accuracy was within 4% of demand. Each functional activity affected may want a different percentage. Negotiation to consensus or top management direction resolves these differences. The forecaster's job is to advise and to develop the best methodology, the one that comes closest to standard as is possible in this uncertain economic world.

The standard selected must be realistic but can have reach. Volatility is also a consideration. If there is normally considerable variability of demand between forecast periods, accuracy can be affected, especially if that variability is not predictable. A standard may be difficult to establish and a forecast technique that averages highly variable demands over time may be the best available. But patterns can also be hidden and sometimes what appears as volatile is reasonably predictable. This subject will be addressed in later chapters.

Above, it is noted that the technique that produces the smallest error is the most accurate. Two other criteria that are material to the selection of a forecasting technique are the number of times that the errors are within the established standard (frequency) and the spread of the forecast errors (consistency). Assume a standard of 4%; now consider the errors for each of the last ten periods for a forecast made by two different methods:

First (%): 3.5, 2.8, 6.5, 5.4, 6.1, 3.8, 3.1, 7.1, 4.0, 3.9.

MAPE = 4.6%, 6 errors 4% or less.

Second (%): 3.5, 4.1, 4.2, 3.9, 4.2, 4.2, 3.9, 4.1, 3.1, 4.1.

MAPE = 3.9%, 4 errors 4% or less.

The second technique produces the lowest average error (MAPE) when compared to the first method. In the first technique more of its errors fall within the 4% standard (frequency). The range of the percentages is closer in the second technique (consistency). Now, computing the standard deviations and the range of probability we find that the first technique has a standard deviation of 3.6% and an error range of zero to 11.7% at 95% probability. The standard deviation for the second technique is 0.3% and the range is 3.2% to 4.6%, thus, consistency is better because all values are grouped closer and, in this case, not too far from the standard. Although the first technique produced more errors that are within the standard, the accuracy and consistency factors conclude that the second forecasting technique is the more appropriate method.

What conclusions can be reached by comparing the error statistics for two other forecasting methods where previously the standard has been set at ±4%?

The first forecasting technique is superior in two categories: average error and frequency, but the second is substantially more consistent. Which of the two is the logical choice? Most, with logic, would tend to the second because the range is compressed. But the choice can only be made by determining the impact on all the functional areas concerned and the estimated results to cost, sales and profit. A simulation to see the impact can be initiated and the results compared. At the same time, a review of the standard can be undertaken.

First (%): 1.2, 9.6, 9.3, 2.4, 2.7, 10.6, 1.4, 3.1, 2.9, 1.1
Second (%): 5.1, 4.8, 5.1, 5.3, 4.8, 4.2, 5.2, 4.9, 4.8, 5.1

A comparison of the error statistics reveals:

	First	Second	
Average error	4.4%	4.9%	
Frequency	7 hits	0 hits	within the 4% standard
Standard deviation	3.6%	0.3%	
Probability Range	0 to 11.7%	4.3% to 5.5%	consistency

The point of the above discussions is to explain that careful review of all pertinent data is necessary, not to consider only one aspect in the forecasting mélange.

Decomposition of a time series into its component parts gives managers and forecasters a tool to better understand the nature of that time series. Applied to sales, it provides a means for understanding why sales act as they do; for example, what part of sales are subject to the seeming capriciousness of the business cycle? If the business cycle is a key player in sales, the company may need to adopt a forecasting technique that considers that factor. Chapter 10 is especially useful in that regard. Knowing the trend and seasonal components are equally important to the planning functions of manufacturing and marketing managers.

One forecasting technique is described above. It may be the best or it may be the least among many. Examine all likely models before making a decision.

Chapter 4

Smoothing and Adaptive Methods

In the last chapter, decomposition was described as a method for dividing a time series into its component parts for the purpose of identifying the factors that influence demand and to ascertain the relative importance of each component. Decomposition is also effective as a forecasting technique, particularly in projecting aggregate demand.

Smoothing and adaptive methods relate to individual products or to product families. Individual components that may be contained in the time series are not knowable unless the demand series is subjected to decomposition. The models described in this chapter are concerned with the short-term future – usually one to six months – most frequently in support of operational planning and scheduling, purchasing, sales planning, and some financial estimates.

These forecasting techniques are classified as time series models because they depend upon the historical pattern of the time series itself. It is assumed that the near-term future at least will be like the past, that is, the historical observations are representative of the future after model manipulation. But the future has a way of fooling mere humans. Although patterns change slowly and generally predictably, forecasting beyond the short-term may be hazardous to accuracy. In this regard, the maximum number of past observations used should be limited to that length of time in which the pattern is relatively stable.

This chapter describes a number of techniques that fall within the categories of moving averages, exponential smoothing, and adaptive filters. These models are related in the sense that each depends upon the historical time series to estimate the future and each averages past demand in one form or another.

There are limitations as well as advantages in time series forecasting, and they are discussed in this chapter.

Moving Averages

Moving averages assume that there is a linear trend. Fluctuations outside the trend may muddy the water and cause inconsistent forecasts in the short-term. A number of techniques are explained in this section and in a way in which the characteristics can be matched to the characteristics of different types of demand patterns. This is not to say that the beauty of absolute accuracy will be attained, but that there are choices.

Simplicity and flexibility in model design are advantages and apply to most (but not all) of the methods described. Conversely, a limitation is that these models do not adapt quickly to changes in the basic pattern. In most instances, forecasts lag actual demand especially when there is an increasing (ascending) or decreasing (declining) trend, with forecast errors tending to accumulate on one side of the average, thus not catching up with the actual demand. As example, it may occur that the forecasts will always be less than the actual demand when the demand pattern is one of an increasing trend. Of course, the reverse is also true.

If there are extreme values in the time series, including more periods in the model will help to minimize the effect that these values have on the forecast. If an extreme value is a one-time event resulting from one of the factors listed at the end of Chapter 1, it may be appropriate to modify the time series to account for the special event; for example, discounting the spike if this is the event. . If the series displays erratic behavior, forecasts may be improved by employing the method detailed in Chapter 6.

Six models have been selected for examination with forecasts made against each of three demand series. Each of the time series has a different pattern so that the goodness of each model can be appraised and conclusions drawn regarding which method is most applicable to each of the time series. Although this is a bunch of forecasts, the number helps to clarify the methodology and provides a guide to the reader when faced with the real world.

The sales histories do not contain seasonal fluctuations. If seasonal variations were a consideration, a seasonal index as described in Chapter 3 would be made and the forecasts based on moving averages calculated from the deseasonalized data.

The three time series are: ascending or increasing trend (AT), declining trend (DT), and changing pattern (CP). Actual demands for these series are displayed in Figure 4-1.

Three Time Series

	1	2	3	4	5	6	7	8	9	10	11	12
AT	100	104	107	110	108	110	112	114	118	110	112	117
DT	130	126	124	120	122	118	115	113	109	107	104	101
CP	140	135	145	127	130	124	131	132	125	136	128	140

Figure 4-1

The number of periods selected to calculate the moving average could be any number of observations more than one. The more observations used in the calculations the greater will be the smoothing effect. For a time series that is stable, the number of periods to incorporate into the model is dependent upon which gives the best results. And that may change with time. When there is much random behavior, many observations may provide the best forecast as that tends to smooth-out the fluctuations. For comparison, three and five period moving averages are used in our examples (except for the double moving average models). A different number of periods, however, could achieve a better (or worse) result. The reader may wish to experiment.

The remainder of this section explains moving average techniques and gives forecasts for one period ahead.

Simple Moving Averages

This technique takes a predetermined number of observations, averages them, and uses that average as the forecast for the next period. Using the AT series in Figure 4-1 as an example a three period moving average totals the three periods and divides by three to obtain the forecast for the next period: $(100 + 104 + 107) \div 3 = 104$ (rounded), therefore, the forecast for the fourth period is 104. The forecast for the fifth period is $(104 + 107 + 110) \div 3 = 107$.

A five period moving average sums the five periods and divides by 5 to get the forecast for the sixth period: $(100 + 104 + 107 + 110 + 108) \div 5 = 106$. Note the lagging effect. Without looking at other moving average procedures, it appears that in the case of an increasing or declining trend simple linear regression may give better results, that is, the equation $Y = a + b(x)$, explained later in reference to double moving averages.

Simple Moving Average Model

Period	Actual Demand	3 Period Forecast	5 Period Forecast
1	100		
2	104		
3	107		
4	110	104	
5	108	107	
6	110	108	106
7	112	109	108
8	114	110	109
9	118	112	111
10	110	115	112
11	112	114	113
12	117	113	113
13	Forecast	113	114

Figure 4-2

Note the forecast for period 13 in Figure 4-2. Actual demand is not known.

Moving Average Difference Model

In this method, averaging is done not to the actual demand but to the difference between the last two actual demands.

Step 1: Subtract demand in period 2 from the demand in period 1, that is, 104 − 100 = 4. This is the difference entered opposite period 2 in Figure 4-3. The entry for period 3 is 107 − 104 = 3. The entry for period 4 is 110 − 107 = 3. Subtraction may result in a negative or a positive number.

Moving Average Difference Model

Period	Actual Demand	Difference	3 Period Moving Av	Forecast	5 Period Moving Av	Forecast
1	100					
2	104	4				
3	107	3				
4	110	3	3.3			
5	108	-2	1.3	113		
6	110	2	1.0	109	2.0	
7	112	2	0.7	111	1.6	112
8	114	2	2.0	113	1.4	114
9	118	4	2.7	116	1.6	115
10	110	-8	-0.7	121	0.4	120
11	112	2	-0.7	109	0.4	110
12	117	5	-0.3	111	1.0	112
13	Forecast			117		118

Figure 4-3

Step 2: For a 3 period moving average, sum the three differences and divide by 3: (4 + 3 + 3) ÷ 3 = 3.3, which is entered opposite period 4 in the moving average column.

Step 3: The forecast is the moving average plus actual demand. The first forecast is for period 5 and is obtained by adding actual demand for period 4 and the moving average for the same period: 110 + 3.3 = 113 (rounded). The forecast is entered for the fifth period.

A five period forecast is computed in the same manner except it is based on a five period moving average. Figure 4-3 illustrates the computational results.

Note the forecasts for period 13 in Figure 4-3. Actual demand is not known.

Percent of Change Model

This model is computed in the same manner as the moving average difference model except the difference is expressed as a percentage.

Step 1: Calculate the difference between demands by subtracting demand for the second period from the demand of the first period as was done above, that is, 104 − 100 = 4. Continue the process.

Step 2: Compute the percent difference by dividing the difference by the first period demand and multiplying by 100: (4 ÷ 100)(100) = 4%. Enter in period 2. Period 3 is calculated as (3 ÷ 104)(100) = 2.88. Period 4 is (3 ÷ 107)(100) = 2.80.

Step 3: The three period moving average is the sum of the three percentages divided by 3, the first being periods 2, 3, and 4: (4.0 + 2.88

+ 2.80) ÷ 3 = 3.2 (rounded). Enter in period 4. Period 5 uses the percent changes from periods 3, 4, and 5: ((2.88 + 2.8 + (-1.82)) ÷ 3 = 1.3 (rounded).

Step 4: Calculate the forecast. The first forecast is for period 5 which is actual demand for period 4 multiplied by the three period moving average and then added to actual demand for period 4: 110 + (110 x .032) = 113.5 or 114. Figure 4-4 gives the forecasts for both three period and five period moving averages.

Percent of Change Model

Period	Actual Demand	Difference	Percent Difference	3 Period Moving Av	Forecast	5 Period Moving Av	Forecast
1	100						
2	104	4	4.0				
3	107	3	2.88				
4	110	3	2.80	3.2			
5	108	-2	-1.82	1.3	114		
6	110	2	1.85	0.9	109	1.9	
7	112	2	1.82	0.6	111	1.5	112
8	114	2	1.79	1.8	113	1.3	114
9	118	4	3.51	2.4	116	1.4	115
10	110	-8	-6.78	-0.5	121	0.4	120
11	112	2	1.82	-0.5	109	0.4	110
12	117	5	4.46	-0.2	111	1.0	112
13	Forecast				117		118

Figure 4-4

Note the forecast for period 13 in Figure 4-4. Actual demand is not known.

Double moving averages as well as single moving averages can be employed as a forecasting tool. The AT time series is used in the explanations that follow.

Basic Double Moving Average

In this technique the second moving average is derived from a previously calculated single moving average. A forecast derived from the second moving average is useful when the first moving average forecast continually lags actual demand. Double moving averages help to correct for the bias and are sometimes better at minimizing the lag. Whenever forecast errors display bias, double moving average techniques are candidates for consideration.

Step 1: Calculate a three period moving average as explained above. These values have been entered into Figure 4-5 rounded to the second decimal, not to a whole number as in Figure 4-2. Note that the first moving average is entered at the third period, not the fourth period as it is in Figure 4-2. When used alone, the moving average is a forecast for the next period. In Figure 4-5, the moving average is not a forecast, thus the numbers are aligned adjacent to the last value of the calculations.

Step 2: Calculate a second moving average from the first one and enter at period 5: (103.67 + 107.0 + 108.33) ÷ 3 = 106.33. For the sixth period, the entry is 108.22, derived from the equation: (107.0 + 108.33 + 109.33) ÷ 3.

Basic Double Moving Average Model

Period	Actual Demand	3 Period Moving Av	Second Moving Av	Value of a	Value of b	Forecast
1	100					
2	104					
3	107	103.67				
4	110	107.00				
5	108	108.33	106.33	110.33	2.00	
6	110	109.33	108.22	110.44	1.11	112
7	112	110.00	109.22	110.78	0.78	112
8	114	112.00	110.44	113.56	1.56	112
9	118	114.67	112.22	117.12	2.45	115
10	110	114.00	113.56	114.44	0.44	120
11	112	113.33	114.00	112.66	-0.67	115
12	117	113.00	113.44	112.56	-0.44	112
13	Forecast					112

Figure 4-5

Step 3: Subtract the second moving average from the first and add the difference to the value of the first moving average: (108.33 − 106.33) + 108.33 = 110.33, or 2(108.33) −(106.33). This is the value of a in the equation $Y = a + b(x)$, with a and b as the values and x representing time. This is the same equation given in Chapter 3 for calculating trend. In these initial calculations, for this method only, time will always be equal to 1. This equation is appropriate for estimating demand more than one period ahead, and the method will be illustrated later.

Step 4: Calculate the b variable. Here are the calculations for the fifth period:(2 ÷ 3-1)(108.33 − 106.33) = 2.0. Note that 3-1 was used in the denominator of the first part of the equation because it represents a three period moving average. For a four period moving average 4-1 is correct, for a five period average use 5-1, etc.

Step 5: Add the a and b values: 110.33 + 2 = 112 (rounded). The x is ignored because it is always 1 in these calculations. The forecast is 112 for period 6.

Double Moving Average Difference Model

In this model, incorporating a second moving average modifies the moving average difference model; thus, the Difference and 3 Period Moving Average columns from Figure 4-3 are transported to Figure 4-6, where we start our calculations. To accommodate further computations, the three period moving averages are rounded to two decimal places.

Step 1: The second moving average is calculated from the original moving average, thus: (3.33 + 1.33 + 1.0) ÷3 = 1.89. Enter opposite period 6. For period 7, the calculations are $(1.33 + 1.0 + 0.67) \div 3 = 1.0$.

Step 2: Prepare the forecasts by adding the second (double) moving averages to the actual demands: for example, $110 + 1.89 = 111.89$, rounded to 112. Enter opposite period 7 as the forecast.

Double Moving Average Difference Model

Period	Actual Demand	Difference	3 Period Moving Av	Second Moving Av	Forecast
1	100				
2	104	4			
3	107	3			
4	110	3	3.33		
5	108	-2	1.33		
6	110	2	1.00	1.89	
7	112	2	0.67	1.00	112
8	114	2	2.00	1.22	113
9	118	4	2.67	1.78	115
10	110	-8	-0.67	1.33	120
11	112	2	-0.67	0.44	111
12	117	5	-0.33	-0.56	112
13	Forecast				116

Figure 4-6

Double Moving Average Percent of Change Model

This is the last of the moving average models to be examined. It extends the percent of change model described above.

Step 1: Copy the data from Figure 4-6; each column through the Difference column and enter in Figure 4-7. Compute the percent difference, for example: period 2 is $(4/100)*100= 4\%$; period 3 is $(3/104)*100=2.88\%$. Compute a three period moving average (round to two places). For period 4 the moving average is $(4 + 2.88 + 2.8)/3$. Then compute a second moving average of the same length as the first (The number of periods in the moving averages may be any number as previously described.).

Double Moving Average Percent of Change Model

Period	Actual Demand	Difference	Percent Difference	3 Period Moving Av	Second Moving Av	Forecast
1	100					
2	104	4	4.00			
3	107	3	2.88			
4	110	3	2.80	3.23		
5	108	-2	-1.82	1.29		
6	110	2	1.85	0.94	1.82	
7	112	2	1.82	0.62	0.95	112
8	114	2	1.79	1.82	1.13	113
9	118	4	3.51	2.37	1.60	115
10	110	-8	-6.78	-0.49	1.23	120
11	112	2	1.82	-0.48	0.47	111
12	117	5	4.46	-0.17	-0.38	112
13	Forecast					117

Figure 4-7

Step 2: Prepare the forecasts. For period 7 it is: 110 + (.0182 x 110) = 112. Note that 1.82% is divided by 100 to allow calculation.

Before leaving moving averages three subjects will be addressed: forecasting the unknown future, evaluating the goodness of the forecasts, and weighted moving averages. First, we will look at the AT series, then the other two time series given in Figure 4-1. Once that discussion is accomplished, explanation will turn to weighted moving averages.

Forecasting with Moving Averages

Only the basic double moving average model contained a method for forecasting more than one period ahead, however, approaches to forecasting several periods ahead will be discussed for each of the moving average models. Frequently, a one period (say, month) forecast is not satisfactory to the planning function. If procurement lead times are three months, for instance, a one-month forecast does not furnish the needed data.

Before discussing forecasting, per se, let's look at the time series relationship between actual demand and the forecasts in the AT time series, especially the last three periods. Purposely a wrench was thrown into the gearbox to illustrate lag and its influence upon the forecasts. In periods 10 and 11 the trend suddenly changes direction and then seems to revert to its former pattern. Note how periods 10 and 11 materially shape the future forecast. Later, the influence on forecasts in periods subsequent to period 12 will be evaluated.

Putting ourselves in the shoes of the forecaster at period 9 (assuming we do not know the demands beyond period 9) we see that all is progressing as expected: no hint of a change unless the sales department has alerted us to a temporary slide or a change in direction, which in a coordinated management environment should occur. By the end of period 11, however, there is reason to be concerned. The forecaster needs to determine if a change is taking place or if the decline is only a blip. Research is required followed by action.

The forecaster's research is done in conjunction with Sales and Marketing to discover the reasons for the drop in demand. What evidence exists? Depending upon the circumstances found there are several options available:

❖ Let the forecast technique take its natural course if the downtrend is expected to continue.

❖ Eliminate periods 10 and 11 from the time series for the purpose of forecasting. This assumes that the up-trend is correct for the future. Do this cautiously.

- ❖ Supply two forecasts (with explanation); one forecasting the down-trend and one the up- trend if there is uncertainty, thus establishing an estimate of the range of probability, but not forgetting the lagging effect. This will trigger management to examine the demand and its underlying causes.

Forecasting One Period Ahead

The procedure for forecasting one period ahead is the same as the practices explained previously. For clarification, the following calculations are provided in forecasting period 13:

- ❖ Simple moving average, Figure 4-2: the 3 period forecast is $(110 + 112 + 117) \div 3 = 113$; for the five period forecast it is $(114 + 118 + 110 + 112 + 117) \div 5 = 114$.

- ❖ Moving average difference model, Figure 4-3: the 3 period forecast is $117 + (-0.3) = 117$; the 5 period forecast is $117 + 1 = 118$.

- ❖ Percent of change model, Figure 4-4: the 3 period forecast is $117 + (117 \times -.002) = 117$; for period 5 the calculations are $117 + (117 \times .01) = 118$.

- ❖ Basic double moving average model, Figure 4-5: the forecast is $112.56 + (-.44) = 112$.

- ❖ Double moving average difference model, Figure 4-6: the forecast is $117 + (-.56) = 116$.

- ❖ Double moving average percent of change model, Figure 4-7: $117 + (-.0038 \times 117) = 117$.

- ❖ Figure 4-8 consolidates the forecasting results.

Period 13 Forecasting Results

Forecasting Models	Forecast
Simple Moving Average, 3 Period	113
Simple Moving Average, 5 Period	114
Moving Average Difference, 3 Period	117
Moving Average Difference, 5 Period	118
Percent of Change, 3 Period	117
Percent of Change, 5 Period	118
Basic Double Moving Average, 3 Period	112
Double Moving Average Difference, 3 Period	116
Double Moving Average % of Change, 3 Period	117

Figure 4-8

Which forecast is most representative in this series? Which will most nearly reflect the actual demand in period 13? Inasmuch as period 13's demand is unknown, it is impossible to determine which method will give the most accurate forecast. Later in this chapter we will explain how to evaluate and rate forecasts. After all of the individual forecasting methods have been explained in the succeeding chapters, two other techniques are described: combined forecasting in Chapter 10 and simulation forecasting in Chapter 13. These procedures allow for the incorporation of several methods into one forecasting model.

A one period misrepresentation may not be critical, but the forecasting method if not on target can distort the picture to the forecasting horizon if it is necessary to forecast more than one period ahead.

Forecasting More than One Period Ahead

Moving averages present a special problem when the forecast must project several future periods (such as when lead-times for buying raw materials or planning production levels are longer than one period). In addition to the problem of accuracy as discussed above, many of the moving average techniques do not lend themselves to estimating more than the next period except where the trend formula $a + b(x)$ can be used in the double moving average models.

Assuming that one period in our time series equals one month, a solution to forecasting more than one period (month) ahead when using single moving average techniques is to forecast by quarter.

The forecasting procedures are identical to those explained except that the demands for three months are first summed; for example: the total for periods 1, 2, and 3 is $100 + 104 + 107 = 311$. For the second three months the total is 328, for the third it is 344 and for the fourth it is 339. The moving averages are computed from these sums. The series needs to be much longer than four quarters, however.

Although the forecast is for the next three months, the process does not allow the three-month forecast to be divided into estimates by month. But it could be divided into months using an eyeball estimate of trend, if absolutely essential. Of course, there is nothing to preclude consolidating more than three months before developing a moving average providing the time series has enough periods to do so. If preparing forecasts by year, one period (year) ahead may be feasible.

Why forecast with single moving averages? The simplicity of single level moving average models may be adequate or one or more may fit well into a simulation or combined model that incorporates several techniques into one forecasting system.

Double moving averages permit the forecaster to look more than one period ahead on a period-by-period basis. First, we will look at the basic double moving average model because it allows a forecast based upon the observed trend; see Figure 4-5.

If this was the forecaster's method of choice, a shortcoming is quickly recognizable: there is a serious lag between actual and forecast (Figures 4-5 and 4-8). If a five period instead of a three period forecast had been used, a small improvement would be recognized. Remember the total number of moving average periods that gives the best result is found through experimentation because "bestness" depends upon many factors including variations within the pattern. Later in this chapter we will test for forecast goodness.

Suppose that the forecaster at the end of period (month) 12 is required to provide a forecast for the next four months. This can be accomplished by employing the trend formula $a + b(x)$ as explained above. For period 13 this is 112 as calculated previously. In each succeeding period the x gains a number, for example period 14's calculation is: $112.56 + (-.44)(2) = 112$; period 15 is $112.56 + (-.44)(3) = 111$; and period 16 is $112.56 + (-.44)(4) = 111$. Note that the model assumes a downtrend.

If there is truly a declining trend or a leveling, the forecast is reasonable. If an increasing trend as previously observed is correct, the forecast will be drifting further from reality. The method is valid but its application may not be appropriate. Again we return to the decision of investigating what is happening to demand (sales) and adjusting our approach to reflect the best estimate of the near-term future.

The double moving average difference and percent change models can also forecast more than one future period. In these models the values $\underline{a}$ and $\underline{b}$ are based on the difference, thus a modification is necessary. Two methods are discussed.

Method 1: forecasting beyond one period in this method is a continuation of the procedure for forecasting one period ahead. In the difference model (Figure 4-6) take the last known demand (in our examples period 12), which is value $\underline{a}$, add to it the product of the second moving average (which is value $\underline{b}$) times the number of periods ahead. Period 13 is 1, period 14 is 2, etc. This is the formula $a + b(x)$. Period 14 forecast is: $117 + -0.56(2) = 116$. In the percent change model (Figure 4-7), the equation for period 14 is $117 + 117*(-.0038*2) = 116$.

Method 2: in the difference model, for instance, the forecast for period 14 is $-0.1 + 0.23(2) + 117 = 117$ (rounded). The values were derived from the moving averages in Figure 4-6; that is, -0.33 and -0.56, calculated as follows: $\underline{a} = ((2*-.33) - (-.56))$ and $\underline{b} = (2/(3-1) * ((-.33-(-.56)))$. The rationale for the percent change model is the same except that percentages are divided by 100 to put them in calculation form. The forecast for period 16, in the difference model is 118; in the percent model it is 117. Note the difference in results between the several models. Like all models, the results need to be tested historically and compared with the results from other models. What is the better forecast? The answer depends upon what has been determined to be the most likely demand pattern, which depends on the reasons for the demands in periods 10 and 11.

A note on the length of time it takes to recover, for the forecast to again be on track if there is truly an increasing trend approximately equivalent to the previous trend: a minimum of two periods of known data but probably longer, depending on the demand pattern.

Methods 1 and 2 give differing results when applied to the same time series, especially when the pattern is not clear-cut. These methods are useful only after careful examination to see if the results are validated by the history: do the forecasts look like the recent past? Also notable is that the equation a + b(x) assumes a linear trend, which is not necessarily the case. It is advisable to use these methods only for the short-term. Possibly, other types of models will give better forecasts.

Forecasting With the Other Time Series

The decline in periods 10 and 11 in the increasing (AT) trend time series illustrated that problems are possible and that forecasting is not just mechanical. In this section we will examine the other two time series in relation to forecasting to see what conclusions can be drawn.

The declining trend time series demonstrates a steady decay in demand. Forecasting with the techniques described above gives the results contained in Figure 4-9. Each of the techniques employed a three period moving average.

Forecasting Results, Declining Trend

Period	Actual Demand	Simple MA	Difference Model	Percent Change	Basic Double MA	Double MA Difference	Double MA % Change
1	130						
2	126						
3	124						
4	120	127					
5	122	123	117	117			
6	118	122	121	121	118		
7	115	120	116	116	116	116	116
8	113	118	113	113	115	113	113
9	109	115	110	110	110	111	111
10	107	112	106	106	106	106	107
11	104	110	104	104	104	104	104
12	101	107	101	101	101	101	101
13	Forecast	104	98	98	98	98	98

Figure 4-9

Unlike the ascending (increasing) trend series, the declining trend does not contain variations that are outside the basic pattern, thus the lagging effect is readily noticeable in the simple moving average forecasts (here, the forecast is consistently larger than demand, but as likely the forecast may consistently be less than demand). As sophistication is added, the estimates more nearly resemble actual demand. Little difference between techniques occurs once the simple moving average is eliminated from consideration. The closeness of the estimates to each other and to actual demand is the result of the purity of the series: the steady decrease in demand resembles a straight line. Whereas five of the techniques are close in their accuracy, this is not usually the norm. Selecting the best technique, therefore, depends upon experimentation.

Long before period 12 management addresses the loss of business. However, from a forecasting viewpoint, it needs to be determined if the decline will continue or if a leveling or increase in business may be expected. With the help of Sales and Marketing and the rest of the management team, the problem needs to be dealt with and decisions made about the future. The forecaster's job may be to prepare forecasts predicated upon different scenarios. In such a case, the forecaster works closely with Finance.

The last of the three time series to be looked at is the changing pattern. The forecasts are given in Figure 4-10.

Just looking at the forecasts, the simple moving average appears to provide the better forecast, a radical departure from the results in Figure 4-9 in which the simple moving average appears to be the least effective forecast.

Forecasting Results, Changing Pattern

Period	Actual Demand	Simple MA	Difference Model	Percent Change	Basic Double MA	Double MA Difference	Double MA % Change
1	140						
2	135						
3	145						
4	127	140					
5	130	136	123	123			
6	124	134	128	129	129		
7	131	127	117	118	117	120	120
8	132	128	132	132	125	129	129
9	125	129	133	133	131	130	131
10	136	129	125	125	130	126	126
11	128	131	138	138	133	137	137
12	140	130	127	127	129	128	128
13	Forecast	135	145	146	140	142	142

Figure 4-10

Measuring forecast reliability was discussed in detail in Chapter 3. Chapter 5 expands upon that discussion. For our purpose here (simplicity), only one measure is computed: mean absolute deviation (MAD), which provides a means of comparing the accuracy of the several forecasts. We will apply it to the CP forecasts in Figure 4-10. The MAD is the average of the sum of the absolute errors; that is, the difference between forecast and actual demand, ignoring the plus and minus signs, for each period divided by the number of observations (periods). Because the forecasts start at different periods, our comparison computes period 7 through period 12 only. The MAD's are: simple moving average is 5.3, single difference moving average is 9.3, the single percent difference moving average is 9.1, the basic double moving average is 8.2, the double difference moving average is 8.5, and the double percent difference moving average is 8.3. In this case, the simple moving average model is the more accurate as it has the smallest average absolute error as measured by the MAD. Its disadvantage is that forecasting more than one period ahead is not mathematically possible.

Before we leave the subject above, there is one more consideration: does the MAD really allow us to ascertaining which model is the most accurate? There are up and down fluctuations in the historical time series. Calculating MSE gets the following results, respectively: 34.3, 108.3, 103.8, 79.3, 80.0, and 81.8. MSE verifies that MAD is valid because it also concludes that the simple moving average model is the most accurate. A last note: only six periods are included in the MAD calculation, which was done for simplicity. Normally, this is not a sufficient number of periods for verify accuracy.

The examples of the moving average models were calculated using three and five period averages. Note that any number of periods greater than one is a possibility, but three should normally be the minimum. To get a better handle on the way that moving averages respond, the reader may wish to experiment with the increasing trend series to see what forecasts result when, say, periods 10 and 11 are discounted or eliminated.

Weighted Moving Average

In the models described thus far equal weight was given to each period in the time series. If a three period moving average is calculated, for example, each of the three periods counts equally in determining the new average. An alternative method is to give more weight or importance to some of the periods in the series. The particular amount of weight that is given to each period is a matter of experimentation. Weights are applied when the forecaster believes that the most recent period of history is more representative of what may occur in the near-term and that other recent history is important but to a lesser degree. The total of the weights always equals one. Of course, reversing the weights is a possibility; that is, the most recent observation receiving the least weight, but this would be rare.

Month	Demand	Weight	Product	Weight	Product
Jan	1651	0.1	165.1		
Feb	1452	0.1	145.2		
Mar	1630	0.2	326.0	0.2	326.0
Apr	1693	0.2	338.6	0.3	507.9
May	1746	0.4	698.4	0.5	873.0
Forecast			1673.3		1706.9

Assume the following demand for the past five months. Using weights, forecast the sixth month. Each demand is multiplied by the weight, and then the results are summed to obtain the forecast. This procedure works best with time series that display at least a general trend or with those that have only moderate movement period to period.

Varying the number of periods or the value of the weights changes the resulting forecast. Exponential smoothing, as will be seen in the next section, automatically weights past data based upon the smoothing factor selected.

Exponential Smoothing

Exponential smoothing models are related to moving average models in the sense that both depend upon the historical time series. The forecast (the average) derived from exponential smoothing is the weighted sum of past demands. The weighting factor can be easily altered to account for changing market conditions. Unlike weighted moving averages, only one weight is applied to the smoothing equation, which automatically weights past demand. The weight that is given to past demand decreases exponentially. Assuming a weight (smoothing constant) of 0.3, the weights given to preceding periods are:

Period	Calculation	Weight
t		0.3
t - 1	0.3(1 - .3)	0.21
t - 2	0.3(1 - .3)(1 - .3)	0.147
t – 3	0.3(1 - .3)(1 - .3)(1 - .3)	0.103

t-4 = 0.072, all others = 0.168

The smoothing constant α, sometimes referred to as alpha, may be any number less than 1. A characteristic of exponential smoothing is that it adjusts for error. The amount of the adjustment depends upon the value of the smoothing constant: the closer that number is to 1 the greater the adjustment. Typical smoothing constant values are depicted in Figure 4-11. The relationship between these alpha values and moving average values are expressed in the equation $2 \div (N + 1)$. A smoothing constant of 0.5, for example, is approximately equivalent to a three month moving average in its response.

Exponential smoothing comes in several flavors and colors. The techniques described in this section, although not everything, should meet all business forecasting needs when exponential smoothing is appropriate. First order exponential smoothing is the fundamental approach; second order considers linear trend; and third order is suitable when the time series exhibits curvature. These equations are often referred to as single, double, and triple exponential smoothing. These methods do not adjust for seasonality. If it exists, Winter's three-parameter model can be employed.

Relationship of Alpha and the Number of Periods

Number of Periods	Alpha
3	0.50
5	0.33
6	0.29
7	0.25
9	0.20
12	0.15

Figure 4-11

First Order Smoothing

Exponential smoothing may be mathematically expressed in several forms. The one given here is simple to apply:

New Forecast = Old Forecast + α(New Demand – Old Forecast).

If the forecast for the current period is 1020 (the old forecast), the actual demand for the current period is 1090 (new demand), and the α being used is 0.3 (the smoothing constant), substituting in the equation gives this result:

$$1020 + 0.3(1090 - 1020) = 1041$$

thus, the forecast for the next period is 1041.

The three time series in Figure 4-1 are our forecasting examples. Because the first two time series display a definite trend, forecasting with first order exponential smoothing provides disappointing forecasts. These series are being saved until later. The changing pattern series is our example for first order smoothing. The estimates for this series are given in Figure 4-12 after rounding.

Demand Estimates for the CP Series

Period	Actual Demand	Forecast @ α 0.2	Forecast @ α 0.3	Forecast @ α 0.5	Forecast @ α 0.7
1	140	140	140	140	140
2	135	140	140	140	140
3	145	139	139	138	137
4	127	140	140	141	142
5	130	138	136	134	132
6	124	136	134	132	130
7	131	134	131	128	126
8	132	133	131	130	129
9	125	133	131	131	131
10	136	131	130	128	127
11	128	132	131	132	133
12	140	131	130	130	130
13		133	133	135	137
MAD		6.25	5.25	5.63	5.75
MSE		50.50	39.80	38.60	39.50
MAPE		4.81	4.02	4.29	4.37

Figure 4-12

The CP time series consists of twelve known values. Theses are the actual demands. The immediate objective is to estimate demand for period 13. To prepare the initial forecast (period 1) that begins the forecasting series, however, requires an old forecast. Since our time series begins with period 1, an old forecast is nonexistent. To overcome this problem the actual demand for period 1 is entered into the equation as both the old forecast and the new demand. Obviously, the forecast for period 2 equals the demand for period 1. (The reader can see the logic by solving the equation.) It takes several periods for the forecasts to settle-in when using this procedure; however, it is satisfactory as the objective is to forecast demand for period 13. More complex procedures for determining the initial old forecast are possible, but generally initializing period 1, as we have done, provides satisfactory estimates.

Following are the computations for several time periods. Note that the forecast for period 4 is rounded at 140 in Figure 4-12. For computing the next forecast, however, the forecast before rounding is applied, that is 140.2.

Period 5: 140.2 + 0.2(127 – 140.2) = 137.56 (rounds to 138)

Period 6: 137.56 + 0.2(130 – 137.56) = 136.05 (rounded to 136)

Period 7: 136.05 + 0.2(124 – 136.05) = 133.64 (rounded to 134)

Which smoothing constant is the logical choice? Forecasts were prepared from four representative smoothing constants to be able to evaluate accuracy. MAD, MAPE and MSE were calculated with α 0.3 being the lowest MAD and MAPE. The MSE results are unclear as α 0.3, 0.5, and 0.7 are roughly the same. MSE by its nature punishes large individual errors more severely, thus it *possibly* may be discounted in this series in light of the other two measures; however, a review of the magnitude of errors may be appropriate; that is, examine the pattern to see what future results may be anticipated. If the objective is to minimize the affect of large errors, MSE may be important in selecting a technique. To give the forecasting method time to adjust, the calculations for accuracy were begun at period 5 and considered the forecasts through period 12. The MAD and MAPE differences between α 0.3 and 0.5 are small indicating that either is a logical choice based upon accuracy; that is either will give estimates, on average, that are percentage-wise roughly the same. Further trials could be conducted, probably between 0.3 and 0.5; however, more accuracy, if achieved, would be minimal.

Remember, MAD is calculated by summing the differences between actual and forecast while ignoring the signs and then dividing by the number of observations. MSE squares the differences, sums, and divides by the number of observations. MAPE is calculated by dividing the absolute error (signs ignored) for each period by the demand and multiplying by 100 to give the result as a percentage, then summing the column and dividing by the number of observations.

The subject of forecast reliability and accuracy was visited in detail in Chapter 3 and is revisited in Chapter 5, together with explanations of tracking and developing a forecasting range.

Second Order Smoothing

Whereas only one period ahead can be estimated with first order exponential smoothing, any number of periods can be forecast with second order smoothing, subject only to practicality. An important limitation is that demand patterns often change over time, thus the forecaster needs to be alert to this probability. As will be seen in Chapter 13, operational forecasts by month are often required for the next twelve months. Methods for forecasting that far ahead will be discussed in Chapters 12 and 13.

The concept of second order smoothing is analogous to double moving averages. Both correct for linear trend by employing a second smoothed average and equations that adjust for trend. To arrive at a forecast for the next period and beyond, a series of five equations are solved sequentially. Figure 4-13, the increasing trend model at α 0.2, is the example illustrated.

Second Order Exponential Smoothing at α0.2

AT Time Series

Period	Demand	First Smoothing Equation	Second Smoothing Equation	Value of a	Value of b	Forecast	Forecast Rounded
1	100	100.000	100.000	100.000			
2	104	100.800	100.160	101.440	0.160		
3	107	102.040	100.536	103.544	0.376	101.600	
4	110	103.632	101.155	106.109	0.619	103.920	
5	108	104.506	101.825	107.186	0.670	106.728	107
6	110	105.605	102.581	108.628	0.756	107.856	108
7	112	106.884	103.442	110.326	0.860	109.384	109
8	114	108.307	104.415	112.199	0.973	111.187	111
9	118	110.246	105.581	114.910	1.166	113.172	113
10	110	110.196	106.504	113.889	0.923	116.076	116
11	112	110.557	107.315	113.799	0.811	114.812	115
12	117	111.846	108.221	115.471	0.906	114.610	115
13						116.377	116

Figure 4-13

Step 1: The first equation is essentially the same as the equation for first order smoothing, recast slightly because it does not constitute a forecast. It is the first essential element.

Old Smoothed Value + α(New Value – Old smoothed Value)

First smoothing equation, period 2: $100 + 0.2(104 - 100) = 100.8$ (new value)

First smoothing equation, period 12: $110.557 + 0.2(117 - 110.557) = 111.846$

Step 2: Compute the second exponential smoothing equation to adjust the value obtained in the first equation.

Old Smoothed Value + α (New Value – Old Smoothed Value)

Second equation, period 2: $100 + 0.2(100.8 - 100) = 100.16$

Second equation, period 12: $107.315 + 0.2(111.846 - 107.315) = 108.221$

Step 3: Compute the value of a which is the first parameter of the forecast equation.

2(First Equation) – Second Equation

Value of a, period 2: $2(100.8) - 100.16 = 101.44$

Value of a, period 12: $2(111.846) - 108.221 = 115.471$

Step 4: Compute the value of b, the trend adjustment factor. In this equation 0.2 represents the smoothing constant. If 0.3 had been the smoothing constant, it would have been used in this equation (as $0.3/(1 - 0.3)$); similarly with other smoothing constants.

(Trend Adjustment)(First Equation – Second Equation)

Value of b, period 2: $(0.2 \div (1 - 0.2))(100.8 - 100.16) = 0.16$

Value of b, period 12: $(0.2 \div (1 - 0.2))(111.846 - 108.221) = 0.906$

Step 5: Prepare the forecast, which utilizes the trend equation a + b(x). In this case the x, which is time, equals 1 because the estimate is for one period ahead. Therefore, the estimate for period 3 is $101.44 + 0.16(1) = 101.6$. For period 13 the estimate is $115.471 + 0.906(1) = 116.377$. Periods that follow 13 take on the next higher x value, thus period 14 is $115.471 + 0.906(2) = 117.283$; period 15's x value is 3, and so forth.

Numbers have been rounded to three places rather than whole numbers to be more exact in our calculations of this series of equations. Slight differences may occur in some of the calculations due to rounding.

Should forecasts be rounded to a whole number? If dealing in units, which are never fractions, rounding to a whole number is appropriate for presentation, but for future calculations, two or more decimals places may be proper. If the forecast represents dollars, most likely several decimal places provides a better picture, as when 116.377 means thousands or millions of dollars. The same is applicable to units if they represent thousands, for instance.

The trend equation presented above is available to forecast more than one period in the future. The method assumes a linear trend. The time factor is modified to signify the number of periods ahead that the forecaster wishes to estimate, as in the examples following. Period 13 is one period ahead, period 14 two periods ahead, and so forth.

$$a + b(x)$$

$$115.471 + 0.906(2) = 117.283 \text{ or } 117 \text{ (period 14)}$$
$$115.471 + 0.906(3) = 118.189 \text{ or } 118 \text{ (period 15)}$$
$$115.471 + 0.906(6) = 120.907 \text{ or } 121 \text{ (period 18)}$$

The forecasts show a continuing rising trend as may be expected with an α of 0.2 (see Figure 4-11). With the decrease in demand in periods 10 and 11 there is the question of whether the trend is continuing or changing, as was previously discussed.

Which smoothing constant provides the most accurate results based upon the accuracy measures previously defined? Figure 4-14 compares the forecasts for the AT series. Calculation of the error measures starts at period 6 to give the series time to "settle-in".

AT Time Series Forecasts and Accuracy Measures

Period	Demand	Forecast 0.2	Forecast 0.3	Forecast 0.5	Forecast 0.7
6	110	108	110	110	109
7	112	109	111	111	111
8	114	111	113	113	113
9	118	113	115	115	116
10	110	116	118	120	121
11	112	115	115	112	109
12	117	115	114	112	111
13		116	116	117	119
14		117	117	118	121
15		118	118	119	123
MAD		3.38	2.85	2.75	3.57
MSE		13.32	13.58	18.09	24.21
MAPE		2.99	2.52	2.44	3.16

Figure 4-14

The forecasting methodology presumes a return to the former increasing trend. If the facts demonstrate or solid judgment agrees, the question becomes which forecast (smoothing constant) is most representative of the near-term future? Both MAD and MAPE suggest that α 0.3 or 0.5 will probably best express the future. The MSE at 18.09, however, is a bit disquieting, but one large error accounts for a substantial part of the MSE. Once the actual demands are known for the next two periods, a more informed decision is possible. For the short-term, a decision is needed.

The company has good reasons to believe that the upward trend will continue and probably with roughly the same pattern. As a result of this review, the forecaster does one more calculation: determines the average gain per period. This was done simply, by finding the difference between each of the actual demands for the first nine periods (pluses and minuses retained), then summing and dividing by the number of differences (which is 8). The average found this way is 2.25 per period, indicating that on average the gain in succeeding periods will be roughly 2.25 units per period. Because of the rule of uncertainty, the forecaster presented a forecast range with 0.5 as the low estimate and 0.7 as the high estimate. This is a one-time forecast. A more mathematically precise way in which to calculate range is standard deviation. The forecasting eyeball will be acutely focused on period 13's actual sales.

How good are the projections for the declining trend and changing pattern time series? Figure 4-15 summarizes the forecasting results.

The smoothing constant 0.5 in the declining trend series has the lowest forecast error in all three categories. The projections for the next three periods are consistent with the historical pattern, thus it is the logical choice. At the close of each demand period, forecast error is reevaluated, but the smoothing constant is not necessarily changed in light of one forecast.

Forecast Summary, DT and CP Series, Second Order Smoothing

Series	α	MAD	MSE	MAPE	Forecast Period 13	Forecast Period 14	Forecast Period 15
DT	0.20	4.40	19.68	4.02	102	100	98
	0.30	2.16	5.12	1.96	99	97	94
	0.50	0.89	1.31	0.80	98	95	93
	0.70	1.10	1.94	0.97	98	95	92
CP	0.20	5.88	48.14	4.44	132	132	132
	0.30	6.43	50.36	4.85	135	136	136
	0.50	7.29	61.41	5.51	140	142	144
	0.70	8.35	89.75	6.32	144	148	153
	0.15	5.49	47.06	4.17	131	131	131

Figure 4-15

In the changing pattern series, the forecaster calculated estimates utilizing the first four smoothing constants depicted in Figure 4-15. It is obvious that the smallest forecast error occurs with α 0.2. Because of this, an additional forecast at α 0.15 was run with an even lower forecast error. Increasing the smoothing constant above 0.3 was considered inconsistent with the historical pattern (it considers to few historical observations). As a further check, the forecaster did a simple pattern review: determining if the difference between each succeeding period was an increase or a decrease in demand. For example: the demand in period two is less than the demand in period one (a minus); demand in period 3 is an increase (a plus). The general pattern derived from this simple approach indicates that usually a decrease is followed by an increase, with the opposite also true. The decision is to determine which of the three forecasts is most likely to produce the smallest error after the next period, especially in light of the historical pattern. Alpha 0.15 was eliminated from consideration because it considers the past twelve periods and only ten periods are available (Figure 4-11). The forecasts do not follow the pattern because the method averages past data, a limitation to be lived with. However, knowing the pattern, it occurred to the forecaster that a high smoothing constant might give better results because it reacts quickly to the last actual demand. A 0.8 constant was tried. It reacted quickly and roughly followed the plus/minus pattern, but the gaps between demand and forecast in the historical series were unacceptably large and the forecasts beyond period 13 increased by six demand unit or more each period. The MAD, for instance, was 9.52. In the end, 0.2 was selected even considering the shortcomings.

In selecting a smoothing constant, a forecaster is not limited to the number of smoothing constants that were tried. Preferably, the historical series used will be longer than twelve periods.

Third Order Smoothing

Third order (triple) exponential smoothing is an appropriate technique when curvature is exhibited in the historical time series. However, there are different varieties of curves, and one technique does not fit all. The process of curve fitting is an attempt to define the parameters of the trend, which allows reasonable forecasts to be developed. Three curves are presented in Figure 4-16. The pattern of these curves is typical of the type in which third order smoothing can be successful, however, this method is viable for other curves. Figure 4-17 provides the data and the forecasts made from one of the three curvilinear models.

Three Demand Series

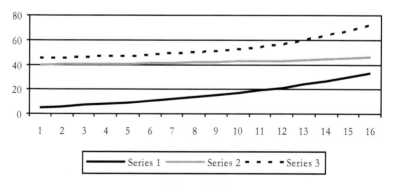

Figure 4-16

Chapter 6 examines other methodologies that may be applied to curve fitting, the technique depending upon the form of the curve. The section describing non-linear trends in Chapter 6 should be read in conjunction with this section.

Recall that in the linear trend model $Y = a + b(x)$ there are two parameters. In the quadratic model, there are three parameters as expressed by the equation $Y = a + b(x) + c(x)^2$.

Initially, the value of each parameter must be estimated from the historical data. This can be accomplished through experimentation until a reasonable fit is obtained. These values form the core of a complex quadratic model that refines the initial values. These values are then exponentially smoothed. However, this forecasting process can be simplified.

Demand in Figure 4-17 is known for sixteen periods. In our initial trial-and-error calculations the first twelve periods are used, with the remaining periods reserved to test the estimated values.

Series 1 Forecast Table

Period	Demand	Difference	1st Forecast	% Difference	2nd Forecast	% Difference	3rd Forecast	% Difference
1	5.1		c=0.1		0.102		0.1027	
2	6.0	0.9						
3	7.0	1.0	6.3	10.0	6.3	9.7	6.3	9.7
4	8.0	1.0	7.1	11.3	7.1	10.9	7.1	10.7
5	9.1	1.1	8.1	11.0	8.2	10.4	8.2	10.2
6	10.6	1.5	9.3	12.3	9.4	11.6	9.4	11.3
7	12.0	1.4	10.7	10.8	10.8	10.0	10.8	9.7
8	13.6	1.6	12.3	9.6	12.4	8.6	12.5	8.3
9	15.5	1.9	14.1	9.0	14.3	8.0	14.3	7.6
10	17.0	1.5	16.1	5.3	16.3	4.1	16.4	3.7
11	19.0	2.0	18.3	3.7	18.5	2.4	18.6	2.0
12	21.0	2.0	20.7	1.4	21.0	0.1	21.1	0.4
13	24.0	3.0	23.3	2.9	23.6	1.5	23.8	1.0
14	27.0	3.0	26.1	3.3	26.5	1.9	26.6	1.4
15	30.0	3.0	29.1	3.0	29.6	1.5	29.7	1.0
16	33.0	3.0	32.3	2.1	32.8	0.6	33.0	0.0

All calculations were done before rounding, data was then rounded, except % differences are those *before* rounding.

Figure 4-17

The first requirement is to assign a value to a. This value is defined as the demand for period 1. The other two values are determined though experimentation. The series beginning with 5.1 (series 1) is used as our example, and period 12 as the initial period of parameter estimation.

The values for b and c are estimated simultaneously. Not knowing a good starting value, begin with a middle value of 0.5, as follows, with the x factors representing time.

$$a + b(x) + c(x)^2$$
$$5.1 + 0.5(12) + 0.5(12)^2$$
$$5.1 + 6 + 72 = 83.1$$

The result is obviously too high as the actual demand for period 12 is 21. The value for c is the primary culprit because of squaring the time value. Various approaches are possible, for example, lower the value for c but not for b: b at 0.5 and c at 0.2, with the resulting estimate being 39.9. Continuing on this track arrive at b and c values equaling 0.1. The estimate is 20.7, reasonably close to actual demand. The estimates for this procedure are contained in the 1st forecast column of Figure 4-17.

The percentage difference between demand and forecast is 2.1% in period 16. Why are the percentage differences much higher in most of the previous periods? Looking at the difference column tells a story of an increasing trend in each succeeding period.

Further refinement can be accomplished mathematically. Below are two examples. The first calculates a new value for c at period 12, the second a new value at period 16. The forecasting results are given in Figure 4-17 in the 2nd and 3rd forecast columns. Calculations were done before rounding. Rounding after calculations resulted in small differences.

$$5.1 + 0.1(12) + (x)12^2 = 21$$
$$5.1 + 1.2 + 144x = 21$$
$$144x = 21.0 - 6.3; x = 0.102$$
$$5.1 + 0.1(16) + (x)16^2 = 33$$
$$x = 0.1027$$

Of course, the forecaster could continue to refine the original estimate, probably with little improvement. Now, the forecaster is ready to forecast demand for periods beyond period 16. If, for instance, a forecast for period 20 is desired the equation is solved as illustrated here:

$$5.1 + .1(20) + 0.1027(20)^2 = 48.2$$

The forecast using 0.1 for the c value is 47.1, using 0.102 it is 47.9. Of concern to the forecaster is the rapidly increasing demand. Assuming that this is a new product introduction, at some point there will be a leveling in sales, which changes the nature of the curve. At that point, it will best respond to growth curve methodology (Chapter 6).

The rate of forecast change can be computed by calculating first and second differences. With series 1, $c = 0.1027$ as example, the arithmetic can best illustrate the procedure. Calculations are made before rounding.

Period 4 minus period 3: $7.1432 - 6.3243 = 0.8189$ and period 5 minus period 4: $8.1675 - 7.1432 = 1.0243$.

These are first differences. Subtracting first differences results in: $1.0243 - 0.8189 = 0.2054$; this is the second difference. The second difference is a constant, the same number in each forecast period, occurring whenever first differences are subtracted. Thus, the forecast for period 6 is $1.0243 + 0.2054 + 8.1675 = 9.3972$.

When $c = 0.1$ the constant is 0.2 and when $c = 0.102$ it is 0.204.

How good is the process when forecasting the other two time series? The slope in time series 2 is not as pronounced as that in series 1, thus the percentage differences between demand and forecast will be lower in this series than it is in series 1. (Percentage differences were calculated before rounding.) The difference in slope is apparent when comparing the difference columns. After refinement, the values for b and c are 0.1 and 0.01719. The forecasts for the first sixteen periods (the periods of known demand) are given in Figure 4-18.

The slope in series 3 is more pronounced than that in series 2. Although somewhat different, it is comparable to the slope in series 1. Trial-and-error resulted in the values for b and c as 0.2 and 0.093. The forecasts are given in Figure 4-18. Note that the parameters b and c always interact; therefore, different combinations that give comparable results are possible whenever this process is used.

Series 2 and 3 Forecast Table

Period	Demand Series 2	Difference	Forecast	Percent Difference	Demand Series 3	Difference	Forecast	Percent Difference
1	40.0				45.0			
2	40.1	0.1			45.2	0.2		
3	40.3	0.2	40.5	0.4	45.8	0.6	46.4	1.4
4	40.6	0.3	40.7	0.2	46.5	0.7	47.3	1.7
5	40.8	0.2	40.9	0.3	47.2	0.7	48.3	2.4
6	41.1	0.3	41.2	0.3	48.0	0.8	49.5	3.2
7	41.2	0.1	41.5	0.8	48.9	0.9	51.0	4.2
8	41.8	0.6	41.9	0.2	49.9	1.0	52.6	5.3
9	42.0	0.2	42.3	0.7	51.0	1.1	54.3	6.5
10	42.5	0.5	42.7	0.5	52.3	1.3	56.3	7.6
11	43.0	0.5	43.2	0.4	54.1	1.8	58.5	8.0
12	43.2	0.2	43.7	1.1	56.5	2.4	60.8	7.6
13	43.8	0.6	44.2	0.9	60.0	3.5	63.3	5.5
14	44.5	0.7	44.8	0.6	63.5	3.5	66.0	4.0
15	45.1	0.6	45.4	0.6	68.0	4.5	68.9	1.4
16	46.0	0.9	46.0	0.0	72.0	4.0	72.0	0.0

Figure 4-18

The curves in these examples are relatively "pure", that is, there is little random fluctuation (noise) in the time series. Frequently, the opposite happens. If there are spikes and dips randomly occurring, the procedure requires that they be discounted. Graph the curve without these fluctuations before applying the process. This provides more accurate initial values. How spikes and dips are added to the forecasts depends upon the reasons they occurred (if that can be determined). A number of possibilities are described at the end of Chapter 1.

If the random fluctuations are moderate, it may be appropriate to calculate the values of the parameters, as the curve exists, without trying to eliminate the noise. In the real world, there are usually unknown factors that are normal and often unidentifiable.

If the forecasts at both periods -- in our example periods 12 and 16 -- do not line up reasonably, it is usually best to align the parameters to the last period. Testing several possibilities will probably indicate a solution. In many instances b = 0.1 will be the best factor at least as a starting value, but not always. Testing others at slightly higher numbers will tell the story.

The process explained in this section has greatly simplified the forecasting of the general order of curves described, thereby avoiding the computational complexity of third order exponential smoothing.

Winters' Model

When a time series contains linear trend and seasonality, Winters' model can be used to predict future demand. Results are comparable to second order exponential smoothing with the added feature of a seasonal coefficient. As new data become available, the model revises the forecasting equations. Winters' model is complex, but like third order smoothing it is possible to simplify and generally get good results, especially when there is at least a minimum of two years of history. In the example provided, a comparison of estimates is made between the simplified approach and Winters' model.

There are three parameters to be estimated: the starting point (intercept), the slope (trend), and the seasonal index.

A graph of the example time series and the estimated trend line appears in Figure 4-19. The time series contains both a linear trend and seasonality.

Linear Trend with Seasonal Effect

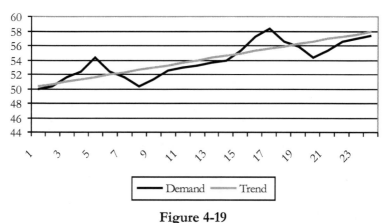

Figure 4-19

Linear trend values and seasonal factors are given in Figure 4-20. The procedure for arriving at these values is explained in steps 2 and 3.

The steps for calculating a forecast with Winters' methodology or with the simplified method are:

Step 1: Plot the demand on a graph as illustrated in Figure 4-19, then free hand, draw the trend (which will be a straight line). The trend line should intersect the demand in a way the divides sthe demand as equally as possible. The trend line at the middle period passes through the average of the demands. To get the average, sum the twenty-four periods of the demand and divide by twenty-four. In our data series the average is 53.95 or 54; therefore, the trend line at period 12 intersects 54 on the vertical scale. Now, draw the trend line. This method should give very good results when testing the forecasts made there from against known demand beyond the twenty-fourth period. Periods 25 through 30 are known demands in the example but are not used in the calculations. It may sometimes be necessary to make more than one attempt before the trend is optimized. A formal procedure for constructing a trend consists of employing regression (least squares) to calculate a trend line after deseasonalizing the data, as explained in Chapter 3. However, this procedure should be unnecessary.

Step 2: Determining the trend line values requires two calculations: first, subtract the value at period 24 (the last period in the series) from the value at period 1 and divide by the number of periods: $(58.5 - 50) \div 24 = 0.3542$. This is the estimated slope. The values for periods 1 and 24 are taken from the graph, not from actual demand; therefore, the vertical scale when drawing the graph should be divided into fractions for accuracy. The graph in Figure 4-19 is not as detailed as is needed. Second, solve the equation $a + b(x)$ to obtain the trend line value: $50 + 0.3542(1) = 50.3542$, which is the value for period 1. For period 2 the equation is $50 + 0.3542(2) = 50.7084$. Note that the trend value increases by 0.3542 each period. In this example the a value (the intercept) is the same as the demand for period 1. This may not always be true.

Step 3: Divide the demand by the trend line value to obtain the seasonal factor: $50 \div 50.3542 = 0.99297$. The seasonal factor for period 2 is: $50.3 \div 50.7084 = 0.99195$.

Data for Linear Trend and Seasonal Effects

Period	Demand	Trend Line Value	Seasonal Factor	Period	Demand	Trend Line Value	Seasonal Factor
1	50.0	50.3542	0.99297	13	53.6	54.6046	0.98160
2	50.3	50.7084	0.99195	14	54	54.9588	0.98255
3	51.6	51.0626	1.01052	15	55.3	55.313	0.99977
4	52.4	51.4168	1.01912	16	57.2	55.6672	1.02754
5	54.4	51.771	1.05078	17	58.4	56.0214	1.04246
6	52.4	52.1252	1.00527	18	56.5	56.3756	1.00221
7	51.6	52.4794	0.98324	19	55.8	56.7298	0.98361
8	50.4	52.8336	0.95394	20	54.4	57.084	0.95298
9	51.3	53.1878	0.96451	21	55.3	57.4382	0.96277
10	52.6	53.542	0.98241	22	56.6	57.7924	0.97937
11	53.0	53.8962	0.98337	23	57.0	58.1466	0.98028
12	53.3	54.2504	0.98248	24	57.4	58.5008	0.98118

Figure 4-20

This is the initial information needed to begin the simplified method of exponential smoothing containing trend and seasonal factors. They update the estimates of the intercept, the slope of the trend line and the seasonal factors. This data is sufficient to forecast demand without further mathematical manipulation. As actual demands become known, the steps above can be repeated to obtain updated values. Here is the method for forecasting with the data that has been developed so far: solve the equation a + b(x), then modify the answer by the seasonal factor. Demands for periods 25 through 30 are known and were saved to test the forecasting technique. The seasonal factors are averaged. Assume the periods are months beginning in January; therefore, period 25 is also a January, as are periods 1 and 13.

$$\text{Period 25: } 50 + 0.3542(25) = 58.855$$

$$[(0.99297 + 0.98160) \div 2] * 58.855 = 58.1$$

$$\text{Period 30: } 50 + 0.3542(30) = 60.626$$

$$[(1.0053 + 1.0022) \div 2] * 60.626 = 60.9$$

By tweaking, the slope of the line can be "fine-tuned". This may or may not improve the forecasts. A slight alteration, for instance, gives a slope of 0.3292. Figure 4-21 compares these forecasts and the one calculated with the complete Winters' method.

Step 4: The above procedure is the simplified method of forecasting. Steps 4 and 5 describe the process of forecasting using the Winters' method, which entails solving three exponential smoothing equations. (Below, another approach to the model is described.) The estimated intercept is represented by the letter $\underline{a}$. The letter $\underline{b}$ represents the estimated slope. The letter $\underline{c}$ (or S) represents the estimated seasonal factor. Each of the equations incorporates a smoothing constant (α). The value(s) selected may be the same or different in each of the equations. At times, forecasters use a higher smoothing constant for the seasonal factor because of fewer data points. The forecaster assigns the values to the smoothing constants. If different α are selected for each of the equations, the rate of change will vary with each equation. However, one α will often be sufficient for all the equations. Experimentation should reveal which value or values are best. Figure 4-11 illustrates the relationship between various smoothing constants (alpha) and the number of periods considered. Period 24 is the forecaster's starting point (see Figure 4-20). The equations are:

a = α(current demand ÷ seasonal factor) + (1 - α)(last trend line value + last estimated slope)

$$0.2(57.4 \div 0.9818) + (1-0.2)(58.147 + 0.3542) = 11.693 + 46.8 = 58.493$$

0.9818 is the average seasonal factor for the previous two Decembers (periods 12 and 24).

b = α(estimated intercept – last trend line value) + (1 - α)(last estimated slope).

$$0.2(58.493 - 58.147) + (1-0.2)(0.3542) = 0.069 + 0.283 = 0.352$$

0.3542 is the slope from Step 2.

c = α(current demand ÷ a) + (1 - α)(seasonal factor).

The seasonal factor is the average for the previously like months. Rather than this procedure, a simple averaging is used below.

0.2(57.4÷58.493) + (1-0.2)(0.9818) = 0.1963 + 0.7854 = 0.9817

Step 5: The forecast result from solving the equation [a + b(x)] (seasonal average). The seasonal average is for the like months of the month being forecast. Forecasting period 25, which is January in this example, means averaging the two previous January's seasonal factors.

Forecast period 25 = [58.493 + 0.352(1)](0.9873) = 58.1

Forecast period 30 = [58.493 +0.352(6)](1.0037) = 60.8

An alternate method for forecasting with Winters' method is to apply the three equations beginning with the first period. This method updates the values in each period. The starting point is period 0. Several techniques exist for determining the values of a, b, and c in period 0. Any logical approach is satisfactory. Although the later values will vary depending upon the period 0 numbers, the forecasts will be essentially the same. The regression equation above is used for forecasting, with period 24 data as the forecasting base and x = 1 for period 25.

Here is a partial series:

Period	Demand	a	b	c
0		50.0	0.3542	1.0
1	50.0	50.2834	0.3400	0.9989
2	50.3	50.570	0.3294	0.9980
23	57.0	57.3676	0.2880	0.9918
24	57.4	57.6937	0.2957	0.9928

Variation because of rounding

In these equations, mathematical notations may vary for the smoothing constants, for example, α in a, β in b, and γ or σ in c (which is also designated S).

To prepare a forecast for known data solve the equation [a+b(x)] (seasonal index), with x always being 1. The forecasts for periods 2 and 24 are:

Period 2: (50.5700 + 0.3294) * 0.9980 = 50.8 (demand = 50.3)

Period 24: (57.6937 + 0.2957) * 0.9928 = 57.6 (demand = 57.4)

The actual demands in the example are fairly straightforward with only minimum random fluctuation. If random fluctuations are significant, the estimates may not be as close to the demands as those in Figure 4-21.

Forecasts

Period	Demand	Forecast 0.3542	% Difference	Forecast 0.3292	% Difference	Winters' Forecast	% Difference
25	57.9	58.1	0.3	57.7	0.3	58.1	0.3
26	58.1	58.5	0.7	58.0	0.2	58.4	0.5
27	59.4	59.9	0.8	59.4	0.0	59.5	0.2
28	61.1	61.3	0.3	60.9	0.3	61.3	0.3
29	62.1	63.1	1.6	62.6	0.8	63.1	1.6
30	61.3	60.9	0.7	60.4	1.5	60.8	0.8

Figure 4-21

Which of the approaches provides the best demand estimates? In most instances the simplified version will give very good results, comparable to the more formal methodologies. If there is a limited demand history, however, the formal Winters' methods will likely provide better forecasts. Comparing results from trials using these methods may be appropriate.

Adaptive Filters

Exponential smoothing and moving average forecasts are grounded in historical data, the assumption being that the future will resemble the past. This is a reasonable expectation when dealing with the near-term (and perhaps mid-term) future. Exponential smoothing has an advantage over most moving average techniques because it weights each past observation automatically, giving more weight to the most recent periods.

Adaptive filtering also depends upon history but its advantage is that it determines during the forecasting process the most appropriate set of weights. The weights are adjusted based upon previous forecast error, with the idea of minimizing mean squared error as it occurs in a number of forecasts. Thus, adaptive filtering is a process of adjusting the weights through the observation of the errors contained in the previous forecasts.

Quarterly Demand

	Year 1	Year 2	Year 3
1st Quarter	1400	1550	1700
2nd Quarter	1450	1600	1750
3rd Quarter	1600	1750	1900
4th Quarter	1500	1650	1800

Figure 4-22

The demands that are used in the adaptive filtering example are given in Figure 4-22. This time series is without randomness in order to show more clearly the methodology. There are two distinct parts to the forecasting procedure: first, the process of training (adjusting) the initial weights until minimum error is achieved; second, forecasting with these optimized weights. Minimization does not necessarily mean reducing error to zero. Rather, it implies bringing error to a level that if further training was undertaken the improvement would be negligible.

Step 1: Specify the number of weights to be used and their value and the value for the learning constant (designated k). If the time series is fundamentally a linear trend without extensive fluctuations between data points, two weights are probably satisfactory, as they depict a straight line. In a monthly time series that displays a cyclical pattern of roughly twelve months, for example, twelve weights are appropriate. If a seasonal aspect is indicated, the number of weights should encompass the total seasonal cycle. Twelve weights are appropriate if demand is expressed in monthly increments. It appears that the demand in Figure 4-22 contains both a trend and a seasonal component. Based on that assumption and because this is quarterly data, four weights are selected. The sum of the weights always equals 1. Individual weights may be equal in value (in this case $1/N$ or 0.25) or more weight may be given to the period closest to the current actual (as when there is an increasing trend). As a start .25 is used for each of the four weights.

The value of the learning constant must be chosen. The larger the value (the closer to 1) the more reactive it will be to finding the optimum set of weights. To choose a value near 1, however, causes the adjustments to overreact to random behavior and defeats the purpose of finding the best weights. Research has revealed that in most cases a reasonable weight is .08 ±.01, especially applicable when there is randomness in the demand, which is usual. With the help of a computer various weights can be tried to see which performs best, that is, which has the most favorable decline in the mean squared error, particularly in the early stages. For this example .08 has been chosen

The process in the steps that follow is the means to adjust the weights by repetitive application of the equation:

$$NW = W + 2ke(x)$$

Where NW = the revised (new) weight
W = the old or initial weight
k = the learning constant
e = the forecast error
x = observed values (actual demand)

Step 2: Solve the forecasting equation below to determine the starting point for adjusting the weights. The beginning application uses the initial weights (.25). Since there are four weights the forecast is prepared for the first quarter of year 2 (the fifth period). The forecast is actually the beginning adjustment of the weights. The forecast for the fifth period is equal to the sum of the actual demands for the first four quarters after they have been multiplied by the initially assigned weights. The actual demands have been offset by three decimal places to keep the weighting factors accurate. This procedure normalizes the data. Had an offset not been made it would be readily apparent that the resulting weighting factors would not be usable.

$$F = W_1 x_1 + W_2 x_2 + W_3 x_3 + W_4 x_4$$

$$F = .25(1.4) + .25(1.45) + .25(1.6) + .25(1.5) =$$

$$0.35 + 0.3625 + 0.4 + 0.375 = 1.4875$$

Since all the weights are equal in value the arithmetic can be simplified by summing the demands and multiplying by 0.25: 5.950 x . 25 = 1.4875.

Step 3: Compute the forecast error by subtracting the forecast from the demand for the first quarter of year 2.

$$e = 1.550 - 1.4875 = 0.0625.$$

Step 4: Determine the weights to be assigned in forecasting the second quarter, year 2, by solving the equation for adjusting weights. Weights are adjusted for each of the first four quarters.

$$NW_1 = 0.25 + 2(.08)(0.0625)(1.400) = 0.264$$

$$NW_2 = 0.25 + 2(.08)(0.0625)(1.450) = 0.2645$$

$$NW_3 = 0.25 + 2(.08)(0.0625)(1.600) = 0.266$$

$$NW_4 = 0.25 + 2(.08)(0.0625)(1.500) = 0.265$$

Adjust the weights to equal 1 by adding the four raw weights and dividing each by the sum: the sum of the weights is 1.0595; 0.264 ÷ 1.0595 = 0.2492. Therefore, the new weights are 0.2492, 0.2496, 0.2511, and 0.2501.

Step 5: Continue to train the weights by repeating the process for each future period in the series. Start the calculations with each succeeding quarter. The forecast above was for the first quarter of year 2 and utilized the four quarters of year 1. The next forecast is for the second quarter of year 2 and utilizes the second, third, and fourth quarters of year 1 and the first quarter of year 2.

$$F = 0.2492(1.45) + 0.2496(1.6) + 0.2511(1.5) + 0.2501(1.55) = 1.5251$$

Compute the forecast error:

$$1.600 - 1.5251 = 0.0749.$$

Find the new weights:

$$0.2492 + 2(.08)(0.0749)(1.45) = 0.2666$$

$$0.2496 + 2(.08)(0.0749)(1.6) = 0.2688$$

$$0.2511 + 2(.08)(0.0749)(1.5) = 0.2691$$

$$0.2501 + 2(.08)(0.0749)(1.55) = 0.2687$$

Adjust the weights: the sum of the raw weights is 1.0732; 0.2666 ÷ 1.0732 = 0.2484. Thus, the new weights are 0.2484, 0.2505, 0.2507, and 0.2504.

Continue the updating process until the improvement obtained with each succeeding iteration is negligible. Once all known data are processed (through the fourth quarter, year 3 in this case) begin again with the first quarter, year 1 using the latest set of new weights. The number of iterations required depends upon the pattern of the demands and the amount of random fluctuation contained in the time series.

Mean squared error (MSE) is a running calculation. For each forecast, square the difference between the demands and forecasts. At the second period, for example, sum the two squared differences and divide by two. At the third period, sum the three squared differences and divide by three, and so on.

With every iteration a new set of weights becomes available, however, throughout the processing in the example series the weights hover near 0.25. After four iterations improvements are only slight, considered inconsequential, thus, in practicality the series is repeating as seen by the MSE's, and it continues to do so indicating that a practical minimum has been reached. If the percent difference between demand and forecast is computed for each period, the percentages are roughly in the 3% to 4% range except for the third quarters when the approximate percentage is 10%. The third quarters are those in which the seasonal component exists. Forecasts made with the computed weights and with 0.25 give the same results. Thus, it is fair to conclude that 0.25 is optimal. This is not a normal situation; this time series is unusual in that only four iterations revealed the best weights to use. Note that the forecasts did not cope with the seasonal nature of the third quarter as these forecasts were off by about 10% because of the large spike in demand. The first five columns of Figure 4-23 illustrate the results of forecasting with adaptive filters. The last two columns show revised forecasts based on the procedure explained below.

Adaptive Filter Forecasts

	Demand	Forecast	MSE	% Difference	Adjusted %	New Forecast
1st Qtr, Yr 1	1400					
2nd Qtr	1450					
3rd Qtr	1600					
4th Qtr	1500					
1st Qtr, Yr 2	1550	1488		4.0	3.8	1545
2nd Qtr	1600	1525	0.0047	4.7	4.5	1594
3rd Qtr	1750	1562	0.0149	10.7	10.25	1722
4th Qtr	1650	1600	0.0118	3.0	2.85	1646
1st Qtr, Yr 3	1700	1638	0.0113	3.6	3.8	1700
2nd Qtr	1750	1675	0.0094	4.3	4.5	1750
3rd Qtr	1900	1713	0.0131	9.8	10.25	1889
4th Qtr	1800	1750	0.0118	2.7	2.85	1800

Figure 4-23

The fifth column of Figure 4-23 is the percentage difference between demand and forecast. By averaging and then applying the average percentages to the forecast, revised estimated are secured. If the procedure proves to be feasible, it can be employed in estimating future demand.

First, average the percentage differences for like periods, for example:

$$1^{st} \text{ Qtr: } (4.0 + 3.6) \div 2 = 3.8\%$$

$$2^{nd} \text{ Qtr: } (4.7 + 4.3) \div 2 = 4.5\%$$

Second, adjust the forecast by the adjusted percentages to get a revised forecast:

$$1^{st} \text{ Qtr: } 1488(1.038) = 1545$$

$$2^{nd} \text{ Qtr: } 1525(1.045) = 1594$$

The new forecasts display accuracy and reliability. The forecaster can confidently apply the procedure to forecasting the near-term future, the periods beyond year 3. Chapter 5 provides more detail about this procedure.

Forecasting is straightforward. The forecasts utilize the optimal weights. However, when actual demands are no longer available, substitute the previous forecast.

1st Qtr, year 4: $1.7(.25) + 1.75(.25) + 1.9(.25) + 1.8(.25) = 1.7875$ or 1788

2nd Qtr, year 4: $1.75(.25) + 1.9(.25) + 1.8(.25) + 1.788(.25) = 1.81$ or 1810

Forecasting results are contained in Figure 4-24. By the fourth quarter, year 4, the original forecasts have drifted substantially away from anticipated reality because, in the equations, forecasts replace demands: actual demands are unknown. Anticipated reality (assumed for the purpose of this exercise) is a continuation of the previous pattern. The adjusted percentages as explained above are the base for computing the revised forecasts (1788 x 1.038 = 1856).

Forecasting the Future

	Demand	Anticipated Demand	Forecast	Adjustment %	New Forecast	% Difference
1st Qtr Yr 3	1700					
2nd Qtr	1750					
3rd Qtr	1900					
4th Qtr	1800					
1st Qtr Yr 4		1850	1788	3.80	1856	0.3
2nd Qtr		1900	1810	4.50	1891	0.5
3rd Qtr		2050	1825	10.25	2012	1.9
4th Qtr		1950	1806	2.85	1857	4.8

Figure 4-24

If a demand series is plagued with random behavior (as is quite normal) the above procedures may not work as well. It may be concluded from this example that the more distant the forecast is from the last known demand the greater will be the error, which may be equally true with some other methods. If more than twelve quarters of history had been available, the system would be substantially improved.

If there is an upward trend as indicated in our example, beginning weights may be assigned to reflect the trend, for example: 0.23, 0.24, 0.26, and 0.27. Applying these weights to the time series resulted in different optimal weights that gave similar forecasts.

By eliminating the seasonal factor and increasing demand by a steady 50 units per quarter, a straight-line trend was created. Forecasting with the optimal weights had an initial 7.8% demand to forecast difference. The difference slightly decreased with each iteration until minimization was realized. Had a learning constant closer to 1 been used, the series would have learned more quickly, but see the explanation below.

Probably, each time series will have features that are unique, therefore, experimentation on a computer is the means of selecting initial weights and a learning constant.

If a seasonal pattern is frustrating the demand series forecasts, the forecaster may take one of several actions: treat the seasonal aspect as spikes as discussed previously, smoothing the series, then adding back to the forecast an additional quantity for the spike, change methods to one that recognizes seasonality specifically, or forecast monthly instead of quarterly as the seasonal increase will be spread over several periods. Remember, adaptive filters may use any length of time for its periods: weekly, monthly, quarterly or yearly, for instance. Likely, seasonality will not be a serious problem except when the seasonal demand is substantially higher than demand in the non-seasonal periods.

There are several important considerations when contemplating the use of adaptive filters:

❖ This method is especially appropriate when there is a definite pattern, such as trend. Random fluctuations disturb the forecasts, but generally this is equally true with other techniques.

❖ The value of the constant k must be chosen. The value must be less than 1, but could be close to 1. The larger the value the more reactive it will be in finding the optimum set of weights. To choose a value near 1, however, may cause the adjustments to overreact to randomness and defeat the purpose of finding the best weights. A reasonable weight is in the range .08 ±.01. As random fluctuation and the number of weights increase, the best constant decreases, therefore, several initial weights should be tried. Generally, but not necessarily exclusively, within the range suggested.

❖ The number of past periods to be used in the forecasts and their initial weights must be specified. Two weights (two past periods) are a possibility if the series displays a steady pattern (as a straight line trend), stability, and little randomness. In a series in which monthly forecasts are desired, twelve weights are usually appropriate because a complete sales cycle is represented. If twelve weights are incorporated, for example, the first forecast is made for the thirteenth month, as the demand for the first twelve months is part of the forecasting equation.

❖ The value of the initial weights must be determined. Unless there is reason to do otherwise, dividing 1 by the number of weights is adequate.

❖ If there is a value (demand) of zero or one very close to zero, the procedure will not work. To overcome this difficulty, add a constant value to each of the values. Because the basic pattern is unchanged, optimal weights will still result.

Because a number of iterations (usually a very large number) are necessary, this technique is not practical without the assistance of a computer.

Conclusions

A host of time series (intrinsic) methods are described in this chapter. Others are presented in Chapter 6. Additionally, combined forecasting is explained in Chapter 10 and simulation forecasting is described in Chapter 13. Because the forecasting base is the historical time series internal to the organization, data are readily available; however, it must be verified that the data are accurate for forecasting purposes. To be successful in projecting the future, history must be representative; that is, the same general pattern must continue to be applicable. This is a reasonable expectation, at least in the near-term. If outside influences, such as economic factors, directly relate to demand, extrinsic (causal) methods may be appropriate, or perhaps a combination of the two.

The forecaster needs to be alert to change. Once it is recognized, many of the forecasting equations can be quickly revised by placing more emphasis upon recent observations. Assigning a higher smoothing constant to an exponential equation or weighting a moving average are examples. However, models cannot predict turning points. If an abrupt change occurs in the most recent observation, it may be an aberration or the beginning of a pattern change. This is a point at which analysis and judgment are essential. What caused the result to be substantially different from the expected? Is this one-time or a real change? At the close of Chapter 1 a list of some of the factors that may account for level changes is provided. Chapter 10 describes the methodology associated with changes in the economy.

The best solution to change is foresight, to recognize in advance that change is in the wind. To discover it after several months of large forecast error is unfortunate, hopefully it can be avoided.

How can an organization anticipate change and avoid surprise, short of having a fantastic crystal ball? It may not be possible, but here are a few suggestions.

- ❖ Although demand may not specifically correlate with outside economic factors, there may be a general but imperfect relationship. This relationship may manifest itself in leading indicators, general economic direction, or information provided by customers or trade associations.

- ❖ Forecasting also has a human side. Much information resides in the minds of the company's general managers and the sales and marketing executives, which often does not filter down to forecasting.

- ❖ Can other methods be joined to the forecasting process that will help to predict turning points? See Chapter 10.

In many time series techniques, forecasts consistently lag demand, especially when there is a definable trend. Calculating adjustment percentages as described above may be a feasible correction solution. More detail is contained in Chapter 5.

Testing methods against known demand is a means of determining goodness. Save several periods of the latest known demands (not to be included in forecast development) and forecast these known periods, then compare actual with estimate and calculate the forecast error by the procedures explained in this book. Also, this is a way to compare results from a variety of techniques.

Chapter 5

Forecast Evaluation and Modification

The objective of this chapter is to provide the forecaster with tools to be used in conjunction with forecasting for the purposes of determining the accuracy and reliability of forecasts, comparing forecasting models, recognizing change in pattern or direction, and establishing a forecasting range. Estimating the future is by itself inadequate. Questions that arise regard the trustworthiness of the projections and whether they are on track. Are they truly representative? Are changes occurring?

The measures of deviation discussed in this chapter are applicable to intrinsic (time series) forecasting techniques. Extrinsic (regression) methods require a different approach and are explained in Chapter 7.

Accuracy and Reliability

Because all of the factors that influence a demand series cannot be known, analyzing error is an essential part of the process. Knowing the magnitude and the distribution or pattern of the deviations from actual is basis for knowledge that leads to better forecasts. Not only is error measurement a means of predicting the range within which forecasts will vary from actual, it is a way in which to compare the results obtained by forecasting the same time series with different methods. The material that follows in this section was previously presented in Chapter 3. That level of detail is not repeated, but new insight should be gained. This section and the section entitled *Testing for Accuracy and Reliability* in Chapter 3 should be read together.

Briefly, here is an explanation of the more important measurements of error. Figure 5-1 is the example time series.

❖ A simple measure of accuracy is obtained by calculating the percentage difference between demand and forecast for each period. Percentages are commonly understood. The average error of the time series is obtained by calculating the arithmetic mean from the sum of the errors. For an unbiased forecasting method it normally will be close to zero because the positive and negative errors tend to cancel each other. Its advantage is that it is easily understood but generally it has limited significance, thus the measures described below (one or more) are recommended for determining accuracy. Although, as will be seen in the section *Correcting for Lag,* average error in conjunction with other measures can serve a purpose.

❖ Mean absolute deviation (MAD) is found by summing the absolute errors for the series being considered and dividing by the number of observations (periods). In Figure 5-1 this is 40 ÷12 = 3.33. Like MSE and MAPE, the MAD can be used to compare the accuracy of competing forecasts. It is also a measure of the average level of accuracy, but it does not estimate a range within which forecasts vary. A better measure for this purpose is standard deviation, which is discussed below.

❖ The mean squared error (MSE) requires that each error be squared, then summed and divided by the number of observations. In Figure 5-1 this is 180 ÷12 = 15. Because the errors are squared, the MSE will be larger than the MAD. MSE assigns more importance to large errors because of squaring. MSE is most useful in comparing time series that display many large errors.

❖ Mean absolute percent error (MAPE) is the average error expressed as a percentage. Divide the absolute error for each period by the demand and multiply by 100 to put the calculation in percentage form. December is (4 ÷111)x100 = 3.6%, for example. Sum the column and divide by the number of periods: 36 ÷12 = 3.0%. The indication is that forecasts will vary on average by 3.0%.

❖ Standard deviation may be expressed in two ways: as numbers or percentages. Each is explained in detail in Chapter 3 along with a discussion of the normal distribution. The standard deviation measures the dispersion around the average (mean) value. Values are distributed more or less equally on each side of the average. A look at the error column in Figure 5-1 shows the difference between demand and forecast, with a difference of 0.17 (2 ÷12), which is close to zero, indicating a normal distribution. Thus, the probability is that an event (value) is just as likely to occur on one side of the average (the mid-point) as on the other. The expectation is that approximately 68% of the errors will fall within one standard deviation. This is roughly 34% on each side of the average. Approximately 95% of the errors are within two standard deviations and 99% within three standard deviations. The standard deviation when calculated in the manner described in Chapter 3 is 1.972. The probable range of error at one standard deviation (sigma) is 1.4 on the lower end and 5.3 on the upper end; therefore, 68% of the time the deviation from actual demand will vary within this range. At two standard deviations the range is between zero and 7.3.

❖ Standard deviation can be expressed as a percentage, beginning with the MAPE. The procedure is explained in Chapter 3. Based on the calculations the standard deviation is 1.8%. The range at 68% is 1.2% (lower end) and 4.8% (upper end). At 95% the range is zero (lower end) and 6.6% (upper end).

Data for Evaluation

Month	Demand	Forecast	Difference (Error)	Average Error %*	Absolute Error	Squared Error
Jan	100	101	-1	1.0	1	1
Feb	110	103	7	6.4	7	49
Mar	106	107	-1	0.9	1	1
Apr	115	110	5	4.3	5	25
May	112	115	-3	2.7	3	9
Jun	112	112	0	0.0	0	0
Jly	109	112	-3	2.8	3	9
Aug	107	109	-2	1.9	2	4
Sep	114	110	4	3.5	4	16
Oct	108	113	-5	4.6	5	25
Nov	116	111	5	4.3	5	25
Dec	111	115	-4	3.6	4	16
Sum			2	36.0	40	180
Average Error			0.17			
MAD = 3.33						
MSE = 15.0						
MAPE = 3.0%						
*Signs ignored						

Figure 5-1

In almost all cases standard deviation based upon an assumption of a normal distribution will be suitable for forecasting purposes. However, forecasts can be skewed so that all or almost all values fall on one side of the average. If this occurs, it is probable that the cause is the lagging effect of the forecasting method itself. Correction for lag as discussed later may be the means to solve this type problem. For biased (skewed) data there are two types of distribution frequencies that describe that condition: the Poisson distribution and Chebyshev's Inequality. In the latter, for instance, at least 75% of the data will fall within two standard deviations and 96% within five standard deviations when applied to frequency distributions. It is also notable that as the sample size increases, the sampling distribution tends toward a normal distribution (Central Limits Theorem). An explanation of the above is found in standard statistics texts. However, to repeat, it is seldom that our process for determining the range of probability will be inadequate, especially after correcting for lag, if it exists.

The measures of error described above are useful in determining the average error that will occur in the forecasting technique being employed. It does not measure the range within which forecasts will vary from actual demand. It can be said, however, that a likely deviation from actual will be ±3.33 or ±3%. A better measure for calculating the range of the errors is standard deviation. A forecaster could, for example, provide three estimates: the forecast itself, an upper end, and a lower end, the latter two being the likely range. Whether one or two standard deviations are selected as the range depends upon what management decides is appropriate for the purposes assigned to the forecast.

The squared errors in Figure 5-1 point to a caution for the forecaster. Three of the last four months are relatively large. Is this indicative of a change in the pattern (a change in sales)? Assuming that there are at least several months of known data not employed in the forecasting technique, forecasting those months will probably answer that question. Under this circumstance the MSE is a useful measure (particularly in comparing competing forecasts).

The measures of forecast error discussed are important criteria in selecting the best-forecast method from several that may be in competition. That which displays the smallest deviation from actual over several periods (the more test periods the better) is the most accurate, at least for that period in time. When testing forecasting methods, periods of known demand are set aside and forecasts calculated to establish which technique gives the most accurate result. Also, these measures can be the basis for setting a standard or target. This subject is explained in more detail in Chapter 3.

The importance of accuracy cannot be over-estimated, but the factor of reliability is equally important. Reliability has two parts: consistency and frequency. Frequency is concerned with the number of times that forecast errors fall within an established standard. Consistency is the spread of the forecast errors, that is, the range of the errors. Chapter 3 gives an explanation and an example. Are all of the factors of accuracy and reliability equal in forecast method selection? If not, what weight should be assigned to each factor? The choice is dependent upon the impact that will be experienced by each of the various functional areas considered in relation to cost, customer service, sales and profit. If different techniques produce different results in these areas, management decides what is most important.

Demand patterns change, thus it is necessary to review forecasting results to see if forecasts are drifting further from demand. Frequent review is essential. If the forecaster believes a change is taking place, he needs to determine the reasons and take corrective action, which may entail retesting different forecasting methods. The next section provides a means of tracking forecast performance that may be useful in evaluating whether the pattern is changing.

With Figure 5-1 as example what conclusions can a forecaster make? Most likely, there would be more than twelve months of history available and that would provide a better base for analysis. Assume that prior to January there was a different demand pattern, therefore, that history is no longer applicable to a study of forecasting accuracy and reliability. The company has established a forecasting standard of no more than a 5% deviation from actual demand. Should the forecaster be concerned with such a tight standard?

Here is the forecaster's analysis. The experience for this year indicates that the average deviation from actual demand for future estimates will be approximately ±3.33 units or about ±3.0%, with some deviations more than the average and some less. This percentage is well within the forecasting standard and could lead management to consider a more stringent standard, however, the range of error (which follows) is a more appropriate measure for this purpose. The errors are fairly evenly distributed, with seven forecasts estimating at a level greater than actual, four under-estimating actual, and one in which forecast and actual are identical. Thus, there does not appear to be a tendency to consistently over- or under-forecast. The range within which forecasts will deviate from actual at 95% probability (based on standard deviation) is from zero on the low end and 6.6% on the upper end. If units are a more understandable measure, the probability range is between zero and 7.3 units. The established standard is the maximum deviation from actual that is allowable. Only once does the forecast error exceed the standard of ±5% (frequency). Consistency is more appropriate when comparing competing forecasting techniques. For this time series the range of the errors is reasonable.

The person who developed the forecasting method is quite pleased with himself or herself, as is fitting.

The way in which this analysis is presented is dependent upon the sophistication of the users of the forecasts. Forecasting presentations should be tailored to the level of "technical" knowledge possessed by the managers and users. It is a turn-off to use forecasting jargon or complex explanations to those not versed in an understanding of forecasting methodology. Keep it simple and adapt to your audience. A good idea is to have a training session to bring those in other disciplines on-board.

Tracking Forecasts

An assumption that is frequently made with regard to the average business series is that forecast errors are as likely to be positive as they are negative, thus they tend to cancel each other. If errors are random, their sum oscillates around zero with short runs of positive errors canceled by negative errors. A change in the character of the series causes errors to collect on one side of zero. If, however, the errors in a series are *always* or *almost always* on one side of zero *without* a shift in the pattern (to a higher or lower average level) a likely cause is the lagging effect of the forecasting method, discussed in the next section. One of the examples that follow addresses this condition.

If forecast errors (not because of lagging) accumulate above or below zero, it may signal a change in the demand pattern, such as a shift in trend, and indicates that forecasting effectiveness may be slipping. Corrective action is needed to bring the forecasts into line.

There are many reasons for a pattern shift. Some examples are: a product price change, realignment of prices relative to competitive products, changing taste or changing technologies, internal actions or competitor actions that affect the salability of a product, market saturation, and the vicissitudes of the economy.

Examining the size of the forecast errors historically may reveal that the pattern is changing; however, the disquieting influence that random fluctuations have on data may obscure the change. Something more is needed. To monitor a forecast's effectiveness, a tracking signal can be constructed. There are several equations, but an effective one is: Algebraic sum of the forecast errors through the current period ÷ mean absolute deviation, which is $TS = \Sigma e_t / \Delta_t$.

If the forecast is tracking properly, the tracking signal will range between ±4, which is roughly three standard deviations. If the tracking signal falls outside these limits for two consecutive months (or several periods if forecasts are updated more frequently), the demand series is reviewed to find out if the pattern is changing. Executives' specialized knowledge should be utilized in reviewing series in which the limits have been exceeded. Marketing and financial managers, for example, can often shed light on the reasons behind a possible change and in many instances they can anticipate the change. If a change is not apparent, watch the forecasts to ascertain if the limits are again exceeded. If so, action is usually indicated to bring the forecasts in line with reality.

Limits more restrictive than ±4 may be set for especially important items or those with an unusually high dollar value; however, be careful that the more restrictive limit does not result in a forecasting series continually out of balance because of "actions" taken. Conversely, the standard may be relaxed for low end, slow movers. In an industrial situation, for instance, items may be categorized according to an ABC (Pareto) analysis. Research has verified that in many industrial environments items can be conveniently classified in three categories according to the value of those items. This equally applies to the value of inventory and the dollar value of annual sales. Pareto's law states that typically ten percent of the products represent eighty percent of the value and thirty percent (includes the first ten percent) represents ninety-five percent of the value. The other seventy percent of the items represents only five percent of total value.

Basing the tracking signal limits on the dollar value of sales, for instance, the most restrictive limits could be assigned to A items, less restrictive limits to B items, and the least restrictive to C items. The A items limit could be, as example, set at ±3 or ±4, B items at ±5, and C items at ±7 with a larger safety stock (if the company maintains safety stock) established for C items, assuming that the total cost of the additional stock is relatively unimportant financially. Note that there is a trade-off between safety stock and customer service. This scheme reduces the number of items that require review after each forecast.

Corrective actions that may be appropriate are adjusting the smoothing constant in exponential smoothing, changing the length of the moving average, changing the weights in a weighted moving average, weighting a moving average, reevaluating the underlying assumptions in decomposition, changing the forecasting method to one that gives better results if an optimal technique is not in place, or as a temporary fix, setting the forecast equal to the actual demand when there is a consistent trend (but see the next section). If a step (ramp) situation is suspected and not verified and setting the forecast equal to demand seems appropriate, follow the demand for two additional periods to ensure that the change is not an impulse. Resetting the forecast to actual when an impulse occurs causes succeeding forecasts to be wild. A step is defined as demand that rapidly increases or decreases to a new level. It is a permanent change. Demand remains in the neighborhood of the new level. An impulse is a sudden rise or fall in demand that lasts for a short time then returns to its previous level, similar to a spike in demand.

When a tracking signal is outside the range, it is an early warning that a pattern change may be taking place. Executive participation in the review, to ascertain possible causes, is indicated. Following demand for an additional two months to verify change is appropriate if causes cannot be identified. However, there is a fine line between action and waiting because change materially impacts operations, marketing, and profits.

Three examples of forecast behavior in relation to tracking are presented below. The first, as illustrated in Figure 5-2, is a distinctive step situation. Demand increases to a new, higher level beginning in September. Exponential smoothing is the forecast base.

❖ The error column is the difference between demand and forecast. February, for example, is $1096 - 1070 = 26$.

❖ The percent error column is the difference between demand and forecast presented as a percent with signs ignored. March is $1052 - 1077.8 \div 1052$, then multiplied by 100 to express the result as a percentage.

❖ The running sum is the algebraic sum of the forecast errors. April is $26 + (-25.8) + 9.9$ which is 10.1. May is $10.1 + (-13) = -2.9$.

❖ The absolute error is the same as the error with signs ignored.

❖ The mean absolute deviation (MAD) is calculated as previously described. May, for example, is the sum of the absolute errors for February through May divided by 4 months.

❖ The tracking signal is the algebraic sum (running sum) through the current month divided by the MAD through the current period. For May the tracking signal is -0.155 rounded to -0.2.

Step Forecasting Series

Month	Demand	Forecast	Error (e)	Error as %	Running Sum (e)	Absolute Error	MAD	Tracking Signal
Feb	1096	1070.0	26.0	2.4	26.0	26.0		
Mar	1052	1077.8	-25.8	2.5	0.2	25.8	25.9	0.0
Apr	1080	1070.1	9.9	0.9	10.1	9.9	20.6	0.5
May	1060	1073.0	-13.0	1.2	-2.9	13.0	18.7	-0.2
Jun	1108	1069.1	38.9	3.5	36.0	38.9	22.7	1.6
Jly	1060	1080.8	-20.8	2.0	15.2	20.8	22.4	0.7
Aug	1069	1074.6	-5.6	0.5	9.6	5.6	20.0	0.5
Sep	1221	1072.9	148.1	12.1	157.7	148.1	36.0	4.4
Oct	1230	1117.3	112.7	9.2	270.4	112.7	44.5	6.1
Nov	1201	1213.8	-12.8	1.1	-12.8	12.8		
Dec	1221	1204.8	16.2	1.3	3.4	16.2	14.5	0.2
Jan	1206	1216.1	-10.1	0.8	-6.7	10.1	13.0	-0.5
Feb	1215	1209.0	6.0	0.5	-0.7	6.0	11.3	-0.1
Mar	1225	1213.2	11.8	1.0	11.1	11.8	11.4	1.0

Figure 5-2

The smoothing constant is set at 0.3 with ±4 as the tracking signal range. Through August the tracking signal indicates that the forecast is well within the range. The percent error column verifies this fact. In September the signal exceeds the limit by a little, indicating caution. October with a tracking signal of 6.1 requires action on the part of the forecaster because the limit has been exceeded two months in a row and review has determined the probable reasons. Of the several options available, the forecaster selects increasing the smoothing constant to 0.7. This action will cause the forecasting equation to react more quickly to actual demand.

September was selected as the starting point for the increased smoothing constant as this was the beginning of the up-step in demand. The sum of the cumulative errors was set at zero. The time now (when the decisions are being made) is October end. The new statistics are:

	Forecast	Error	e as %
September	1070.7	150.3	12.3
October	1175.9	54.1	4.4

By going back to the beginning of the trend change, the forecaster allows the equation to "catch-up" so that the forecast for November will respond appropriately. The forecaster does not know the actual demands for November forward, of course. The forecasts in Figure 5-2 from November forward are those calculated at α 0.7. At some point, the forecaster intends to reevaluate the smoothing constant's performance and return to a smaller constant, after referring to the chart that indicates the number of periods each smoothing constant considers (Figure 4-11).

As long as the cumulative sum of the forecast errors is within the tracking range, that is, the confidence limit, it can be assumed that the errors arose from random fluctuations. Outside the range indicates that there is a change and the forecasting technique is failing.

It should be noted that the first calculations for MAD and the tracking signal (February, March) were for two periods since it was the start of the series. Having only two or three periods as the beginning of the computations may cause erratic results. Generally, the forecaster will have a longer series thus avoiding this possible problem.

If there had been good integration of the forecasting activity with the other divisions of the company, especially Marketing and Sales, the jump in demand likely would have been anticipated and forecasting action taken. Possible actions are: basing the forecast on an item or group of items that previously had experienced a similar situation or applying one of the qualitative methods detailed in this book. Also, Sales may know the reason and the approximate amount or the percentage of the expected increase if it is based, say, upon the addition of new customers who have committed, but not ordered.

Increasing Trend Forecasting Series

Month	Demand	Forecast	Error	Error as %	Tracking Signal
January	1053	1050.0	3.0	0.3	
February	1053	1051.5	1.5	0.1	2.0
March	1055	1052.3	2.7	0.3	3.0
April	1054	1053.6	0.4	0.0	4.0
May	1058	1053.8	4.2	0.4	5.0
June	1065	1055.9	9.1	0.9	6.0
July	1068	1060.5	7.5	0.7	7.0
August	1070	1064.2	5.8	0.5	8.0
September	1074	1067.1	6.9	0.6	9.0
October	1078	1070.6	7.4	0.7	10.0

Figure 5-3

The next demand series represents a different situation, one in which there is a steadily increasing trend, as depicted in Figure 5-3.

The characteristics of the time series in Figure 5-3 are: demand steadily increases, forecasts consistently trail demand, errors accumulate on one side of the distribution, error measured as a percentage is very good, always less than one percent, and tracking signals increase consistently (rounded to whole numbers) and exceed the tracking signal limit after three months. For the purposes of this illustration, exponential smoothing with a smoothing constant of 0.5 is used.

The peculiar tracking signal increase results because of the relational nature of the running sum to the sum of the absolute errors. They are identical. By June the forecaster is wondering about the validity of the tracking signal and what it may be revealing. It indicates that forecasts are always less than demand but that is obvious from the other data. The percentage difference (error as percent) is very small as are the differences (error) between forecast and actual. Since estimates are close to demand, the forecaster is reluctant to make a change. Because forecasts are consistently below actual demand, however, there is concern. Perhaps a change is called for, perhaps not, at the June period. One possibility is to adjust the forecast in the manner explained in the next section. If this option had been exercised in this type of situation, it is probable that the tracking signal would be in line in the future periods. Other possibilities are changing the forecasting method or the smoothing constant, but this is unlikely considering the goodness of the results. (The example is not the result of testing different techniques, as we needed a series to illustrate tracking and lagging. Look back to Chapter 4 for methods better designed to forecast consistent trends.) This example demonstrates that tracking signals as well as other measures of accuracy and reliability must be tempered by analysis of the forecasting series.

Figure 5-4 gives another example of tracking signals. This is from the double moving average difference model in Figure 4-6. Note how the series is balanced and that the tracking signal in period 12 is zero because the running sum of the errors is zero although there is a 4.3% forecast shortfall.

Tracking Model

Period	Demand	Forecast	Error	Error as %	Tracking Signal
7	112	112			
8	114	113	1	0.9	2.0
9	118	115	3	2.5	3.0
10	110	120	-10	-9.1	-1.7
11	112	111	1	0.9	-1.7
12	117	112	5	4.3	0.0

Figure 5-4

It is possible that the number of demand items that exceed the tracking signal limits in a period may be more than can be reasonably evaluated in the time available. One way to reduce the number of out of control items is by applying the ABC procedure described earlier. Another way is to program the computer to sort the tracking signals by numerical magnitude. The item with the largest tracking signal number exceeding the established limit (as measured in absolute terms) is put at the top of the list. Others in which the established limits have been exceeded are ranked in order of size. This permits the reviewer to identify the critical items for evaluation. If items are grouped by different limits, separate lists are prepared for each grouping.

A tracking signal outside of its limits for two successive periods indicates the need to take a deep look at the demands, the pattern, and the forecasts to determine if action is necessary. Not every out-of-limit situation will call for immediate change, but it may portend an upcoming radical change. A series can have both positive and negative deviations (errors) and still exceed in one or more periods the tracking limit as when the sum of the errors is not close to zero.

Correcting for Lag

As seen in the New Forecast column of Figure 4-23 and the explanation, forecasts can be revised to give an outcome closer to reality. In that scenario, the percent differences were averaged and then used to adjust the forecast to provide a modified (new) estimate. The averaging was limited to two periods because of the limited data available. Because of the unusual nature of the demand series, a two period average was sufficient. Of course, having more periods available is better as the forecaster can try a number of periods for averaging to ascertain the optimal number.

The increasing trend series depicted in Figure 5-3 is another type of time series that responds well to modifying the forecast. The new estimates in Figure 5-5 result from modifying the original forecasts. Rather than using error as percent, the calculations were made from the error column itself. Percentages can be the base for the calculations but the resulting forecasts are the same. A three-month moving average of the errors was calculated to arrive at the adjustment:

$$\text{April adjustment: } (3.0 + 1.5 + 2.7) \div 3 = 2.4$$

$$\text{May adjustment: } (1.5 + 2.7 + 0.4) \div 3 = 1.5$$

Revised Forecast

Month	Demand	Original Forecast	Error	Error %	TS	New Forecast	Error	Error %	TS
Jan	1053	1050.0	3.0	0.3					
Feb	1053	1051.5	1.5	0.1	2.0				
Mar	1055	1052.3	2.7	0.3	3.0				
Apr	1054	1053.6	0.4	0.0	4.0	1056.0	-2.0	-0.2	2.3
May	1058	1053.8	4.2	0.4	5.0	1055.3	2.7	0.3	3.3
Jun	1065	1055.9	9.1	0.9	6.0	1058.3	6.7	0.6	4.7
Jul	1068	1060.5	7.5	0.7	7.0	1065.1	2.9	0.3	5.7
Aug	1070	1064.2	5.8	0.5	8.0	1071.1	-1.1	-0.1	5.8
Sep	1074	1067.1	6.9	0.6	9.0	1074.6	-0.6	-0.1	6.1
Oct	1078	1070.6	7.4	0.7	10.0	1077.3	0.7	0.1	6.9
		MAD original forecast: 5.9 (Apr – Oct)				MAD new forecast: 2.4 (Apr – Oct)			

Figure 5-5

The number of periods appropriate for the moving average is determined by experimentation. Next, add the adjustment to the forecast. April, for example, is 1053.6 + 2.4 = 1056.0. If there are negative errors, they are subtracted.

This example illustrates the method and the problems that may be encountered. The forecasts were adjusted each month based on the latest data, so they represent one period forecasts. The tracking signal is computed on all periods through the current period. If in April the adjustment of 2.4 was used for all forecasts through October, the results would be materially different and not as good but better than the original forecasts. This procedure is not a sure fire solution. Remember, that the forecaster does not know real demands.

Correcting for lag improves forecasts: estimates are closer to actual demand, and the error and tracking signal are smaller. At October end the MAD is also smaller in our example. Unfortunately, the tracking signal still exceeds the limit in the later months. There is one additional option available, which is calculating a second revision. Results are shown in Figure 5-6. Adjustments are calculated from a three-month moving average of the forecast errors as before; new forecast errors are used when available.

April adjustment: $(3.0 + 1.5 + 2.7) \div 3 = 2.4 + 1056 = 1058.4$

May adjustment: $(1.5 + 2.7 - 2.0) \div 3 = 0.7 + 1055.3 = 1056.0$

June adjustment: $(2.7 - 2.0 + 2.7) \div 3 = 1.1 + 1058.3 = 1059.4$

The forecaster has three options to consider in deciding which will supply the best forecasts. First, we will look at forecasts from April through October, and then a review assuming it is the end of July.

The original forecast resulted in very small errors; however, they are all on one side of zero (an unbalanced condition). Perhaps this is unimportant because of the closeness of forecast to actual, perhaps not. Had each of the differences (errors) been larger, it would be of concern as the errors would accumulate, not be offset by errors on the other side of zero. Now, considering the period April through October, which forecast is best?

Second Forecast Revision

Month	Demand	Forecast	Error	Error %	Tracking Signal
April	1054	1058.4	-4.4	-0.4	1.0
May	1058	1056.0	2.0	0.2	1.8
June	1065	1059.4	5.6	0.5	3.3
July	1068	1067.6	0.4	0.0	3.9
August	1070	1075.2	-5.2	-0.5	1.8
September	1074	1077.4	-3.4	-0.3	0.7
October	1078	1077.7	0.3	0.0	0.9
					MAD 3.0 (Apr – Oct)

Figure 5-6

The first revision has the lowest MAD, but the tracking signals for the second revision are within standard. Both revisions are balanced between positive and negative errors whereas the original forecast's errors are not. The MAD treats an error as an error regardless of sign, so; in this case, the MAD must be taken into account but along with other data.

Another data set of importance in this situation is the average error. Summing the errors, signs considered, and dividing by the number of months gives the average error. Results follow:

Original forecast: $41.3 \div 7 = 5.9$

First revision: $9.3 \div 7 = 1.3$

Second revision: $-4.7 \div 7 = -0.7$

The accumulation of errors in the original forecast, at 41.3, is substantially higher than it is in the two revisions. Also, the average in the revisions is close to zero, as it should be in a balanced series (positives and negatives tend to cancel each other). In the periods August through October, the errors are somewhat less in the first revision. The MAD's in the revised forecasts are close, but the first revision's MAD is slightly smaller. Overall, the tracking signal is far superior in the second revision. The interpretation and choice is with the forecaster who considers the consumer's specific requirements. However, the second revision is the probable choice.

Assume that it is the end of July and the forecaster in the previous section is going to make a decision about which of the three forecasts will be adopted. Of course, demand beyond July is not known. The average errors and MADs for April through July follow:

Original forecast: average error $21.2 \div 4 = 5.3$; MAD 5.3

First revision: average error $10.3 \div 4 = 2.6$; MAD 3.6

Second revision: $3.6 \div 4 = 0.9$; MAD 3.1

Reviewing MAD's, average errors and tracking signals and examining the data itself convinces the forecaster to select the second revision for future forecasts. As more months of data become available a different decision is possible.

The demand as seen in Figures 5-5 and 5-6 is a relatively straight-line increase month to month. In Chapter 6 the least squares method of forecasting is discussed. A demand pattern such as this may respond well to least squares. Often, however, a trend is only a part of the pattern that is revealed by decomposition. In developing a forecasting methodology, it is appropriate to review all of the techniques described in this book.

Chapter 6

Other Time Series Techniques

Chapters 3 and 4 described many of the time-series (intrinsic) methods used in forecasting. Chapter 3 is important because it explains decomposition, the method by which a time-series is divided into its component parts. The knowledge gained from this technique is a valuable tool in understanding the factors hidden in the demand pattern and therefore helpful in selecting candidates for forecasting consideration.

The models described in this chapter complete time-series forecasting. The first part of the chapter explains the least complex techniques. Non-linear time series analysis and forecasting and an introduction to the Box-Jenkins methodology follow.

Least Squares Trend

Forecasting with the least squares trend model is appropriate for linear time-series. If there is curvature in the series under consideration, the methods described later are better choices. The purpose of this procedure is to reveal movement over-time, that is, the straight-line trend, which may be increasing, decreasing, or horizontal. It is a good choice for forecasting the longer term as once the trend-line is identified it can be extended a reasonable distance into the future; however, remember that the further into the future one delves, the less accurate the forecasts. There are limitations to its applicability, however. Seasonal data can affect the slope of the trend-line resulting in inaccurate or less accurate forecasts. The seasonal factor may be eliminated by estimating sales for that period less the seasonal factor. In new product introductions, sales may increase rapidly before reaching maturity; therefore, a trend computed on this rapid growth is only of value for a limited time. An S-curve or logistics curve is probably a better approach. If economic conditions or product acceptance is expected to change, the trend line will not account for the change.

The trend equation and the method of calculating the trend line were explained in Chapter 3 as part of the decomposition method. This is the same process as previously described. Figures 6-1 and 6-2 are our examples.

Least Squares Forecast Model

Month	Y (demand)	X	XY	X²	Trend Line
January	1892	-7	-13244	49	1846.1
February	1935	-6	-11610	36	1892.9
March	1878	-5	-9390	25	1939.7
April	1937	-4	-7748	16	1986.5
May	2003	-3	-6009	9	2003.3
June	2100	-2	-4200	4	2080.1
July	2118	-1	-2118	1	2126.9
August	2200	0	0	0	2173.7
September	2244	1	2244	1	2220.5
October	2288	2	4576	4	2267.3
November	2333	3	6999	9	2314.1
December	2288	4	9152	16	2360.9
January	2400	5	12000	25	2407.7
February	2481	6	14886	36	2454.5
March	2509	7	17563	49	2501.3
Sum	32606		13101	280	

Figure 6-1

Least Squares Forecast Model

Month	Y (demand)	X	XY	X²	Trend Line
January	2030	-11	-22330	121	2021.9
February	2041	-9	-18369	81	2028.5
March	2052	-7	-14364	49	2035.1
April	2001	-5	-10005	25	2041.7
May	2009	-3	-6027	9	2048.3
June	2088	-1	-2088	1	2054.9
July	2091	1	2091	1	2061.5
August	2030	3	6090	9	2068.1
September	2093	5	10465	25	2074.7
October	2053	7	14371	49	2081.3
November	2133	9	19197	81	2087.9
December	2077	11	22847	121	2094.5
Sum	24698		1878	572	

Figure 6-2

The least squares or linear regression model is a relationship between the values a (a constant number called the intercept), b (the slope of the line), and x the coded time period. When time is the independent variable a simplified method of fitting a trend line is available in the equation: $Y = a + b(x)$, with Y as the demand or the forecasted demand and N the number of months.

$$a = \Sigma Y/N = 32606/15 = 2173.7$$

$$b = \Sigma XY/\Sigma X^2 = 13101/280 = 46.8$$

The forecast for April, second year is $Y = a + b (x)$ which is 2173.7 + 46.8(8) = 2548. The time factor (x) is the next number in the coded sequence; here March is 7. May forecast is 2173.7 + 46.8(9) = 2595. Note that the sequence of demands and forecasts increases by *exactly* the

<u>b</u> value each month: January/February, first year is 1892.9 − 1846.1 = 46.8. This illustrates that the slope is a straight line. It is also the rate of change between periods.

Figure 6-1 consists of 15 months of known demand, which is an odd number of periods, thus the coded sequence began with zero at the middle month of August and increased or decreased by 1 each month. With an even number of periods, the sequencing is by 2 each period, starting with −1 and +1 as formatted in Figure 6-2.

The values to be substituted in the equation are a = 2058.2 and b = 3.3. The forecast for January is 2058.2 + 3.3(13) = 2101. Note that the trend increases by twice 3.3 to 6.6 each period because the coded values increase by 2.

This equation is also the basis for simple linear regression forecasting as explained in the next chapter. That model is more complex because time is not the independent variable.

Percent of Sales Model

The percent of sales model is a time series forecasting method in which sales may be projected for one period (frequently a month) or one year or for any number of periods. Its basic requirement is that there is a generally repeatable pattern. The method assigns a percentage to each period (month or quarter usually) based upon previous annual sales and the periodic distribution of those sales. The method is not affected by seasonality and usually not by trend unless there is a step situation. Random influences if significant and truly random befuddle the pattern. With reasonable stability, this method is effective, either as a stand-alone method or in conjunction with another technique. It is not only useful in sales forecasting, it may also be applied to financial analysis.

Figure 6-3 gives three years of history: the actual sales (demand) and monthly sales as a percent of yearly sales. For example, the percent of sales for January, year 1, is 1.0%, derived by dividing 1010 by 101000. The sum of all monthly percentages equals 100%. In January, sales were 1.0% of the total sales for the year; in May sales were 13.9% of total year 1 sales. It may occur that the percentages will not sum to 100%. In this case, percentages can be tweaked if the difference is not significant. A formal method of bringing the percentage total to 100 is described in Chapter 3 as regards adjusting the seasonal index (see Figure 3-6). The average percentage is the sum of the percentages for the three years divided by 3. For example:

January is (1.0 + 1.2 +1.1)/3 = 1.1; May is (13.9 + 12.7 + 13.8)/3 = 13.5.

What can be concluded by examining the data in Figure 6-3?

* ❖ The time series is stable, that is, there are only small percentage differences year to year in any one month. Frequently, this is not true. Larger differences do not negate the validity of the method. In that case, the magnitude of the deviations between actual and forecast will probably be larger. Percentages can change from year to year for many reasons: random fluctuation, an unexpected large order as when a customer opens a new store, a downturn in a customer's business, competitor bankruptcy or fire, etc.

* ❖ There appears to be a trend or at least total yearly sales are increasing year to year. The trend will not materially affect forecasting as the methodology accounts for trend.

* ❖ There is seasonality. Months with low percentages are consistent for all three years as are months in which there is high demand. Sales can slide, however, from one month to the next as when a customer(s) places his order for a later delivery date than was his practice in previous years, or when a company's annual promotion is scheduled in a different month than previously. Once identified, a correction can be made as was done with seasonality in Chapter 3.

Percent of Sales Model

Month	Year 1 Sales	Sales as %	Year 2 Sales	Sales as %	Year 3 Sales	Sales as %	Average %
January	1010	1.0	1250	1.2	1151	1.1	1.1
February	3939	3.9	4064	3.9	4079	3.9	3.9
March	7272	7.2	7398	7.1	7322	7.0	7.1
April	11110	11.0	13338	12.8	12134	11.6	11.8
May	14039	13.9	13233	12.7	14435	13.8	13.5
June	16665	16.5	16985	16.3	17364	16.6	16.5
July	9393	9.3	9378	9.0	9623	9.2	9.2
August	2020	2.0	1771	1.7	1569	1.5	1.7
September	10706	10.6	10837	10.4	11401	10.9	10.6
October	5959	5.9	6356	6.1	5753	5.5	5.8
November	12827	12.7	13338	12.8	13493	12.9	12.8
December	6060	6.0	6252	6.0	6276	6.0	6.0
Total	101000		104200		104600		

Numbers rounded

Figure 6-3

Once the average percentages have been calculated, an annual sales projection and estimates for each succeeding month can be made. In the early months of the new year (the year being forecast) there is a paucity of actual demand data, which can cause the forecasts to be out-of-tune with reality as when random fluctuations are especially active.

Here is a forecasting scenario based on the data in Figure 6-3 (three zeros dropped from demand).

❖ The time is December end of year 3. What is the forecast for year 4? Determining a forecast is more speculation than science at this point because there are no sales in the new year. Initially, the forecaster can assume that sales will be the same as year 3, thus the forecast is 104,600 for the year and 1151 for January year 4. When January sales are known, the forecast may change. The forecaster can also assume that year 4 sales will be higher than year 3 because of the increasing demand in the past years. But by how much? Most likely the conclusion would be about 105,000, which replicates the increase from year 2 to year 3. Under that rationale January sales will be 105000 x .011 = 1155. (.011 is the percentage expressed as a ratio.) Perhaps, in coordination with the Sales Department, the forecaster has a good feel for the direction of sales, which would be incorporated into the forecasting explanation.

❖ The time is January end, year 4. January sales are 1180. What are the annual and monthly forecasts? The annual projection is January sales divided by January ratio: 1180 ÷ .011 = 107272. February's estimate is 107272 x .039 = 4184. These may be quite disturbing estimates unless there is information to substantiate this magnitude of the increase. However, the percentage difference is not large and thus may be an acceptable interim forecast. Believing an annual forecast of 107,000 to be too high, the forecaster could present monthly estimates based upon a 105,000 and 107,000, with whatever caveats are appropriate. Impact is especially grave for purchasing and manufacturing. Probably, the forecaster has also prepared a projection by another technique that will mitigate the dilemma. An alternate and probably better scheme is to include December in the forecast, it being close to year 4 should represent the near term sales level. The sales forecasts are: annual = (6276 + 1180) ÷ (.06 + .011) = 105014 and February = 105014 x .039 = 4096. If judgment dictates November could also be included in the formula, in which case the forecasts are: annual, (13493 + 6276 + 1180)/(.129 + .06 + .011) = 104745, February, 104745*.039 = 4085.

❖ The time is February end, year 4. February sales are 4070. From this point, sales and percentages are cumulative. The forecasts are: annual = (1180 + 4070) ÷ (.011 + .039) = 105000 and March = 105000 x .071 = 7455. The process is continued for each month in the year. At this point in time it may or may not be feasible to include December in the forecast.

❖ At the end of March, the annual forecast is 105372 when March sales are 7500; that is:(1180 + 4070 + 7500) ÷ (.011 + .039 + .071). To estimate monthly sales, the average percentage for the month being forecast is multiplied by the annual projection. This cumulative process is utilized for each succeeding month and updated at the close of each month.

❖ A light bulb lit up the forecaster's brain and he decided to try other models, specifically least squares, basic double moving average, and second order exponential smoothing. All the forecasts were totally out of sync with reality because of the nature of the pattern, which illustrates the importance of pattern analysis. Perhaps, decomposition would be useful.

Erratic Demand

Sometimes demand does not appear to have a definable pattern because historically the sales in a given month vary wildly from year to year. Such irregular demands can be caused by random fluctuations, customers placing orders when goods are needed but not on a fixed schedule, or a customer base consistently in flux. It may be that when all customers' orders are aggregated the demand will be smoothed, but this is not necessarily true. What can be done? There are several options.

❖ Average the demands by month for several past years and forecast the averages.

❖ Rather than monthly forecasts, forecast quarterly, perhaps subdividing the quarterly estimates by month. It is even possible to aggregate demand for longer periods, but with caution.

❖ Aggregate individual end item sales and forecast by product group or family.

More than one forecast can be developed to serve different purposes. A product group forecast may satisfy the needs of the financial, sales and marketing, and top management communities. In a manufacturing company, for instance, production planning and purchasing need forecasts by individual end-item.

Figure 6-4 is a five-year history of an end-item. What can be concluded from the data? A look, by year, of total sales for the five years indicates the there has been a general up-tick in sales that may suggest a long-term trend. It is appropriate to assume that sales in year 6 will equal or exceed year 5 but this is not assured because there is some up/down fluctuation, with year 3 the lowest in total sales. The average sales per month range between 260 (year 3) and 342 (year 4). Take any year and the sales spread between the months in each of the years is significant and dramatic and does not follow a pattern; rather it seems random as to when high and low sales will occur. In like manner, the sales for each of the months appear to be random; January, for example has low sales of 50 and high sales of 520. Taking the average sales for five years (Januarys are 292) shows that the range between months (January through December) when averaged for five years are within a relatively narrow range. Another interesting statistic is that there may have been some growth during the five-year period.

The forecasting rationale is to provide the most accurate estimates possible to satisfy consumer needs, realizing that the results may have variations that are sizeable.

What are some of the forecasting possibilities?

An Erratic Time Series

	Year 1	Year 2	Year 3	Year 4	Year 5	Total for Month	Average Month
January	400	50	200	520	290	1460	292
February	100	390	400	500	100	1490	298
March	50	280	390	120	600	1440	288
April	300	400	50	260	500	1510	302
May	450	350	50	500	200	1550	310
June	50	50	700	100	600	1500	300
July	190	500	100	450	390	1630	326
August	370	100	500	60	550	1580	316
September	620	100	50	450	290	1510	302
October	120	590	250	480	40	1480	296
November	500	90	400	320	200	1510	302
December	360	550	30	340	210	1490	298
TotalYr	3510	3450	3120	4100	3970		
Average	293	288	260	342	331		

Figure 6-4

❖ Develop estimates for a product group rather than for individual end items if this smoothes demand. Divide the aggregated demand into end-items by the percentage that each is to the product group, if needed. The divided forecast may still have large errors in some periods.

❖ Rather than forecast by month, forecast for an extended period such as quarterly. Divide the quarterly forecast into monthly segments, if required, for production and purchasing. Each segment could be equal or weighted based upon what is vital for insuring production and delivery. Although inventory may not be minimized, it would be controlled. Here is an example:

assume a quarterly forecast is 650. Average of the demands for the like periods the last several years, which, say, results in percentages of 20%, 70%, and 10%. Estimates, therefore, are: 130, 455, and 65. From this information a purchasing and manufacturing plan can be developed that considers meeting an on-time shipping objective or anther important criterion. Plans could entail making a larger portion in the first month than indicated by forecasted sales or a plan could be developed that chooses to optimize customer service, manufacturing efficiency and utilization, or inventory management or that strikes a balance. Of course, this same reasoning can be applied without dividing the forecast into monthly segments. Calculating a range of error based on the standard deviation serves the same purpose (see Chapter 5). Looking at both options simultaneously will be enlightening.

❖ Use the average monthly demands as the forecasting base. In Figure 6-4 this is the five year average per month (January is 292, February is 298, etc.). Note that the range is a low of 50 to a high of 520 in January with similar conditions existing in each of the months. A stable forecast is likely because there is not much variation month to month, but the forecast could be misleading in any one month because of the probable range of demand.A production and purchasing plan as above is essential.

With averages, it is important to understand that actual demand will vary greatly from the average and needs to be addressed in appropriate plans. A range of error computed from standard deviation should be helpful to all forecast consumers. It has to be computed from the actual monthly demands and not from the averages. Arriving at the right forecasting method is a matter of experimentation and works in conjunction with the reasoning above.

Another forecasting difficulty is forecasting items that have only sporadic demand. An item in this category may have only occasional sales at unpredictable times, either high or low volume. An attempt to forecast the timing of sporadic demands is futile. A better approach is to estimate the annual demand, possibly by qualitative methods or simply averaging past annual demand over a period of several years. Determining a stock level could be based upon a criterion of having product available to equal a predetermined stockage objective, a cost comparison between producing one or several lots a year, or the cost of maintaining inventory compared with it profit. Perhaps, make-to-order is feasible.

Once an estimate is made, a production or a distribution plan can be formulated to stock these items. In a manufacturing company manufacture should be planned to disrupt production as little as possible. It may be more cost effective to make the entire estimate at one time or to manufacture to order. There is a trade-off between the carrying cost of inventory and set-up/disruption cost of manufacture. It may be more profitable not to sell those products if they represent an incidental part of the profit picture.

The Box-Jenkins Forecasting Method

This methodology, developed by Professors Box and Jenkins, is designed to examine complex situations in which the underling pattern of a time series is veiled. It is mathematically complex. It is particularly applicable for forecasting the short-range and possibly the mid-range. Box-Jenkins is a procedure that systematically scrutinizes the data to arrive at the most suitable model while eliminating those that do not adequately explain the historical time series. It is a good choice for consideration when less complicated techniques fail to produce the desired results. However, it is involved and feasible only when a software package specifically designed to forecast employing the Box-Jenkins model is used. The process of identifying the pattern and selecting an appropriate model requires experience on the part of the forecaster. Because of the intricacy involved in the process, it is not possible to provide a detailed explanation; thus, the following paragraphs are introductory only.

Initially, the forecaster assumes a tentative pattern rather than beginning with a known pattern. Through iteration, incremental improvements lead to an optimized model that defines the pattern while minimizing error. To have an effective forecasting model necessitates having a minimum of fifty data periods, probably more if a seasonal factor is present.

Frequently, the acronym ARIMA is seen in descriptions of autoregressive models such as Box-Jenkins. It stands for the basic elements of the procedure: autoregressive (AR), integrative or differencing (I), and moving averages (MA).

In a sense, Box-Jenkins is comparable to regression. Both depend upon independent variables. The dependent variable and the independent variable(s) are in consort. Whereas an independent variable(s) in regression is acquired from data not a part of the time series, in Box-Jenkins the independent variable is a past value of the time series. Correlation is a function (correlation coefficient) between +1 and -1. The closer a value is to +1 the more positive the relationship.   When the independent variable moves the dependent variable moves in the same direction, how closely depends upon the degree of correlation (how close to +1).   When there is a negative correlation, the same applies except that an increase in one results in a decrease in the other. A zero coefficient means that there is an absence of correlation. An autocorrelation coefficient describes the dependence of values at different time periods. A key element in Box-Jenkins, therefore, is autocorrelation between successive values. An important consideration is that the data must be stationary; that is, a time series without trend (basically horizontal) with values that fluctuate around a mean. If there is trend and/or a seasonal function, the time series can be manipulated to render it stationary. In its application, Box-Jenkins can be considered a partnership between multiple regression and time series (intrinsic) methods.

By creating artificial variables A and B and changing the time origin we create a simple representation of autocorrelation. In this case, the B variable is the A variable lagged one time period, and the two would be the basis for computing the autocorrelation coefficient, which is done in the same manner as if there was an independent variable rather than the same value lagged one or more periods.

Variable   Variable

Figure 6-5 represents a time series in which there is trend. By the process of differencing, the series can be converted to stationary data. First differences are the result of subtracting successive values. The differences become the new variable.

Differencing a Time Series

Period	Value	1st Difference	2nd Difference
1	206		
2	212	6	
3	216	4	-2
4	220	4	0
5	226	6	2
6	228	2	-4
7	230	2	0

Figure 6-5

Figure 6-5 is a partial series, which illustrates the method of differencing to establish a stationary series from a series with trend. The first difference at period 2 is 212 – 206 = 6. The second difference at period 3 is 4 – 6 = -2. Second differencing is calculated when the first difference does not result in a stationary series. In a complete series, it is likely that the first differences in Figure 6-5 will convert the series. The forecasting process uses the first or second differences, not the original values.

In the historical context, the method uses an iterative approach to identify an appropriate model, thus not assuming a predetermined pattern. The model selected is verified against historical data to see if there is a good fit. If not, the process is repeated until a best model is found. There are three general categories of models: those whose basis is autoregressive (AR) only, those employing only a moving average of the error terms (MA), and those using a combination of the two types of models.

Conducting forecasting with the Box-Jenkins methodology requires model estimation and testing, which is done utilizing a Box-Jenkins software package. The complexity of the procedure precludes a detailed explanation beyond this point in our discussion. Some texts provide more detail, but without the availability of the software program, a comprehensive example is not practical.

Non-linear Trend Analysis

Not all patterns are created linear. In Chapter 4, one method of curve fitting was described, a modified form of third order exponential smoothing. In this section several other techniques for analyzing non-linear trends are explained. Mathematically, demand patterns can be analyzed and a model developed specifically for that pattern; however, the methods described in this section will be adequate in most situations.

Second-Degree Parabolic Trends

The expressed form of the polynomial equation is written as: $Y = a + b(x) + c(x^2) + d(x^3) + ...$ In its most simple form it is written as $Y = a + b(x) + c(x^2)$. This is the form that we will use for describing the parabola, which with this equation is a second-degree parabolic trend. There are three equations to solve:

$$a = [\Sigma(Y) - c\Sigma(X^2)] \div n$$

$$b = \Sigma(XY) \div \Sigma(X^2)$$

$$c = [n\Sigma(X^2Y) - \Sigma(X^2) \bullet \Sigma(Y)] \div [n\Sigma(X^4) - (\Sigma X^2)^2]$$

To be able to compare methods, this example will utilize the demand in Figure 4-17.

Step 1: Construct a table of values that are used to solve the three equations. The table is contained in Figure 6-6. The Y column is the demand. The X column represents the coded periods, the sum of which always equals zero. Begin numbering with the middle period. If there are an odd number of periods, enter a zero and number the earlier periods −1, -2, etc. and the later periods +1, +2, etc. If there are an even number of periods, number the two middle months −1 and +1. Numbering is by two's as illustrated. XY is the product of the X and Y values (5.1 x −15 =-76.5). The remaining columns follow the same arithmetic rules.

Step 2: Sum each of the columns. These totals are the values needed to solve the three equations.

Step 3: Solve for c: note that n represents the number of observations, which, in this case, is 16. Substitute numbers in the equation and solve

$$[16(23867.5) - (1360)(257.9)] \div [16(206992) - (1360)^2] =$$
$$(381880 - 350744) \div (3311872 - 1849600) =$$
$$31136 \div 1462272 = 0.0213 \text{ (or } .021)$$

Computation, Second-Degree Parabolic Curve

Period	Demand Y	X (coded)	XY	X^2	X^2Y	X^4	Trend (Forecast)
1	5.1	-15	-76.5	225	1147.5	50625	5.4
2	6.0	-13	-78.0	169	1014.0	28561	6.0
3	7.0	-11	-77.0	121	847.0	14641	6.8
4	8.0	-9	-72.0	81	648.0	6561	7.8
5	9.1	-7	-63.7	49	445.9	2401	9.0
6	10.6	-5	-53.0	25	265.0	625	10.3
7	12.0	-3	-36.0	9	108.0	81	11.8
8	13.6	-1	-13.6	1	13.6	1	13.4
9	15.5	1	15.5	1	15.5	1	15.2
10	17.0	3	51.0	9	153.0	81	17.2
11	19.0	5	95.0	25	475.0	625	19.4
12	21.0	7	147.0	49	1029.0	2401	21.7
13	24.0	9	216.0	81	1944.0	6561	24.2
14	27.0	11	297.0	121	3267.0	14641	26.9
15	30.0	13	390.0	169	5070.0	28561	29.7
16	33.0	15	495.0	225	7425.0	50625	32.7
Total Σ	257.9	0	1236.7	1360	23867.5	206992	257.5

Some rounding

Figure 6-6

Step 4: Solve for a: $[257.9 - .0213(1360)] \div 16 = 14.31$ (or 14.3).

Step 5: Solve for b: $1236.7 \div 1360 = 0.909$ (or 0.91).

Step 6: Calculate a forecast for each of the past periods. Period 1 forecast is:

$$a + b(x) + c(x^2) = 14.3 + 0.91(-15) + 0.021(225) = 5.4.$$

Forecasts for future periods are calculated by substituting the x factor for that period. For instance, period 17 (coded x equals 17) and period 20 (coded x equals 23) forecasts are:

$$\text{Period 17: } 14.3 + 0.91(17) + 0.021(17^2) = 35.9$$
$$\text{Period 20: } 14.3 + 0.91(23) + 0.021(23^2) = 46.3$$

In Chapter 4, the forecasts for period 20 ranged between 47.1 and 48.2 depending on the c factor applied. Which of these forecast methods is best? Probably that which is most accurate as calculated by the measures in Chapter 5. However, accuracy must be recalculated every few periods.

Gompertz Curve

The Gompertz curve is another form that is useful in new product introductions in which there is slow growth in the initial stage, quick growth during the middle stage, and a decline in demand as when a market becomes saturated. It often takes an "S" shape. It can also be an effective forecasting method where there is a non-linear pattern (growth curve), as explained in the procedure that follows.

This method is complex and is tedious when worked by hand. It is adaptable to computer forecasting. The steps are explained in detail to facilitate an understanding of the methodology. Figure 6-7 consolidates the steps that result from solving the equations. The procedures necessitate the use of logarithms. Logarithm tables are available in most statistical and college mathematical textbooks together with an explanation of their properties. The demand in Figure 6-7 is the same as the demand in Figure 6-6, thus allowing a comparison of several forecasting models.

The equation for the Gompertz curve in logarithmic form is:

$$\text{Log } y = \log a + \log b(c^x)$$

Columns 1 through 3 are the basic data. The x column sets the origin at zero against the first period. The value of 1/5 in the equations represents that each subgroup consists of five periods. Had the subgroups had eight periods, for example, 1/8 would be used.

Step 1: Divide the series in three equal parts. There are sixteen periods in the time series, but only fifteen are used in order to have each series of three equal in number. Each subgroup has five periods of data.

Step 2: Find the logarithm for each demand and enter it in column 4. A logarithm consists of two parts: the characteristic and the mantissa.

The characteristic is the number of digits before the decimal point. The number 5.1 has a one-digit whole number; the number 30 (period 15) has a two-digit whole number. The characteristic reflects the number of whole number digits and is always one less than the number of digits. Thus, 1 through 9.9999 has a zero characteristic, 10 through 99.9999 has a 1 characteristic, and so on. The mantissa is the number obtained from the table of logarithms. The logarithm for 300, for example, is 2.4771 (rounded to 4 places). The whole number 300 is three digits (thus 2) and .4771 is the mantissa. The mantissa is the same for any number beginning with 3; the characteristic determines the number of whole number digits. For numbers less than one, the rule is different. In Figure 6-7, the logarithm for 5.1 is 0.7076 (rounded to 4 places).

Step 3: Sum each of the three subgroups in column 4. The total for periods 1 through 5 is 4.1930; subgroup 2 is 5.6587; and subgroup 3 is 6.8897.

Step 4: solve the following two equations:

$$S_1 = \Sigma_2 \log Y - \Sigma_1 \log Y$$
$$S_1 = 5.6587 - 4.1930 = 1.4657$$

$$S_2 = \Sigma_3 \log Y - \Sigma_2 \log Y$$
$$S_2 = 6.8897 - 5.6587 = 1.2310$$

Step 5: Find the value for c. Solve for c^5 by dividing the answers obtained in step 4: $1.2310 \div 1.4657 = 0.8399$. Thus, the c value is $\sqrt[5]{0.8399}$. The fifth root of c may be found by using logarithms, to six places to avoid interpolation, thus 0.8399 is 0.924228 (N column 839, column 9).

$$\log c = 1/5(\log 0.8399) = 1/5(-1 + 0.924228) =$$
$$1/5(-0.075772) = -0.0151544 \text{ which is } 9.984846 - 10$$

Note if 10 is added to −0.0151544 it is 9.984846 − 10. The value of c is the antilogarithm of .984846, which is .9657. An antilog is the inverse of the logarithm, readable from the log table: find 98 in the 0 column, then find 4846, which in 965 in the N column plus the number 7 in the seventh column.

Step 6: Find the value of log b:

$$\log b = S_1 (c - 1) \div (c^5 - 1)^2 =$$
$$1.4657(0.9657 - 1) \div (0.8399 - 1)^2 =$$
$$1.4657(-0.0343) \div -(0.1601)^2 = -1.9614$$

Step 7: Find the value of log a:

$$\log a = 1/5[\Sigma_1 \log Y - (S_1 \div c^5 - 1)] =$$
$$1/5[4.1930 - (1.4657 \div 0.8399 - 1)] =$$
$$1/5[4.1930 - (1.4657 \div -0.1601)] = 2.6696$$

Note: log Y is found in Figure 6.7

Step 8: Complete column 5 in Figure 6-7. Enter 1.0000 for period 1, the x factor being zero. Each succeeding period is a function of the c value. Period 2, therefore, is 0.9657; period 3 is 0.9657^2, which is 0.9326; period 4 is 0.9657^3, which is 0.9006; and so forth. The simplest way to calculate the values is to multiply the last value in the column by 0.9657.

Step 9: Complete column 6. Multiply log b by the value in column 5. Period 1, column 6 is 1 (-1.9614) = -1.9614; period 2 is 0.9657 (-1.9614) = -1.8941.

Step 10: Complete column 7, which is obtained by adding the value in column 6 to the value of a: 2.6696 + (-1.9614) = 0.7082 for period 1; period 2 is 2.6696 + (-1.8941) = 0.7755.

Step 11: Complete column 8, which is the trend or forecast. Column 7 is the logarithms for determining the values in column 8. Find the antilog for each of the logs from the logarithmic table. The antilog of 0.7082 is 511 (4 place mantissas table) or 5108 (6 place table). The characteristic is zero; therefore, the value is 5.1 rounded. The trends (forecasts) for the first fifteen periods are close to actual demands, which verifies the validity of this forecasting method.

Gompertz Curve Calculations

Period	Demand Y	Period Code X	Column 4	Column 5	Column 6	Column 7	Column 8
1	5.1	0	0.7076	1.0000	-1.9614	0.7082	5.1
2	6.0	1	0.7782	0.9657	-1.8941	0.7755	6.0
3	7.0	2	0.8451	0.9326	-1.8292	0.8404	6.9
4	8.0	3	0.9031	0.9006	-1.7664	0.9032	8.0
5	9.1	4	0.9590	0.8697	-1.7058	09638	9.2
		$\Sigma_3 \log Y$	4.1930				
6	10.6	5	1.0253	0.8399	-1.6474	1.0222	10.1
7	12.0	6	1.0792	0.8111	-1.5909	1.0787	12.0
8	13.6	7	1.1335	0.7832	-1.5362	1.1334	13.6
9	15.5	8	1.1903	0.7564	-1.4836	1.1860	15.4
10	17.0	9	1.2304	0.7304	-1.4326	1.2370	17.3
		$\Sigma_3 \log Y$	5.6587				
11	19.0	10	1.2788	0.7054	-1.3836	1.2860	19.3
12	21.0	11	1.3222	0.6812	-1.3361	1.3335	21.6
13	24.0	12	1.3802	0.6579	-1.2904	1.3792	24.0
14	27.0	13	1.4314	0.6353	-1.2461	1.4235	26.5
15	30.0	14	1.4771	0.6135	-1.2033	1.4663	29.3
		$\Sigma_3 \log Y$	6.8897				

Rounding in some numbers

Figure 6-7

Logarithms can be found in Excel: go to f_x in the tool bar or in insert, to math and trig, then to log 10.

The forecasting equation is: forecast $= \log a + \log b(c^x)$. The value of log a is 2.6696 (step 7 above). The value of log b is –1.9614 (step 6 above). The value of c is 0.9657 (step 5 above). Recall that the c value is multiples of itself, thus, period 3 is .9657², period 4 is .9657³ and so forth (see the X column). The simplest way is to take the last known number in column 5 as a starting point and multiply that number by . 9657 once for each future period. To forecast periods 17, for instance, solve the following equation:

Period 17: $2.6696 + (-1.9614)[(0.6135)(0.9657)(0.9657)] = 1.5474$

Find the antilog of 1.5474, which is 35.3, the forecast

Applying the same logic, the forecast for period 20 is 45.6.

Comparing forecast results for period 20 reveals that the forecasts in Chapter 4 ranged from 47.1 to 48.2, the parabola model forecast is 46.3, and the Gompertz model forecast is 45.6. Which is best? The measures described in Chapter 5 can be used in making that determination. But also look at periods 12 through 16 only, as the actual increase is exactly three units of demand between periods (in this case).

Exponential Curve

Another way in which to forecast a non-linear curve is the exponential trend. It is especially applicable when demand changes at a somewhat constant, compounded rate. The equation in logarithm form is:

$$\log y = \log a + \log b(x)$$

Again, the same demands are used to illustrate the method. Initially, computations are made and entered in Figure 6-8. Columns 1 through 3 are basic information. The origin in the X column (column 2) is set at the middle period. If there are an odd number of periods, the middle period is zero and numbering proceeds by one's: -1, -2, -3, etc and +1, +2, +3, etc. However, if there are an even number of periods, the two middle periods are designated +1 and –1 and numbering is by two's, as in Figure 6-8.

Step 1: Find the logarithms for each of the demands and enter them in column 4. These are the same as those in Figure 6-7.

Step 2: Multiply column 2 by column 4 and enter in column 5; for example period 1 is: -15 times 0.7076 = -10.6140.

Step 3: Square the numbers in column 2 and enter in column 6.

Step 4: Calculate the constants log a and log b by solving the following equations:

$$\log a = \Sigma \log Y \div N = 18.2599 \div 16 = 1.1412$$

$$\log b = \Sigma X(\log Y) \div \Sigma X^2 = 36.3127 \div 1360 = 0.0267$$

Step 5: For each period, compute the demand as a logarithm and enter in column 7, using the log equation, for example:

Period 1: $1.1412 + 0.0267(-15) = 0.7407$

Find the antilog of 0.7407, which is 5.5

Period 16: $1.1412 + 0.0267(15) = 1.5417$

Find the antilog of 1.5417, which is 34.8

Enter the results of each calculation in column 8

The next succeeding log in column 7 may be obtained by adding log b to the last number in column 7. If the codes in column 2 are coded by one's, add log b to the preceding number. If coded by two's (as here), add twice log b, for example: $0.0267(2) + 0.7407 = 0.7941$.

The forecasting equation is the log equation given above. Examples of forecasts follow:

Period 17: $1.1412 + 0.0267(17) = 1.5951$, antilog 39.4

Period 20: $1.1412 + 0.0267(23) = 1.7553$, antilog 56.9

Note the forecast for period 20. It is totally out-of-line with the other forecasts made in this section although the same demands were used. By plotting the demands and forecasts on a graph the exponential nature of this method becomes apparent and suggests it specialized nature, generally, an unending compounded increase.

Exponential Curve Calculations

1	2	3	4	5	6	7	8
Period	Code X	Demand Y	Log Y	X(log Y)	X²		
1	-15	5.1	0.7076	-10.6140	225	0.7407	5.5
2	-13	6.0	0.7782	-10.1166	169	0.7941	6.2
3	-11	7.0	0.8451	-9.2961	121	0.8475	7.0
4	-9	8.0	0.9031	-8.1279	81	0.9009	8.0
5	-7	9.1	0.9590	-6.7130	49	0.9543	9.0
6	-5	10.6	1.0253	-5.1265	25	1.0077	10.2
7	-3	12.0	1.0792	-3.2376	9	1.0611	11.5
8	-1	13.6	1.1335	-1.1335	1	1.1145	13.0
9	1	15.5	1.1903	1.1903	1	1.1679	14.6
10	3	17.0	1.2304	3.6912	9	1.2213	16.7
11	5	19.0	1.2788	6.3940	25	1.2747	18.8
12	7	21.0	1.3222	9.2554	49	1.3281	21.3
13	9	24.0	1.3802	12.4218	81	1.3815	24.1
14	11	27.0	1.4314	15.7454	121	1.4349	27.2
15	13	30.0	1.4771	19.2023	169	1.4883	30.8
16	15	33.0	1.5185	22.7775	225	1.5417	34.8
Total Σ	0	257.9	18.2599	36.3127	1360		

Figure 6-8

The forecasts of the several series may be compared. Although one may be the best for a given time series, it does not hold that it will always be the best for every time series. The forecaster must also be alert for change in a given series that could materially affect the outcome. Change indicates review and analysis and possibly a need for a change in the model. If there are factors such as seasonality or cyclical considerations, the time series may require modification to eliminate their influence, with those factors added back after forecasting. Decomposition is a good way in which to determine the make-up of a time series.

Growth curves (non-linear trends) are revisited in Chapter 11 with regard to forecasting when the pattern is not positively known but known "probably".

Chapter 7

Causal Models

The rationale for the forecasting methods described thus far is that the historical time series is of itself representative of at least the near-term future.

Causal models are a different breed. These models assume that the value to be forecast is related to one or more independent (explanatory) variables. The equations quantify that relationship. The forecast is not based upon past observations but upon the cause/effect relationship between the dependent variable (the value to be forecast) and the independent variables. However, it is inaccurate to say that one is the cause of the other, more correctly one moves in approximate agreement with the other.

An independent variable may be any demand determinant that is statistically related to the value being forecast. Some examples are the Dow Jones average, new housing starts, time, industry advertising expenditures, demographic data, total production in an industry group, the gross domestic product or its subdivisions such as disposable income, leading indicators, the prime or other interest rates, other economic data, the average performance of company sales representatives, or other internally generated indicators. In fact, any series that moves in at least approximate agreement with the demand being forecast is a candidate as long as it is not a nonsense association, such as, comparing the number of storks nesting in chimneys of some European villages and the number of human births in those villages.

Which demand determinants are pertinent is found through research. The first step is to learn as much as possible about the product to be forecast and the independent variables that may be associated with it. If sales are being forecast, for instance, the research is directed to finding an affinity between the sales of that product and independent series. The look can be directed inward as well as outward. The level of sales may be influenced by the advertising budget, the sales of the industry that your company supports, the product price, the ratio of company price to competitor price, or a segment of the economy (interest rates, wholesale prices, the jobless rate, etc.). Probably, the connection is complex. A part of the problem is to identify those few independent variables that move in close proximity with demand and that adequately describe the relationship.

The correlation between variables may be positive or negative. When one variable increases as the other increases, a positive relationship exists. If one variable decreases and the other increases, a negative (inverse) relationship exists. Either is useful in forecasting. Variables may move simultaneously or one may lead the other.

Simple regression implies one dependent and one independent variable. Multiple regression consists of two or more independent variables. Relationships may be linear or curvilinear. To better illustrate the procedures, independent variable examples in this chapter may be a bit different than the actual historic data.

Two significant problems arise when contemplating the application of regression:

- ❖ Finding historical data that are in the form needed, for example, in monthly or quarterly segments as opposed to yearly. Finding up-to-date data. Frequently, government figures lag significantly behind the current period.

- ❖ Having good forecasts of independent variable data, especially when actual data lag the current period. The reliability of professionally prepared economic forecasts when numbers are attached to their predictions is suspect and should be historically tested to determine reliability.

Sources are government statistics (Statistical Abstract of the United States, Commerce Department publications, etc.), trade organizations, professional societies, and professional services specializing in providing economic data and forecasts, and the web. More information regarding sources is contained in the introductory part of the Multiple Regression section.

Simple Linear Regression

Simple linear regression when time is the independent variable is described in Chapter 6 (least squares trend). In the explanation that follows, the independent variable may be any variable except time. The forecasting (trend) equation is: $a + b(x)$.

Regression analysis requires that there be a statistical relationship between two or more variables. If the movement of the variables is concurrent, the accuracy of the forecast depends not only on the closeness of the relationship but also upon the predictability of the independent variable should actual data not be available for the latest periods. If the independent variable is a leading indicator, actual data may sometimes be applied to the forecasting model. The following examples illustrate the method.

Assume that a company produces a line of products (such as plumbing fixtures) that are used primarily in private residences. It sells to building contractors for installation in residences that they are building. Renovation projects, as in home remodeling, constitute a secondary market. The company also sells replacement parts for its products.

The company has studied its relationship to the marketplace and has found that its ultimate customers are private contractors who build single-family dwellings or small apartment buildings. Replacement fixtures are an incidental consideration. Replacement parts are a function of the age of the equipment in use.

Research also revealed that initial sales are closely related to new housing starts. Housing starts are a three-month leading indicator for the company because the contractor buys the fixtures after the exterior of the house is enclosed and the distributor reorders after his sale is made. Thus, first quarter sales of 62 (Figure 7-1) are ordered for delivery in the second quarter (three months later). Replacement fixtures are ignored in the formulation because of their insignificant influence. They become part of the random fluctuation. Replacement parts sales are related to the age of the end items in use. That forecast is based upon the age of the end items that have been sold.

Pertinent data and extensions are shown in Figure 7-1 for end item forecasting. In this example, the exact product is not identified. It could be a single end item, a product group, or an entire line, as may be appropriate. It may be expressed in units (as it is here) or in constant or current dollars if one of those measures is the most meaningful for the purpose being served by the forecast.

Assume the product line is bathroom fixtures. Multiple fixtures per house or apartment are more likely than dwellings with only one bathroom. The company has considered this and after research has increased new housing starts to the estimate of bathroom fixtures. This may be an unnecessary step, however.

Step 1: Prepare a table in the format illustrated in Figure 7-1. Y as a percentage of X is not part of the following calculations. It is discussed separately. The X quantity (new housing starts, modified) is unadjusted, not modified for cyclical or seasonal considerations. Source data for new housing starts comes from government and trade association publications.

Step 2: Solve for b by substituting the totals in Figure 7-1 into the equation:

$$n\Sigma(XY) - \Sigma(X)\Sigma(Y)/n\Sigma X^2 - \Sigma(X)^2 =$$

$$11(527151) - (7996)(719)/11(5859694) - 7996^2 =$$

$$5798661 - 5749124/64456634 - 63936016$$

$$b = 0.095$$

Step 3: Solve for a:

$$(\Sigma Y - \Sigma X(b)) \div n$$

$$(719 - 7996(0.095))/11$$

$$a = -3.69 \text{ or } -3.7$$

Note that the last four columns of Figure 7-1 were not used in these calculations, but are applicable to the correlation analysis, which follows.

Simple Regression Computations

Time Period	Starts X	Sales Y	XY	X²	Y²	Y%X	Y_c	$Y-Y_c$	$(Y-Y_c)^2$
1st Qtr	661	62	40982	436921	3844	9.38	59.105	2.895	8.38100
2nd Qtr	790	74	58460	624100	5476	9.37	71.360	2.640	6.96960
3rd Qtr	757	66	49962	573049	4356	8.72	68.225	-2.225	4.95060
4th Qtr	700	61	42700	490000	3721	8.71	62.810	-1.810	3.27610
1st Qtr	654	52	34008	427716	2704	7.95	58.440	-6.440	41.47360
2nd Qtr	811	76	61636	657721	5776	9.37	73.355	2.645	6.99600
3rd Qtr	735	65	47775	540225	4225	8.84	66.135	-1.135	1.28823
4th Qtr	658	66	43428	432964	4356	10.03	58.820	7.180	51.55240
1st Qtr	633	57	36081	400689	3249	9.00	56.445	0.555	0.30800
2nd Qtr	822	77	63294	675684	5929	9.37	74.400	2.600	6.76000
3rd Qtr	775	63	48825	600625	3969	8.13	69.935	-6.935	48.09420
Total	7996	719	527151	5859694	47605				180.05000

Figure 7-1

Housing starts and company sales in thousands of units. In absolute terms (signs ignored) Y – Y_c sums to 37.06.

Forecasting with Simple Linear Regression

Once the values have been determined, the forecasting equation is ready to estimate future sales. Because of the lead-time for reorders of equipment, the company can forecast sales for the fourth quarter of year 4, as new housing starts are known. Fourth quarter starts, translated to fixtures, are 667. Substitute the values in the forecasting formula a + b(x): -3.7 +0.095(667) = 59.7 or 60. The fourth quarter estimate of 60 will be delivered for first quarter sales.

It is likely that an estimate for the next quarter would not include enough of the future for planning purposes, especially for purchase of materials and production planning. Options are discussed below. The reader should generalize the rationale as it may be applied in many situations. Planning for the long-term is discussed later with regard to strategic planning and forecasting (see Chapter 12).

It may be that satisfactory forecasts for housing starts for periods beyond the current period (here quarterly) are available through government, trade association, or professional forecasting services. If so, the forecast of housing starts is used because actual data is not available. The reliability of those forecasts is suspect and should be tested historically.

Perhaps housing starts correlate with other economic data that through regression analysis will result in reasonable forecasts of housing starts. If so, a forecast of housing starts can be generated.

Regression analysis (least squares trend) with time as the independent variable may provide a reasonable forecast of the near-term. The objective is to calculate a trend line based on known data and extend that line into the future. Figure 7-2 illustrates the methodology with calculations as explained in Chapter 6.

Least Squares Trend Line

Quarter	Y (Starts)	X (Code)	XY	X^2	Trend
1st Qtr, Yr 1	661	-11	-7271	121	722.17
2nd Qtr	790	-9	-7110	81	722.13
3rd Qtr	757	-7	-5299	49	722.08
4th Qtr	700	-5	-3500	25	722.04
1st Qtr, Yr2	654	-3	-1962	9	721.99
2nd Qtr	811	-1	-811	1	721.94
3rd Qtr	735	1	735	1	721.90
4th Qtr	658	3	1974	9	721.85
1st Qtr, Yr 3	633	5	3165	25	721.81
2nd Qtr	822	7	5754	49	721.76
3rd Qtr	775	9	6975	81	721.71
4th Qtr	667	11	7337	121	721.67
Total	8663			-13	572	

a = 721.92, b = -0.023

Figure 7-2

If the trend line is accepted as typical, the forecast for the first quarter of year 4 is 721.62. Is this acceptable? Not for the purpose of forecasting the first quarter since there is a seasonal aspect to new housing starts, thus the trend is not representative of the first quarter. Also note that the trend depicted in Figure 7-2 varies only slightly from the first to last quarter. Dividing 8663 by 12 periods is 721.92, which is the average for the three years. The data could be deseasonalized as described in Chapter 3 or available deseasonalized data used, but first look at the following to see if a simplification is available. Note that there is a slight downward trend overall.

1st quarter: 661, 654, 633 for an average of 649

2nd quarter: 790, 811, 822 for an average of 808

3rd quarter: 757, 735, 775 for and average of 756

4th quarter: 700, 658, 667 for an average of 675

The averages verify the seasonal nature of new housing starts. In the first quarter there is a declining trend the past three years, but this is not necessarily true for the other quarters. Is it possible to make an estimate of housing starts for the first quarter, year 4 without involving forecasting equations? It is logical to assume that housing starts will be somewhere between 661 and 633, and possibly less than 633 as there is a decrease year to year. Assuming a continuation of the economic trend, a projection of 633 or less is not unreasonable. Translating this to company sales can be done by determining the average past relationship between sales and housing starts. The Y as % of X column in of Figure 7-1 shows the percentage that company sales are to housing starts. If the first three quarters is averaged, the percentage is 8.78%. Thus, 8.78% of 633 equals 56, the estimate the forecaster chose for the first quarter. The rationale in this paragraph can be extended to forecasting further into the future.

What has not been done is to determine the goodness of the forecasting methodology, which is the subject of the next section. Validation would normally be done before forecasting to insure that there is an appropriate relationship between the variables.

Correlation Analysis

There are several statistical techniques designed to measure the goodness of a regression equation, that is, they evaluate or validate the model. Specifically, it is important to know the range of accuracy that may be expected and the closeness of the relationship that exists between the variables. These measures indicate the confidence that may be assigned to the regression equation.

Standard Deviation of Regression

The standard deviation of regression, alternately known as the standard error of the estimate, measures the errors of the Y values in relation to the regression (straight) line, that is, the probable variation that may occur. The closer that the data points are to the regression line the smaller the standard deviation of regression, thus the more reliable the estimates. Following are two formulae for extracting the standard deviation. Both examples utilize data from Figure 7-1.

The standard deviation may be found from the equation $\sqrt{\Sigma(Y - Y_c)^2 \div n}$, where Y_c is the forecast, thus, $\sqrt{180.05 \div 11} = \sqrt{16.3682} = 4.05$ or 4.1 rounded. (Y_c for the first quarter, year 1, for example, is found by solving the equation $a = b(x)$, which is $-3.69 + 0.095(661) = 59.105$.

The second formula is as follows.

$$SE = \sqrt{(\Sigma Y^2 - a\Sigma Y - b\Sigma XY)/n}$$

$$\sqrt{[47605 - (-3.7)(719) - 0.095(527151)]} \div 11$$

$$\sqrt{[47605 - (-2660.3) - 50079.3]} \div 11$$

$$\sqrt{186} \div 11 = \sqrt{16.9} = 4.1$$

The reader will recall that approximately 68% of the values fall within ±1 standard deviation in a normally distributed pattern and approximately 95% fall within ±2 standard deviations. This relationship may be expressed by the equation $Y_c \pm SE$ for the 68% area and $Y_c \pm 2SE$ for the 95% area. Therefore, the deviation 68% of the time will be, roughly, within ±4 units and 95% of the time within ±8 units, as rounded. Because the units are in thousands, the variation equals 4,000 and 8,000 units. Knowing the range is important for planning purposes and as an indicator of reliability. The forecast as previously determined for the fourth quarter is 60,000 ±8,000 at 95% probability. The first quarter forecast is 56,000 ±8000 at 95%. Our example is in units, but the procedure applies equally if the data were current or constant dollars. Note that the forecast errors $(Y - Y_c)$ are all contained within the 95% area, the largest being 7.18. When Y values are compared with the average of Y, $(Y - Y_{av})$, see Figure 7-4, the range of values is greater.

In Chapter 3's section *Testing for Accuracy and Reliability* standard deviation and the range of error was explained. Those calculations for range are equally applicable here. Applying that procedure, the probable range of error is calculated as follows, with the average forecast error being $37.06 \div 11 = 3.37$.

At 68%: 3.37 – 4.1 = -0.73 (lower end)

3.37 + 4.1 = 7.47 (upper end)

At 95%: 3.37 – 2(4.1) = -4.83 (lower end)

3.37 + 2(4.1) = 11.57 (upper end)

Since the error cannot be less than zero, the negative numbers are changed to zero. Note that the probability range is larger when this procedure is employed. The range of the forecast error at 95% will fall somewhere between zero and 11.57.

Another procedure for predicting the interval between actual and forecast is to calculate the **standard error of the forecast (Sf)**. In the equation, N is the number of observations (time periods), which are 12 because for X (housing starts) data for all twelve periods are known. SD is the standard deviation of regression. The other data are taken from Figure 7-3. Since the fourth quarter is being forecast, housing starts for that quarter are incorporated into the equation. The average (721.9) is the total (8663) divided by 12 periods.

$$\text{SD } \sqrt{[1 + (1 \div N)] + [(X - X_{av})^2 \div \Sigma(X - X_{av})^2]} =$$

$$4.1 \sqrt{[1 + 0.0833] + [(667 - 721.9)^2 \div 50618.9]} =$$

$$4.1\sqrt{1.0833 + 0.0595} = 4.38$$

In the equation, 667 is the value of X at the 4th quarter of year 3. The standard error of the forecast measures the variability of the estimated values of Y in relation to the true value of Y for a given value of X. Because we are predicting future values (unknown after the last period) this is an appropriate measure.

Standard Error of the Forecast

Time Period	X	X − X$_{av}$	(X - X$_{av}$)^2
1st Qtr Yr 1	661	-60.9	3708.81
2nd Qtr	790	68.1	4637.61
3rd Qtr	757	35.1	1232.01
4th Qtr	700	-21.9	479.61
1st Qtr Yr 2	654	-67.9	4610.41
2nd Qtr	811	89.1	7938.81
3rd Qtr	735	13.1	171.61
4th Qtr	658	-63.9	4083.21
1st Qtr Yr3	633	-88.9	7903.21
2nd Qtr	822	100.1	10020.01
3rd Qtr	775	53.1	2819.61
4th Qtr	667	-54.9	3014.01
Total	8663		50618.92

Average of X = 8663/12 = 721.9

Figure 7-3

To compute the range, from the probable point estimate (the forecast) solve the equation $Y_c \pm ZSf$ where Y_c is the fourth quarter, year 3 forecast and Z is a value of the normal curve. The Z values (confidence coefficients) of interest are: 1.0 for 68% (actually 68.27%) probability, 1.96 for 95%, and 2.58 for 99%. For example:

$$60 + 1.96(4.38) = 68.6$$

$$60 - 1.96(4.38) = 51.4$$

The assumptions made for this procedure are that the relationship is linear, that the Y values are normally distributed around the population, and that the number of observations (samples) is sufficient to give an accurate reading. The sample size is generally expected to be in the neighborhood of 30 or more. Inasmuch as our sample size is smaller the shortcoming can be overcome by computing the range using the *t* distribution. The t value is derived from the table at the end of this chapter. The equation is $Y_c \pm Sf$. In this example, .05 is applied, which is a 95% probability. The D column indicates the degree of freedom and it is explained below in conjunction with the F test. For this purpose $D = n - k$. with n as the number of observations, which is 12, and k as the number of constants; there are two, the a and b parameters in the regression equation. So, $D = 12 - 2 = 10$. D at 10 is the appropriate row.

$$60 + 1.812(4.38) = 67.9$$
$$60 - 1.812(4.38) = 52.1$$

The procedures above can be applied to any number that falls within the range of the numbers in Figure 7-3, that is between 633 (low) and 822 (high). If the forecaster wants to know the forecast and range if housing starts are 800 (perhaps this is an estimate of what the forecaster expects for the second quarter), a forecast is made (a + b(x)), which is 72.3; then, using the t distribution a range of 64.4 to 80.2 is calculated. The procedure may be used with any series, of course, but predictions outside of the range of numbers in the series should be avoided.

Several methods of calculating the range within which the forecast is likely to vary from actual have been presented. Which is the most appropriate is a judgment call based upon an examination of the historical time series: the one that provides the best fit. A caution: the more observations the better, but those observations are applicable only if there has not been a change in the series. Are the oldest data as representative as the newest data?

Of course, the objective in forecasting is to obtain precision in the estimates. Because estimates will seldom be exactly on the money, a probable range of variation is calculated. A caution in forecasting is not to assume that because a procedure is statistically valid, it must be adopted without fear and without reproach. The experience of the forecaster may lead to a conclusion that it needs modification. The keys are knowledge, objectivity, and prudence.

Coefficient of Determination (r^2)

The coefficient of determination measures the degree of closeness of two variables. Expressed as a percentage, it indicates how much of the variation is explained by the independent variable.

Step 1: Prepare a table in the format illustrated in Figure 7-4. Column 2 is company sales (see Figure 7-1). Column 3 is the difference between sales and the arithmetic mean for the series; for example, the first quarter of year 1 is $62 - 65.36 = -3.36$. Column 4 is column 3 squared.

Step 2: Divide the total in column 4, Figure 7-4, by the number of observations (quarters in this case): 608.5456 ÷11 = 55.32.

Computations for r^2

Time Period	2 Y	3 $Y- Y_{av}$	4 $(Y - Y_{av})^2$
1st Qtr, Yr 1	62	-3.36	11.2896
2nd Qtr	74	8.64	74.6496
3rd Qtr	66	0.64	0.4096
4th Qtr	61	-4.36	19.0096
1st Qtr, Yr 2	52	-13.36	178.4896
2nd Qtr	76	10.64	113.2096
3rd Qtr	65	-0.36	0.1296
4th Qtr	66	0.64	0.4096
1st Qtr, Yr3	57	-8.36	69.8896
2nd Qtr	77	11.64	135.4896
3rd Qtr	63	-2.36	5.5696
Total	719		608.5456

Arithmetic average (mean) of sales: 719/11 = 65.36

Figure 7-4

Step 3: Find r^2, which is $1 - [16.9 \div 55.32] = 1 - .3055 = 0.6945$ or 69.5%. 16.9 is the radical found when solving the equation for the standard deviation of regression.

What meaning may be attached to the answer in step 3? About 70% of the variability in company sales is attributable to new housing starts. Approximately 30% of the variability is unexplained. It is due to factors not identified. An explanatory factor may be competitor sales, for example. Remember, only about 9% of the fixtures sold are this company's product. From time-to-time builders may choose a competitor's or this company's product more frequently than is the norm. There may be other economic factors at play that have not been discovered. Competitors or the company may lower or raise prices at various times. Some of the variability may be due to replacement fixture sales, which are only a small part of company sales, however.

The coefficient of determination is always a positive number. Is there a positive or negative relationship between company sales and new housing starts? This may be determined by calculating the coefficient of correlation. A much easier way is to look at the b value in the regression equation. In our example, it is 0.095, a positive number, thus a positive relationship exists. Had there been a negative number an inverse relationship would prevail. The range of the r^2 values will always be between 0 and 1. Zero indicates no relationship and 1 indicates a perfect relationship. The relationship may be positive or inverse, that is zero to plus or minus one.

If more independent variables are added to the equation, r^2 increases, but this does not mean that there is an increase in the goodness of the relationship. In such cases, an adjusted r^2 is computed, as with multiple regression, to compensate for this condition (explained later).

Coefficient of Correlation (r)

The correlation coefficient is not frequently used as a measure as it is more difficult to understand than r^2 in the context of the relationship between dependent and independent variables, however, there is a specific use for r in multiple regression as described in the next section. Coefficients of correlation are discussed later with regard to multicollinearity between independent variables in multiple regression.

The simplest way to determine r is to find the square root of r^2, thus r is $\sqrt{0.6945} = 0.833$ or 83.3%. Another way is to solve the product-moment formula from the data in Figure 7-1.

$$n\Sigma(XY) - (\Sigma X)(\Sigma Y)/[\sqrt{n\Sigma X^2 - (\Sigma X)^2}][\sqrt{n\Sigma Y^2 - (\Sigma Y)^2}]$$

$$11(527151) - (7996)(719)/[\sqrt{11(5859694) - (7996)^2}][\sqrt{11(47605) - (719)^2}] =$$

$$49537/59036.4 = 0.839$$

To find r^2 square r: $0.839 \times 0.839 = 0.704$ or 70.4%. The slight number difference in the two approaches is due to rounding.

The reader can construct a chart that compares r and r^2 values (side by side columns). The table will illustrate the dynamic nature of the relationship. For example, a coefficient of correlation of 0.80 is twice that of 0.40, but the coefficient of determination is four times stronger.

When r = 0.40 r^2 = 0.16

When r = 0.80 r^2 = 0.64

Determining Significance

The r^2 indicates the degree of association between the dependent and independent variables. Although a high degree may be indicated, the possibility that chance plays a major role in the association must be considered. When there are a limited number of data points, the possibility grows. Procedures are available that test the significance of the relationship. One such test is the F test. It measures the significance of the relationship by comparing explained and unexplained variances. The term variance signifies that both the number of observations (data points) and the number of variables are included in the calculations.

Step 1: Prepare a chart in the form of Figure 7-5, as follows:

Column 1 is company sales and column 2 is new housing starts.

Column 3 is Y_c which equals a + b(x). For example, the first quarter year 1 is $-3.69 + 0.095(661) = 59.105$; second quarter year 1 is $-3.69 + 0.095(790) = 71.36$. These are the equivalent of forecasts.

Column4 is company sales minus column 3. The first period is 62 – 59.105 = 2.895.

Column 5 is column 4 squared, that is 2.895 x 2.895 = 8.381025.

Column 6 is company sales minus the mean (arithmetic average) of sales, that is 62 – 65.36 = -3.36.

Column 7 is column 6 squared, that is –3.36 x –3.36 = 11.2896.

Computations for F

Time Period	1 Sales Y	2 Starts X	3 Y_c	4 $Y - Y_c$	5 $(Y - Y_c)^2$	6 $Y - Y_{av}$	7 $(Y - Y_{av})^2$
1st Qtr Yr 1	62	661	59.105	2.895	8.381025	-3.36	11.2896
2nd Qtr	74	790	71.360	2.640	6.969600	8.64	74.6496
3rd Qtr	66	757	68.225	-2.225	4.950625	0.64	0.4096
4th Qtr	61	700	62.810	-1.810	3.276100	-4.36	19.0096
1st Qtr Yr 2	52	654	58.440	-6.440	41.473600	-13.36	178.4896
2nd Qtr	76	811	73.355	2.645	6.996025	10.64	113.2096
3rd Qtr	65	735	66.135	-1.135	1.288225	-0.36	0.1296
4th Qtr	66	658	58.820	7.180	51.552400	0.64	0.4096
1st Qtr Yr 3	57	633	56.445	0.555	0.308025	-8.36	69.8896
2nd Qtr	77	822	74.400	2.600	6.760000	11.64	135.4896
3rd Qtr	63	775	69.935	-6.935	48.094230	-2.36	5.5696
Total Σ	719	7996			180.049900		608.5456

a = -3.96; b = 0.095 as previously computed

Mean of sales: 719/11 = 65.36

Figure 7-5

Step 2: Determine variation. Total variation is the total of column 7, unexplained variation is the total of column 5, and explained variation is the total variation minus the unexplained variation, which is 608.5456 – 180.0499 = 428.496.

Step 3: Determine the degree of freedom, which is defined as the number of variables that can vary freely in the equation. For our purposes it is solving these two equations: $D_1 = k - 1$ where k is the number of constants in the sample regression. Because our regression formula contains the a and b constants, k = 2. D_2 incorporates both k and the number of observations (n). Thus, the equation is: $D_2 = n - k$.

Explained variation: $D_1 = k - 1 = 2 - 1 = 1$

Unexplained variation: $D_2 = n - k = 11 - 2 = 9$

Step 4: Calculate the estimate of population variance, as follows:

Unexplained: variation $\div D_2 = 180.05 \div 9 = 20$

Explained: variation $\div D_1 = 428.496 \div 1 = 428.496$

Step 5: Find F: 428.496 ÷ 20 = 21.42.

An informal rule says that when the F value is 5 or more there is a significant regression model, that is, there is a significant relationship between the dependent and independent variables. It assumes, however, that there are thirty-six or more observations. Because interpretation may mislead, it is better to refer to a table of F values. Generally, there are two tables: one at 5% probability (95% level of confidence), one at 1% probability. Abbreviated charts are given at the end of this chapter.

Referring to the charts, the computed F value is larger than the values in the charts at both the 5% and 1%, thus, there is a significant relationship and the regression model is valid. The degree of freedom for the numerator (D_1) is the numbers horizontally on the chart; the degree of freedom for the denominator (D_2) is the numbers vertically on the chart. The value is at the intersection of 1 and 9. At 5% the value is 5.12; at 1% it is 10.6. F is 21.42, which is above the minimum chart values. The forecaster can conclude with practical certainty that the relationship between the dependent and independent variables is sound.

It may occur that F is larger than the chart value at 5% but smaller at 1%. In this case, it is more accurate to conclude that the correlation is probably significant.

A related test of significance is the *t test*. Symbolically $t = \sqrt{F} = \sqrt{21.42} = 4.628$. It may also be calculated from r and r^2 directly: $r\sqrt{(n - 2)/(1 - r^2)}$. Once the value of t is computed, the table of t distributions is consulted. The symbol df is the same as D_2, thus the intersection of row 9 at column 0.05 is 1.833. Because 4.628 is greater than 1.833, the coefficient of the independent variable is significant. The F and t tests almost always reach the same conclusion, indicating that only one of the procedures is necessary (but it does no harm to do both).

The last procedure to be examined is the **Durbin-Watson test**. In this test the forecaster analyzes the residuals (errors). These are the unexplained differences that occur because the forecasts computed by the regression equation do not equal the actual values. The idea is to determine whether the residuals are random. If there is autocorrelation present, a pattern of some sort is indicated, which suggests that the dependent variable is influenced by outside factors. The result of autocorrelation is possibly inaccurate forecasts; therefore, it is necessary to test for this condition.

Step 1: Prepare a table as given in Figure 7- 6. Column 2 lists sales or actual values and column 3 the estimates (forecasts). Column 4 are the errors for each period, that is, the difference between columns 2 and 3; for example, the first quarter is $62 - 59.105 = 2.895$. Column 5 is the difference between the current error and the previous error, thus the second quarter is $2.64 - 2.895 = -0.255$. Column 6 is the square of column 5, so 0.255 x 0.255 = 0.0650. Column 7 is the square of column 4.

Computations for Durbin-Watson Test

1 Period	2 Y	3 Y_c	4 e_t	5 $e_t - e_{t-1}$	6 $(e_t - e_{t-1})^2$	7 e_t^2
1st Qtr, Yr 1	62	59.105	2.895			8.381
2nd Qtr	74	71.360	2.640	-0.255	0.0650	6.969
3rd Qtr	66	68.225	-2.225	-.4.865	23.6682	4.950
4th Qtr	61	62.810	-1.810	0.415	0.17220	3.276
1st Qtr, Yr 2	52	58.440	-6.440	-4.630	21.4370	41.474
2nd Qtr	76	73.355	2.645	9.085	82.5370	6.996
3rd Qtr	65	66.135	-1.135	-3.780	14.2880	1.288
4th Qtr	66	58.820	7.180	8.315	69.1390	51.552
1st Qtr, Yr3	57	56.445	0.555	-6.625	43.8910	0.308
2nd Qtr	77	74.400	2.600	2.045	4.1820	6.760
3rd Qtr	63	69.935	-6.935	-9.535	90.9160	48.094
Total					350.2960	180.050

Figure 7-6

Step 2: Divide the total in column 6 by the total in column 7: 350.3/ 180.05 = 1.95. Note that the sum of column 7 includes all 11 periods. 1.95 is the Durbin-Watson score. A table of DW test bounds is given at the end of this chapter (explained in the section about multiple regression), however, a general rule states that if the score is between 1.5 and 2.5 the residuals are randomly dispersed and no autocorrelation exists.   The best score is 2.0 as the value range is between zero and four.

The DW score computed above is 1.95, in the range and close to 2, thus the series is without autocorrelation and the regression equation is valid.

In reviewing the results of the various tests, what can the forecaster conclude?

$$F \text{ test} = 21.42$$

$$t \text{ test} = 4.628$$

$$\text{Durbin-Watson} = 1.95$$

$$\text{Coefficient of determination} = 69.5\%$$

The F test measures the relationship between the independent and dependent variables, specifically the significance of that relationship. Because the F value is above the chart values at both the 5% and 1% levels, the forecaster concludes that the relationship is significant. The finding is verified by the t distribution.

Next, the forecaster determines if the residuals are randomly distributed. If not, a pattern is indicated; therefore, the independent variable does not explain the dependent variable differences. The DW score of 1.95 is within the box of 1.5 to 2.5. There is no autocorrelation and forecast accuracy will not be affected. The residuals are random.

The relationship between variables, that is the goodness of the forecasting technique, is valid. How well do the forecasts perform? First, the forecaster reviews the coefficient of determination (r^2). At 69.5% (or 70%), about 30% of the variation between forecast and actual is *not* explained by the independent variable. As will be seen in the next paragraph the historical spread between forecast and actual is a consideration. If the MAPE is calculated as described in Chapter 5 the average percentage is 5.31%. This is the average error as a percentage indicating that forecasts will vary from demand on average about 5.3%. This is a reasonable result. The forecaster notices that at least three of the quarterly percentages are quite high. Some reasons for the 70% relationship were explained above and the forecaster may consider them for the future, especially to see if there are other economic factors that may be added to the regression equation. Overall, the 70% indicates a fair but not a stellar relationship between the variables, which may, however, be improved by the addition of other independent variables.

Now, the forecaster considers the range within which the forecasts will fluctuate from actual demand. Several options have been described. Which is most likely to be representative in the future? Because of the limited number of time periods, the decision is made to use the standard error of the forecast as modified by the *t* distribution at .05. The methodology is described above in *Correlation Analysis*. The *t* value is 1.812 times 4.38 (the value of S*f*), which equals ±7.94. All errors (difference between demand and forecast (Y_c)) are within this range (e_t, Figure 7-6).

In the next section there is an explanation of how to use Microsoft Excel to calculate the regression equation and several of the tests described above.

Multiple Regression

Multiple regression is an extension of simple linear regression, the difference being that there is more than one independent variable. Normally, multiple regression will give better forecasts than simple regression if the demand determinants (independent variables) are valid and carefully selected. In the simple regression example in the last section, r^2 was about 70% meaning that the independent variable explained 70% of the variability in company sales. However, by adding other meaningful independent variables, a higher coefficient of determination might be realized.

The multiple regression equation may comprise any number of variables, however, the goal is to select those few that describe adequately that portion of the business world being studied. The minimum number of data points (observations) is usually determined to be five observations for each independent variable. However, some authorities suggest that ten observations are needed. The more the better if the dependent variable has not changed over time in a direction or with a magnitude not represented by the independent variables. Too few data points may negate the trustworthiness of the results.

A not uncommon frustration is locating data series in the format needed for forecasting. The historical series needs to be as current as possible and good forecasts of the independent variables are essential from the date of the last actual observation to the forecasting horizon. There are many sources for obtaining data. One source is internal company records for promotional data, advertising expenditures, and pricing at different periods of time. Trade associations and professional organizations frequently collect data. Trade associations, for example, gather data concerning the industry and the products that are sold within its area of interest. Government is a rich but frustrating source because of a lag time in some series (not real time data). Some sources are the Census Bureau, the Bureau of Economic Analysis, and the U. S. Bureau of Labor Statistics (go to the web). The Conference Board is another excellent source; their web sites are www.conference-board.org and www.globalindicators.org. A search of the web will reveal other sources such as professional organizations, for example, Micrometrics, which is found at www.micrometrics-inc.com and The Financial Forecast Center at www.forecasts.org.

There are several basic requirements that must be met in a multiple regression relationship as explained below and in the examples following.

- ❖ A straight-line relationship between the dependent and independent variables must exist. This is called linearity. Curvilinear series cannot be incorporated into the mix unless they can be converted into a linear form (perhaps through logarithms).

- ❖ The difference between each actual value and the related predicted value (called the residual) must be independent of those residuals before and after it. Residuals (errors) are disturbance terms that may change slowly with time, therefore, they may be related to nearby observations. Measuring residuals was discussed earlier in this chapter and will be incorporated in the examples that follow.

❖ Each of the independent variables must be correlated with the dependent variable but not with each other. Intercorrelation may be tolerated if the relationship is weak or the pattern is stable – does not change radically. This condition is called multicollinearity. Its existence may reduce accuracy. Its influence upon the results should be estimated to determine if it is a significant problem. Available economic and business data often tend to be correlated because many of the elements react to the same basic economic pressures. Transformation, as discussed later, is a means of correcting for multicollinearity.

❖ The variance of the errors must be finite and constant over the range of the observations. This means that the proportional difference, not the absolute difference of the errors, is constant. When the relationship is proper, the condition is referred to as homoskedasticity. When the condition is not met, the problem of heteroskedasticity exists. If data points were plotted on a scatter diagram and were fan shaped, for instance, that would constitute heteroskedasticity. Another type resembles a wave that fluctuates above and below the regression line as would occur when a curvilinear relationship is estimated by a linear one. Transformation may solve the problem.

❖ The dependent and independent variables must be related in time. It is not correct to assume that the movement of the dependent and independent variables should be concurrent. Although this is not uncommon, it is by no means exclusive. One variable may lag another requiring that it be offset as to time. As the time periods become smaller – months rather than years – this condition becomes more likely. Although this may be a serious mathematical problem in econometrics, offsetting is an appropriate avenue to take in sales forecasting. Recognizing that a lag exists is the problem.

❖ The model must be carefully formulated to include those variables that are relevant and exclude those that are extraneous. The rule of parsimony applies. The goal is to select those few independent variables that best reflect that segment of the business world being captured. There may be many series that could be used, but do they add significantly to the explanation of the series? Testing is possible to determine how much an independent variable adds to the result.

❖ The observations used in formulating the model must come from the same population, that is, there must be continuity. It is desirable to incorporate as many observations as possible;

however, if economic conditions at a given time are radically different than the past range of normality, that difference may constitute a separate population that is better excluded. If the number of data points covers a sufficient period to include, say, recession and boom times, that may be normal. Differences of wartime and peacetime economics may constitute separate populations. Using sales statistics for an industry that suffered a major strike for an extended period may be misleading. This condition is frequently referred to as structural break.

The Multiple Regression Model

The multiple regression equation is an extension of the model for simple regression and takes the form

$$Y = a + b_1(x_1) + b_2(x_2) + \ldots + b_n(x_n)$$

Each of the x values are independent variables. If there are five independent variables, the x factors are x_1 through x_5.

The model is fashioned by first selecting a number of possible independent variables. Each is tested to determine how close a relationship exists with the dependent variable. There are several ways in which to approach the building of the model: total regression investigates all possible equations that can be developed from the independent variables and judges which is most appropriate by comparing the changes in the R^2 value or changes of some other statistic; backward elimination begins with incorporating all possible variables then eliminating them one at a time to see the impact on the R^2 value; and stepwise regression introduces one independent variable at a time and evaluates how much of the variance is explained by the introduction of that independent variable, the one with the highest R^2 value is entered first. These procedures are complex and are usually handled by regression software packages. Microsoft Excel has a program that performs the calculations and determines validity (described below). However, it is important that the forecaster understands the fundamentals of building and using a multiple regression model; therefore, a level of explanation is provided.

Assume for the first example a company that manufactures and imports non-durable, consumer type products that are sold to retailers. The forecaster has identified five independent variables that may influence company sales. Of course, there may be others. The variables are gross domestic product (GDP), designated as x_1, personal consumption expenditures for non-durable goods (PCE) as x_2, retail sales as x_3, disposable personal income (DPI) as x_4, and the consumer price index for urban consumers (CPI) as x_5. For purposes of multiple regression we will designate the independent variables with capital X's and r-values with capital R's.

The first order of business is preparing a correlation matrix. The matrix contains the correlation coefficients (R) for all variables. The R-value is derived by solving the product-moment formula explained earlier in this chapter (see the formula below) or as done here by employing the regression tool in Excel (explained later). There are 27 quarterly periods of data, of which 24 are used in the calculations and the final three reserved for testing the model.

$$n\Sigma(XY) - (\Sigma X)(\Sigma Y) \div [\sqrt{n\Sigma X^2 - (\Sigma X)^2}][\sqrt{n\Sigma Y^2 - (\Sigma Y)^2}]$$

It is unnecessary for our purposes to chart the sales and independent variable data, as the columns would look like the appropriate columns in Figure 7-1. Note, however, that the R-values in Figure 7-7 are not only those that compare the independent variables with the dependent variable but they also compare each independent variable with the other independent variables. In determining the R-value for X_1 and X_2, for example, X_1 becomes the Y value for the purpose of calculation.

Correlation Matrix

	Y	X_1	X_2	X_3	X_4	X_5
Y	1.000					
X_1	.954	1.000				
X_2	.952	.991	1.000			
X_3	.984	.907	.904	1.000		
X_4	.950	.993	.986	.899	1.000	
X_5	.956	.987	.991	.905	.992	1.000

Figure 7-7

In reviewing the Correlation Matrix, first notice that all independent variables have a high correlation with the dependent variable (Y). There is also high correlation between each of the independent variables, a condition previously defined as multicollinearity. Because each of the independent variables react similarly to changing economic conditions, correlation between the independent variables is not surprising. In selecting independent variables the objective is to find those that correlate with the dependent variable but not strongly with each other.Multicollinearity can cause problems because it explains the same variance in the dependent variable. When multicollinearity occurs, one of the independent variables should be dropped from the formula. The logical choice is to retain the one that has the highest correlation with the dependent variable.

The forecaster's problem, however, is more serious than just one or two instances of multicollinearity. All of the independent variables display the disease.

Another caution: when the correlation between two independent variables is larger than the correlation of the independent variable with the dependent variable, that independent variable, generally, should not be incorporated into the formula. This is an almost universal situation in our example series; for example, X_2, X_1 compared to X_2, Y.

It appears that simple regression will provide reliable forecasts using variable X_3 (retail sales). The coefficient of determination (R^2) is .968 or 96.8% (.984 x .984). Thus, about 97% of the variation is explained by the independent variable. To feel secure, the forecaster will run a few tests as described previously in this chapter, then test the equation against known data (the known sales figures for the last three quarters).

The F value at both 5% and 1% is substantially larger than the chart values. There is a significant relationship between the dependent and independent variables, thus the relationship is sound. The Durbin-Watson test indicates that there is no autocorrelation and the regression equation is valid. Considering the three factors (F test, DW test, and R^2), it is apparent that the technique is valid. As a final test, the forecaster will forecast known sales data that were not a part of the original 24 periods that comprised the development stage. The final three quarters of data (periods 25 through 27) for company sales and retail sales are tested to determine the goodness of the methodology.

Period	Company Sales	Retail Sales	Forecast	Error
25	24.6	748.2	23.5	1.1
26	26.4	876.9	27.0	0.6
27	27.0	875.6	27.0	0.0

In period 25 there was a decline in both company sales and retail sales, which may account for the larger error (given here in absolute terms). The forecasting equations are solved below. As computed by Excel, the a value is 3.047 and the b value is 0.0273.

$$Y = a + b(x)$$
$$3.047 + 0.0273(748.3) = 23.5$$
$$3.047 + 0.0273(876.9) = 27.0$$
$$3.047 + 0.0273(875.6) = 27.0$$

The forecaster can be confident that the technique will provide good company sales estimates. However, forecasts may be improved by finding other independent variables, and then again they may not.

Another approach that may allow the dismissed independent variables to be incorporated is to transform several of them, as explained in the second example. And there is a forecasting caveat: if the independent variable must be forecast (by the company or by an economic forecasting agency), the resulting company sales forecast will only be as good as the accuracy contained in the independent variable's forecast. Accurate point economic forecasts are not a given and may be difficult to come by.

Before examining a second example of multiple regression, Excel's regression program will be explained. It is equally applicable to simple or multiple regression.

One of several statistical functions that can be accessed by Microsoft Excel is regression. Select "Data Analysis" in the toolbox. If it is not there click "Add-ins" in the toolbox. It may be that Add-ins is not there which means Microsoft Office needs to be incorporated into your computer. Once Add-ins is installed, select "Analysis Tool Pak". In the Analysis Tool Pak select Regression. Now you are ready to indicate the range for the Y and X values, indicating where each begins and ends. The easiest way is to drag the cursor through the range. For multiple regression, the first value is the first value of X_1 and the last value is the last value of the final X. In addition to the following there are other boxes that will provide additional information that may be of value. *See addendum

Some of the useful data (that which we use in our examples, and explained previously) are:

- ❖ Multiple R. This is R, the coefficient of correlation. It is referred to as multiple because it is the R-value for all X variables in the equation.

- ❖ R^2, the coefficient of determination, and adjusted R square, which is adjusted for the number of independent variables, thus rendering the true R^2.

- ❖ Standard E, the standard error of the estimate (standard deviation of regression).

- ❖ Observations, the number of periods in the equation.

- ❖ In the ANOVA section are several columns of data:

- ❖ There are three columns of interest: the top labeled Regression, next Residual, and last Total. The statistics are computations for finding F. Entries are in descending order. Under *df* are the degrees of freedom: explained, unexplained, and the total of the two, followed by SS: explained and unexplained variation, followed by MS: D1 and D_2, and the F value in the next column, which is the statistic of interest. These are the numbers that were explained previously.

❖ In the next section are the coefficients: the first is the intercept (the $\underline{a}$ value) followed by the X variables (these are the values for each of the independent variables, that is the $\underline{b}$ values).

As versions of Microsoft are updated, the instructions for calling forth data analysis may be different.

The second multiple regression example concerns a durable goods manufacturer. Research indicates that sales may respond to the external factors of gross domestic product and personal consumption expenditures for durable goods and to the level of company advertising. Realistically, there are likely to be others, but for the purposes of illustration these three will be considered. The company believes that there is also some seasonality.

Dependent and Independent Variables

Periods In Qtr	Y Sales	X_z GDP	X_2 PCE	X_3 Co Ads	X_4	X_5	X_6
Yr 1, 1st	80.0	76.30	6.06	1.05	1	0	0
2nd	81.3	77.83	6.21	1.10	0	1	0
3rd	84.0	78.59	6.17	1.30	0	0	1
4th	72.6	79.81	6.22	1.42	0	0	0
Yr 2, 1st	83.4	81.24	6.35	0.90	1	0	0
2nd	81.9	82.80	6.24	1.08	0	1	0
3rd	88.1	83.91	6.52	1.53	0	0	1
4th	79.0	84.79	6.58	1.14	0	0	0
Yr 3, 1st	87.8	86.28	6.67	1.18	1	0	0
2nd	86.8	86.97	6.89	1.20	0	1	0
3rd	97.0	88.20	6.92	1.44	0	0	1
4th	91.0	89.85	7.25	1.20	0	0	0
Yr 4, 1st	100.2	90.93	7.32	1.41	1	0	0
2nd	98.8	91.61	7.55	1.46	0	1	0
3rd	106.3	92.97	7.68	1.51	0	0	1
4th	95.9	95.23	7.89	1.10	0	0	0
Yr 5, 1st	109.4	96.69	8.21	1.41	1	0	0
2nd	109.0	98.58	8.14	1.40	0	1	0
3rd	114.0	99.38	8.25	1.81	0	0	1
4th	99.4	100.28	8.12	1.30	0	0	0
Yr 6, 1st	111.7	101.42	8.38	1.52	1	0	0
2nd	110.0	102.03	8.45	1.61	0	1	0
3rd	115.0	102.25	8.41	1.90	0	0	1
4th	117.0	102.63	9.10	1.50	0	0	0
Yr 7, 1st	116.8	104.31	8.77	1.50	1	0	0
2nd	115.2	104.71	8.80	1.51	0	1	0
3rd	130.1	115.11	9.66	1.96	0	0	1

Figure 7-8

Relevant data are given in Figure 7-8. Sales are in millions, GDP and PCE in billions of dollars and company advertising in millions of dollars. To facilitate calculation and to make reading the numbers easier, dollars have been decimalized. For the first quarter, year 1, for example, GDP in billions is generally abbreviated 7630. Figure 7-8 reduces it to 76.30. Similarly, PCE becomes 6.06 (from 606), and advertising and sales are in millions expressed as 1.05 and 80, respectively. This does not change the results or the relationship between variables. It does change the $\underline{b}$ values. X_4 through X_6 are dummy variables explained later.

A correlation matrix is prepared as was done in the previous example (Figure 7-9). Regardless of the approach, a correlation matrix is advised. The forecaster first notices that there is a condition of multicollinearity between X_2 and X_1, which indicates that one of those variables should be dropped. X_2 has a higher correlation with Y than does X_1, however, the correlation of X_2 and X_1 is higher than it is with Y. The forecaster realizes that more in-depth analysis is needed. What should be done? Can multiple regression be applied and can forecasts be improved?

The forecaster decides to try a number of possible equations to determine which provides the most satisfactory forecasting results. There are many ways in which to transform the independent variables and their explanations follow. For judgment purposes, the forecaster will look at the correlation coefficient R, the adjusted coefficient of determination R^2, standard error, and F. The last three quarters of sales are held aside (not used in the formulations) for the purpose of testing. The Durbin-Watson test will be calculated for those candidates running in the finals.

Correlation Matrix

	Y	X_1	X_2	X_3
Y	1.000			
X_1	.929	1.000		
X_2	.945	.982	1.000	
X_3	.735	.658	.642	1.000

Figure 7-9

Before continuing with our example, a short explanation of the way in which the constants (the $\underline{a}$ and $\underline{b}$ values) are calculated will be presented. This is done by solving a set of normal equations, a sample of which follows. The number of normal equations relates to the number of constants, which includes the $\underline{a}$ and $\underline{b}$ values. If there are four constants, for instance, there are four normal equations. To derive the X values for the equations requires that a table be prepared and the sums of the columns applied to the equations. The columns are the squares of each independent variable (X), each YX and each X multiplied by each of the other X's; also, the sum of the Y (dependent variable) and the sum of each X is needed. With four independent variables there are nineteen columns of data to calculate and sum. Once the data are entered into the equations they are solved simultaneously or by matrix algebra. As can be envisioned this is a giant undertaking if done with pencil and calculator, but Excel solves this problem. The equations below represent three constants (two independent variables). The equations can be easily expanded to accommodate more variables.

Normal equations for three constants:

$$\sum X_1 = na + b_2\sum X_2 + b_3\sum X_3$$

$$\sum X_1X_2 = a\sum X_2 + b_2\sum X_2^2 + b_3\sum X_2X_3$$

$$\sum X_1X_3 = a\sum X_3 + b_2\sum X_2X_3 + b_3\sum X_3^2$$

Transforming a Data Set

If a model needs to be improved or to try alternate approaches to model building, modifying data is a method that is available. Many of the most useful methods are described in the literature, see Professor Chaman L. Jain's *Practical Guide to Business Forecasting*. Only selected independent variables need be converted, not all variables.

❖ Converting an independent variable with logarithms, explained in Chapter 6. This is especially appropriate in changing nonlinear data to a linear format.

❖ Dividing an independent variable into its component parts, thus creating possible additional independent variables. An example is dividing advertising expenditures into subcategories.

❖ Combining independent variables, for example, combining several subcategories into one variable. This is especially useful when there are too many variables compared with the number of observations.

❖ Adding a constant number to an independent variable, such as adding 10 to each observation.

❖ Converting current dollars to constant dollars or the reverse, particularly to have each data set in the same unit of measure.

❖ Multiplying two independent variables, using their product as the new independent variable.

❖ Dividing one by an independent variable, that is, $1/X$ or dividing one independent variable by another, that is, X_1/X_2 etc.

❖ Squaring each value of an independent variable (or adding a quadratic term).

❖ Using different transformations for the same variables, as dividing one variable by another and also multiplying the same two variables to create two new variables.

❖ Differencing as explained in the Box-Jenkins section or percentage change rather than actual change are possibilities.

❖ Ratios of one variable to another, such as advertising dollars per retail customer, rather than two independent variables.

With a little imagination other forms of modification can be called forth. An independent variable can be used in its original form and in a modified form. A few variables could be changed into many variables or vice versa.

Dummy Variables

Another method of improving regression models is to incorporate dummy (independent) variables to account for unusual situations. If a variable cannot be quantified, a dummy variable can be added. For example, a threatened strike, a strike, or a fire has a material affect upon sales, thus they are candidates for dummy variables. An unusual (not typical, not repetitive) increase or decrease in sales in a period calls for a dummy variable. (See the last example in Chapter 10 for a further explanation.) Values for dummy variables are either 1 or 0. In those periods when the unusual event occurs a 1 is entered as a dummy variable and a 0 is applied to all other periods. It may occur that there is more than one type of unusual event in, say, a year. A dummy variable is added to the equation for each different unusual situation. For instance, if there is a strike in one or more periods, a new dummy (independent) variable is added. A 1 is entered in the period(s) in which the strike occurred, a zero in all other periods. If there is a second unusual occurrence (say, a fire), a second dummy independent variable is added. For example, two different types of unusual incidents call for two additional variables. The value of 1 incorporated in the equation compensates for the unusual event(s). A 0 indicates that its effect is to be ignored.

Another situation in which dummy variables are useful is when there are two or more variable levels. For example, if the company advertises in three publications but at different times it may wish to know its success rate for each medium. Three dummy variables are established. A 1 is entered in those periods in which there is an advertisement in a particular publication, a zero in all other periods. Another condition using the same reasoning is when it is important to know the breakout between female and male (or any two groups), a 1 is assigned to one group and 0 to the other. If age breakout is significant, the same rationale applies.

If there is seasonality, dummy variables can be added to mitigate the impact. In Figure 7-8 three dummy variables are added to the quarterly data (X_4 through X_6), which is one less than the number of quarters in a year. Monthly data (twelve periods in a year) require eleven dummy variables. Figure 7-8 illustrates the manner in which the 1's and 0's are assigned for seasonality.

Seasonality in this example is a factor, and to determine the possible influence that it may have on forecasting, the forecaster prepared an historical chart of sales. The results are given in Figure 7-10. The percentages were derived by dividing quarterly sales by total sales for the year.

Seasonal Sales Chart, in Percentages

	1st Qtr	2nd Qtr	3rd Qtr	4th Qtr
Year 1	25.2	25.6	26.4	22.8
Year 2	25.2	24.7	26.6	23.8
Year 3	24.2	23.9	26.8	25.1
Year 4	25.0	24.6	26.5	23.9
Year 5	25.3	25.2	26.4	23.0
Year 6	24.6	24.2	25.3	25.8
Average	24.9	24.7	26.3	24.1

Figure 7-10

The quarterly averages indicate a steady pattern except that there is a seasonal aspect in the third quarter. This pattern is generally repeated throughout the six years of sales history. The forecaster will test a number of multiple regression models, some using the seasonal variables, some without because the seasonal pattern is only somewhat prominent. Figure 7-11 contains the results.

Selecting the Forecasting Model

Each of the columns in Figure 7-11 represents a factor that will be examined by the forecaster in selecting the sales forecasting model. The company needs a forecast of two quarters to plan and execute the purchase of raw materials, to schedule production, and to accomplish financial planning. It prefers three quarters ahead, with the third quarter tentative, not for making firm commitments.

❖ In theory, the model with the highest coefficient of correlation (R) will give the best forecasting results; however, it is appropriate to examine the other factors before making a decision. R is a relative measure of the relationship between variables. Remember that the R^2 value as adjusted indicates the percentage of variation in sales that is explained by independent variables, therefore, it is a meaningful (and critical) statistic.

❖ The adjusted R^2 is the R^2 value adjusted for the degrees of freedom (the number of independent variables). Recall that R^2 (coefficient of determination) can be computed by multiplying R by R. For example, the R squared value for the first period in

Figure 7-11 is .929 x .929 = .863. After adjustment it is .857 or 85.7%. This adjusted value correlates with R. The two are examined together. In multiple regression, the unadjusted R^2 value misleads because as variables are added to the model, the R^2 value increases, therefore, the need for the corrective action of the adjusted R^2.

Results of Different Regression Models

	X Variables	R	Adjusted R^2	Standard Error	F Test	% Ave.	Ave. Difference
1	GDP only	.929	.857	5.06	138.6	0.9	1.1
2	PCE only	.945	.888	4.48	182.5	1.5	1.8
3	Advertising only	.735	.519	9.27	25.8	-	-
4	GDP, PCE, Ads	.959	.909	4.04	77.4	0.9	1.0
5	GDP, PCE, Ads, S	.994	.984	1.70	237.3	1.5	1.8
6	GDP, Ads	.943	.879	4.64	84.8	1.2	1.9
7	GDP, Ads, S	.972	.929	3.57	60.9	2.4	3.0
8	(GDP)(PCE), Ads	.955	.904	4.15	109.1	1.8	2.3
9	(GDP)(PCE)	.942	.882	4.58	173.7	1.8	2.2
10	(GDP)(PCE) Ads, S	.989	.972	2.24	160.9	3.5	5.5
11	(GDP)(PCE), S	.989	.973	2.19	209.3	4.4	5.4
12	In(GDP)(PCE)Ads,S	.977	.941	3.25	74.4	2.3	2.9
13	In GDP	.921	.841	5.33	122.9	2.8	3.5
14	In GDP, Ads	.934	.860	5.00	71.4	2.9	3.6
15	In GDP, S	.964	.914	3.90	62.5	0.8	1.0
16	In GDP,Ads, S	.965	.912	3.97	48.6	0.9	1.1
17	In (GDP)(PCE)	.931	.862	5.00	145.0	4.4	5.5
18	In (GDP)(PCE), S	.976	.943	3.18	96.9	2.4	3.0
19	GDP, PCE*, Ads, S	.994	.984	1.70	237.3	1.4	1.8
20	GDP, PCE*, S	.994	.985	1.60	299.4	1.4	1.8
21	PCE*, S	.994	.985	1.60	372.8	1.7	2.1

Abbreviations: **GDP** is gross domestic product, **PCE** is personal consumption expenditures for durable goods, **PCE*** indicates that 10 was added to each value (6.06 becomes 16.06), Ads is company expenditures for advertising, S is seasonal dummy variables, and In indicates inverse $(1/X_2,$ for example). (GDP)(PCE) indicates that the two variables were multiplied and the product thereof is the new variable. Percent Average is the percent of difference (error) between actual sales and forecast for the final three quarters in **Figure 7-8**, the test periods; Average Difference is the numerical difference.

Figure 7-11

❖ The standard error of the estimate measures the accuracy of the forecasts that will issue from application of the model being examined. It is the base for calculating the range of the error: the smaller the error the closer that forecasted values (sales) will be to the actual values. In our example (Figure 7-11), a standard error of 5.06 at 95% confidence level indicates that 95% of the time the estimates will be within an accuracy range of ±10.12 units (5.06 x 2), that is, an actual sales value of 80 should forecast between 69.88 and 90.12. Because sales are in millions, 10.12 is also in millions. Previously, several methods of determining range were described, which the reader may wish to review.

❖ The F statistic (test) answers the question: how significant is the relationship between the dependent and independent variables? As learned earlier, the higher the F value the more relevant the association. By referring to tables of F distributions at the 5% level (95% level of confidence) and the 1% level, the minimum values for F to be significant are determined. If the F value exceeds the value in the tables, there is a significant relationship between the dependent and independent variables.

❖ The last two columns measure error, the difference between actual and forecast in absolute terms, for the last three periods of known sales, the three quarters of year 7. The second to last column expresses the error as a percentage, the last column as the numerical difference. Both are averages of the three forecasts. In setting aside actual data for test purposes it is best if that data is reasonably typical of the series as a whole.

The first look by the forecaster is a perusal of the first three entries in Figure 7-11. They are the three independent variables that are being considered. Both GDP and PCE have high R-values whereas advertising expenditures is not very high, especially when looking at the Adjusted R^2. Although the correlation between advertising and sales is lacking substance (standard error of 9.27), there is some relationship; therefore, it will not be eliminated as a candidate for inclusion in some models. On the other hand, the forecaster is reluctant to include PCE, which has a good (but not terrific) correlation with sales, because it has a stronger correlation with X_1 than it does with Y.

Because the forecaster is developing a multiple regression model, the more independent variables incorporated into the model the better providing that each contributes to forecasting reliability and accuracy. Thus, a number of possibilities were developed, some of which build-in transformations of PCE and GDP. This is not an exhaustive list and other combinations can be added if the forecaster deems it appropriate, as he probably would on his first try.

As the forecaster studies the data in Figure 7-11, the universal rule becomes obvious: nothing is as clear-cut as it should be!

Because there are a number of combinations with high R-values and R^2-values, the forecaster chooses those to examine further. They are lines 5, 7, 10, 11, 12, 15, 16, 18, 19, 20, and 21. Lines 5 and 19 contain the same variables except that line 19 has transformed PCE. The resulting factors are identical as expected inasmuch as the same independent variables are present. Because PCE, not transformed, is suspect as a variable to be used long-term, line 5 is eliminated (see earlier reasoning). Lines 7 and 12 are dropped because *comparatively* the standard error is high and the F value low. Lines 15 and 16 give the most accurate forecasts for the last three periods of known sales, but the F value is *comparatively* low and the standard error high. Lines 10 and 11 look good but the forecasts for the last three periods of known sales are less accurate than the best of the remaining candidates. Line 18 does not make the cut for reasons given above. Lines 19, 20, and 21 remain. Each has high R and R^2 values, low standard errors that signify reliable forecasts, high F values, and good forecasts of known sales. Judging upon the values of F as the major criterion, line 21 would be selected. But is it better to include more independent variables? The future is unknown. What will be the contributions of each variable in the future? Before decision time, a Durbin-Watson test is conducted for each of these three candidates.

The Durbin-Watson statistic tests for autocorrelation among the residuals (the errors; that is, the differences between sales and forecasted sales). Score values range from 0 to 4, with 2 as the mean and the best value in the informal test. Recall from the previous discussion that an informal rule states that any DW test score between 1.5 and 2.5 is assumed to be free of autocorrelation. However, there are more exacting ways to evaluate the DW test scores. The computations for arriving at the scores are summarized in Figure 7-6. Once the score is calculated, reference is made to a table of Durbin-Watson test bounds. Abbreviated tables are available at the end of this chapter. The test scores are:

Line 19: 1.72

Line 20: 1.79

Line 21: 1.35

In the tables, the appropriate lower (L) and upper (U) bounds are at the intersection of the number of periods (n) and the number of variables. In the example, there are 24 periods; for line 21 there are four independent variables (PCE* and three seasonals). At a level of significance of .05, the bounds are L = 1.01 and U = 1.78. Similarly, in the table for .01 significance, the bounds are 0.8 to 1.53. Here are the results for the three candidates:

$\alpha = .05$ $\alpha = .01$

Line 19: 0.85 to 1.92; 0.64 to 1.79 (6 variables)

Line 20: 0.93 to 1.90; 0.72 to 1.66

Line 21: 1.01 to 1.78; 0.80 to 1.53

Frequently, the .05 level of significance is the test vehicle. Sometimes, however, it is more revealing to view both.

Some authorities conclude that any score outside the bounds automatically indicates autocorrelation, however, there is a range of uncertainty that needs to be explored before drawing a conclusion. Here are the DW statistics at both the .05 and .01 levels:

.05 level	Line 19	Line 20	Line 21
Positive autocorrelation	0 to 0.85	0 to 0.93	0 to 1.01
Uncertain area	0.85 to 1.92	0.93 to 1.90	1.01 to 1.78
No autocorrelation	1.92 to 2.08	1.90 to 2.10	1.78 to 2.22
Uncertain area	2.08 to 3.15	2.10 to 3.07	2.22 to 2.99
Negative autocorrelation	3.15 to 4.0	3.07 to 4.0	2.99 to 4.0
.01 level			
Positive autocorrelation	0 to 0.64	0 to 0.72	0 to 0.80
Uncertain area	0.64 to 1.79	0.72 to 1.66	0.80 to 1.53
No autocorrelation	1.79 to 2.21	1.67 to 2.34	1.53 to 2.47
Uncertain area	2.21 to 3.36	2.34 to 3.28	2.47 to 3.20
Negative autocorrelation	3.36 to 4.0	3.28 to 4.0	3.20 to 4.0

Values for the statistics above are derived as follows, using line 20 at 0.05 as illustration.

Positive autocorrelation is zero to the lower table value (.93)

Uncertain area is lower to upper table value (.93 to 1.90)

No autocorrelation is upper level to 4 minus upper value (1.90 to 2.10; 4 − 1.9)

Uncertain area is 2.10 to 4 minus lower value (2.10 to 3.07; 4 - .93)

Negative autocorrelation is 3.07 to 4

On the way to decision, the forecaster drew the following conclusions: the F statistic indicates that there is a significant relationship between the dependent and independent variables in each of the three equations, with line 21 the highest score; however, its DW score was outside the range of 1.5 to 2.5. The forecaster thinks that GDP is an important contributor. On the other hand, advertising does not seem to be essential. By deduction, line 20 appears the most appropriate. The adjusted R^2 represents that more than 98% of sales is explained by the independent variables; the error rate is very low; and the significance of the equation is validated. Considering DW at the .05 level, both lines 19 and 20 are in the uncertain zone; at .01 line 19 is in the uncertain zone and line 20 is in the no autocorrelation zone. It must be noted, however, that both are well within the 1.5 to 2.5 range. With the other factors as favorable as they are, the forecaster would, if considered necessary, discount the formal statistics. In conclusion, line 20 is considered the best of the three.

The forecaster is cautious, however, and is concerned because GDP and PCE had a very high correlation (see Figure 7-9). The objective is to find variables that correlate with the dependent variable but not strongly with each other. Adding 10 to each observation transformed PCE, but perhaps this was not sufficient to preclude inadequate forecasts in the future. A different transformation for GDP was considered pertinent. Thus, each GDP observation was squared, (GDP multiplied by itself) and new values calculated with the results that follow: GDP squared, PCE plus 10, and seasonals: R at .994, adjusted R^2 at .985, standard error at 1.6, F at 305.5, percent average at 0.7 and average difference at 0.9. This is a nice improvement. The DW score increased to 1.89. The boundaries are the same as calculated above because there are still 24 periods and 5 independent variables. The DW test determines if the residuals (errors) are randomly dispersed. If so, the residuals suggest that the most critical factors are included in the equation. The forecaster concludes that they are random. If the residuals are summed (pluses and minuses retained) the total should be close to zero, which it is at 0.348.

No doubt the forecaster has found his forecasting vehicle. As can be visualized, the twenty-one equations plus the new one is not exhaustive of the possibilities. The final one selected, however, is about as good as it gets.

Serious shortcomings attend the use of independent variables of the economic persuasion. Government figures for the current period may not be finalized or they may not exist. The preliminary numbers may change upon finalization. Because company forecasts are dealing with an unknown future, actual economic data will not be available at the close of the time period necessitating the infusion of forecasts of the independent variables. Thus, company projections will only be as good as the forecasts of the independent variables. The goodness of professionally prepared economic forecasts should be determined historically so that the forecaster knows the depth of the puddle into which he is jumping.

One way in which to mitigate the shortcoming is to find leading economic indicators that can function as independent variables. Another possibility is that a concurrent indicator can act like a leading indicator for the company; that is, company sales react but only at a later time. An example is given in the section that explains simple linear regression.

Business cycle indicators are classified as leading, those series that move in advance of the business cycle; concurrent (coinciding), those that move in relation to the business cycle; and lagging, those that trail the business cycle. The Conference Board publishes *Business Cycle Indicators* monthly. Each series published therein consists of a composite index and a number of sub-series plus other data series.

The following tables are abbreviated versions of complete tables, provided for illustration. Complete tables can be found in statistical texts and books of statistical tables.

Tables of F Distributions

Values of F at .05 (upper 5% probability)

D_1 D_2	1	2	3	4	5	6	7	8	9	10
1	161	200	216	225	230	234	237	239	241	242
2	18.5	19.0	19.2	19.2	19.3	19.3	19.4	19.4	19.4	19.4
3	10.1	9.55	9.28	9.12	9.01	8.94	8.89	8.85	8.81	8.79
4	7.71	6.94	6.59	6.39	6.26	6.16	6.09	6.04	6.00	5.96
5	6.61	5.79	5.41	5.19	5.05	4.95	4.88	4.82	4.77	4.74
6	5.99	5.14	4.76	4.53	4.39	4.28	4.21	4.15	4.10	4.06
7	5.59	4.74	4.35	4.12	3.97	3.87	3.79	3.73	3.68	3.64
8	5.32	4.46	4.07	3.84	3.69	3.58	3.50	3.44	3.39	3.35
9	5.12	4.26	3.86	3.63	3.48	3.37	3.29	3.23	3.18	3.14
10	4.96	4.10	3.71	3.48	3.33	3.22	3.14	3.07	3.02	2.98
11	4.84	3.98	3.59	3.36	3.20	3.09	3.01	2.95	2.90	2.85
12	4.75	3.89	3.49	3.26	3.11	3.00	2.91	2.85	2.80	2.75
13	4.67	3.81	3.41	3.18	3.03	2.92	2.83	2.77	2.71	2.67
14	4.60	3.74	3.34	3.11	2.96	2.85	2.76	2.70	2.65	2.60
15	4.54	3.68	3.29	3.06	2.90	2.79	2.71	2.64	2.59	2.54
16	4.49	3.63	3.24	3.01	2.85	2.74	2.66	2.59	2.54	2.49
17	4.45	3.59	3.20	2.96	2.81	2.70	2.61	2.55	2.49	2.45
18	4.41	3.55	3.16	2.93	2.77	2.66	2.58	2.51	2.46	2.41
19	4.38	3.52	3.13	2.90	2.74	2.63	2.54	2.48	2.42	2.38
20	4.35	3.49	3.10	2.87	2.71	2.60	2.51	2.45	2.39	2.35
21	4.32	3.47	3.07	2.84	2.68	2.57	2.49	2.42	2.37	2.32
22	4.30	3.44	3.05	2.82	2.66	2.55	2.46	2.40	2.40	2.34

Values of F at .01, selected values

	1	2	3	4	5	6	7	8
1	4,052.00	5,000.00	5,403.00	5,625.00	5,764.00	5,928.00	5,928.00	5,982.00
2	98.50	99.00	99.20	99.20	99.30	99.30	99.40	99.40
3	34.10	30.80	29.50	28.70	28.20	27.90	27.70	27.50
8	11.30	8.65	7.59	7.01	6.63	6.37	6.18	6.03
9	10.60	8.02	6.99	6.42	6.06	5.80	5.61	5.47
10	10.00	7.56	6.55	5.99	5.64	5.39	5.20	5.06
13	9.07	6.70	5.74	5.21	4.86	4.62	4.44	4.30
14	8.86	6.51	5.56	5.04	4.70	4.46	4.28	4.14
15	8.68	6.36	5.42	4.89	4.56	4.32	4.14	4.00
18	8.29	6.01	5.09	4.58	4.25	4.01	3.84	3.71
19	8.19	5.93	5.01	4.50	4.17	3.94	3.77	3.63
20	8.10	5.85	4.94	4.43	4.10	3.87	3.70	3.56

Durbin-Watson Test Bounds

Level of Significance = .05 Selected values
Numbers 1 through 5 are the number of independent variables; n is the number of observations

n	1 lower	1 upper	2 lower	2 upper	3 lower	3 upper	4 lower	4 upper	5 lower	5 upper
20	1.20	1.41	1.10	1.54	1.00	1.68	0.90	1.83	0.79	1.99
21	1.22	1.42	1.13	1.54	1.03	1.67	0.93	1.81	0.83	1.96
22	1.24	1.43	1.15	1.54	1.05	1.66	0.96	1.80	0.86	1.94
23	1.26	1.44	1.17	1.54	1.08	1.66	0.99	1.79	0.90	1.92
24	1.27	1.45	1.19	1.55	1.10	1.66	1.01	1.78	0.93	1.90
25	1.29	1.45	1.21	1.55	1.12	1.66	1.04	1.77	0.95	1.89
26	1.30	1.46	1.22	1.55	1.14	1.65	1.06	1.76	0.98	1.88
27	1.32	1.47	1.24	1.56	1.16	1.65	1.08	1.76	1.01	1.86
28	1.33	1.48	1.26	1.56	1.18	1.65	1.10	1.75	1.03	1.85
29	1.34	1.48	1.27	1.56	1.20	1.65	1.12	1.74	1.05	1.84
30	1.35	1.49	1.28	1.57	1.21	1.65	1.14	1.74	1.07	1.83

Level of Significance = .01

n	1 lower	1 upper	2 lower	2 upper	3 lower	3 upper	4 lower	4 upper	5 lower	5 upper
20	0.95	1.15	0.86	1.27	0.77	1.41	0.68	1.57	0.60	1.74
21	0.97	1.16	0.89	1.27	0.80	1.41	0.72	1.55	0.63	1.71
22	1.00	1.17	0.91	1.28	0.83	1.40	0.75	1.54	0.66	1.69
23	1.02	1.19	0.94	1.29	0.86	1.40	0.77	1.53	0.70	1.67
24	1.04	1.20	0.96	1.30	0.88	1.41	0.80	1.53	0.72	1.66
25	1.05	1.21	0.98	1.30	0.90	1.41	0.83	1.52	0.75	1.65
26	1.07	1.22	1.00	1.31	0.93	1.41	0.85	1.52	0.78	1.64
27	1.09	1.23	1.02	1.32	0.95	1.41	0.88	1.51	0.81	1.63
28	1.10	1.24	1.04	1.32	0.97	1.41	0.90	1.51	0.83	1.62
29	1.12	1.25	1.05	1.33	0.99	1.42	0.92	1.51	0.85	1.61
30	1.13	1.26	1.07	1.34	1.01	1.42	0.94	1.51	0.88	1.61

Critical Values of t

Abbreviated table

D or df	t .100	t .050	t .025	t .010
1	3.078	6.314	12.706	31.821
2	1.886	2.920	4.303	6.965
3	1.638	2.353	3.182	4.541
4	1.533	2.132	2.776	3.747
5	1.476	2.015	2.571	3.365
6	1.440	1.943	2.447	3.143
7	1.415	1.895	2.365	2.998
8	1.397	1.860	2.306	2.896
9	1.383	1.833	2.262	2.821
10	1.372	1.812	2.228	2.764
11	1.363	1.796	2.201	2.718

Chapter 8

Short Life Cycle Forecasting Models

It is not uncommon to encounter companies that manufacture, distribute, or sell at retail items that have relatively short product life cycles. Two variations are discernable: the product is no longer saleable at the close of a selling season but may be resurrected during the next comparable season and the product that never again becomes saleable. Typical categories are toys, specially items associated with a holiday (Easter, Christmas), food items, textiles, and clothing. Not all items within these classifications have short life cycles, but many do.

If the methods described in the preceding chapters cannot be effectively employed, the techniques that follow should provide reliable forecasts.

Forecasting demand for these products is divisible into two distinct parts: forecasting before the beginning of the selling season and forecasting during the selling season. Each situation presents a different problem, but the important point is to secure reliable forecasts as early as possible because of the limited selling period and the vulnerability of these products to obsolescence.

Consider the case of a clothing manufacturer or importer of styled garments with a life cycle of one season and a maximum order booking period of fifteen weeks. The reader may consider sales as bookings or shipments. A sale is booked when the order is received and accepted. Normally, each order has a requested delivery date, which is the date that the customer wants the goods. The requested delivery date (as accepted) is the shipping date. For products with short life cycles, bookings data are especially important because it is essential to know as early as possible the quantity of an item that will be sold. The effective booking period – the length of time within which the majority of orders and reorders are received – is frequently less than the length of the selling season. Typically, orders come in slowly at first, and then order receipt accelerates rapidly before it declines. To increase the chances of manufacturing or importing the right product mix, it is imperative that accurate forecasts are available early in the game.

Before Season Forecasting

There are several methods for setting initial forecasts for individual end items that help in determining a start-up level for production, for allocating capacity, and for purchasing the initially needed raw materials. If the company imports its products, forecasts establish first purchase orders. In some import situations, however, first orders may predate first sales to customers. The primary techniques are:

❖ Qualitative methods of the type discussed in Chapter 11. In practice, these methods generally reduce to judgment expressed either as executive opinion (sales manager, merchandiser) or panel consensus (sales force, company executives, selected customers). (However, see the section concerning growth curves in Chapter 11.) These are methods of last resort because of their subjective nature. In apparel manufacturing, for instance, the line is designed with the hope that every style will be a winner, each being the best work of the designers. But the company knows from experience that some will be losers and that many surprises will occur on both sides of the ledger. The firm has done its best in the design stage; its judgment is unlikely to improve before orders are received. For this reason, judgmental end item forecasts have limited value. Judgment cannot be disparaged, however, when considered in its proper context of managerial review and modification. Management frequently knows of circumstances not considered in the forecasting methodology, such as pre-existing contracts or customer intentions. In reality, judgment may be the only feasible option for initial sales projections.

❖ Regression or trend models of the types described in the preceding chapters. Regression may be selected if there are demonstrable relationships. In trend analysis (exponential smoothing, etc.), the prevailing trend of sales is continued into the future. Again, some form of aggregate forecasting is the norm unless there is comparability for individual items. In our example, aggregate may mean grouping items using like raw materials. Care must be exercised in applying the trend approach. Because there is a gap between selling seasons, there is opportunity for general economic conditions to change thus invalidating the trend. If the economic situation changes significantly, the changed condition must be considered to insure comparability.

❖ A direct comparison with last season, in the aggregate, subdivided into individual end items, if necessary. The estimates are projected into the future only as far as necessary to meet initial requirements although this may be the total of a short season.

It may be necessary to begin production well in advance of the selling season, as may occur for products associated with a specific holiday. In some instances, the product line will be a repeat and the danger of producing the wrong items is unlikely, but when the items take on a new face, the menace is real. If early start up is unavoidable, the before season estimates may be crucial. Probably, regression or trend models are the best opportunities if they can actually be applied. Be cautious, however, a slippery slope may await.

Early manufacturing start-up and the purchase of raw materials presents different problems for different products. If the materials used are basically the same season-to-season early planning mistakes are probably not critical. If, as in apparel, the designs and colors are different from previously, a problem may exist in determining the initial quantities. It may be possible to order (if ordering in advance is required by vendors) materials in some semi-finished state to be held in the supplier's inventory until finishing instructions are received. Many companies may be able to shift the timing of manufacture to later start-up with the length of the production period remaining unchanged. To accomplish this good requires an in-place, class A production and material control system that integrates all functions related to manufacture. The reduction of risk that accrues from later start-up makes this approach one of considerable importance. There are many systems advances in the area of production and material planning and control.

In-Season Forecasting

Once bookings begin, information becomes available from which forecasts may be revised. The approach discussed is relational analysis, which consists of several techniques.

Relational Analysis

Relational analysis assumes that there is a quantitative relationship between sales this season and sales in one or more previous seasons; for example, that spring sales this year are comparable to sales in the preceding spring seasons. The objective is to obtain reliable estimates as soon as possible after the selling season starts so that resources can be committed to the products that are most likely to be winners. Four techniques are discussed. Remember that bookings lead the requested delivery dates. Figure 8-1 shows an approximate relationship between sales by received date and sales by requested delivery date that is typical in some industries.

Trade Show Approach

If a company's products are sold at trade shows as well as by a sales force calling upon customers and these shows are held early in the season or before the sales force begins selling, there may be an historical relationship between the quantity of an item sold at the show(s) and total season sales. Assume that trade shows in which the company participates are held at the beginning of the selling cycle and historically 7% to 11% of total sales by individual item are sold at the shows. If sales are 1,800 at the shows, the range of anticipated sales for the season is:

$$1800 \div .07 = 25714 \text{ maximum}$$

$$1800 \div .11 = 16364 \text{ minimum}$$

This is a forecasting and planning starting point, later to be modified by another technique. Care is needed to assure that history supports the procedure and that conditions are the same as previously, no significant change in the business climate.

Bookings History

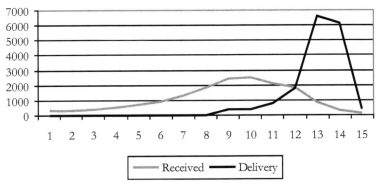

Figure 8-1

The same rationale applies if sales to key accounts are accomplished early in the season. Key accounts are defined as large accounts that buy directly from the line; such accounts may be retail regional or national chains, for example, or other manufacturers to whom the company supplies materials.

Direct Sales Comparison

Another technique is a direct comparison between sales to date and sales from previous seasons. Different groupings of products may have different patterns. For example, some items in a line may book earlier than other items. This procedure is closely related to the Percent of Sales Model described in Chapter 6.

Figure 8-2 is a three-year, cumulative bookings history for an end item or for a product group, as may be appropriate, which has shown excellent sales continuity the past three years. Often, the relationship between the years will not be as good as that given in our example; however, that does not negate the validity of the model nor preclude it from being used to forecast. An important consideration is that week 1 represents the first week of sales regardless of when that week actually occurs. Year-to-year, week 1 may actually take place in different calendar weeks but it is still week 1. Another important consideration is that key account sales (those customers who buy large amounts) be entered in the same relative period each year. If this is not possible because an individual account has decided to place its order later, an estimate from the customer can be used or as a last resort, an estimate from the sales department. Be wary: do not enter the quantity twice (once for the estimate, later for the order). Flag the estimate for future year processing.

Bookings History by Date Received, Cumulative

Week	Sales Year 1	Percent of Total	Sales Year 2	Percent of Total	Sales Year 3	Percent of Total	3 Year Average %
1	300	1.82	360	1.97	360	1.88	1.89
2	650	3.93	770	4.22	810	4.23	4.13
3	1050	6.36	1260	6.90	1225	6.40	6.55
4	1550	9.38	1800	9.85	1885	9.85	9.70
5	2260	13.68	2625	14.37	2825	14.77	14.27
6	3200	19.37	3685	20.18	3800	19.86	19.80
7	4510	27.30	5135	28.11	5400	28.23	27.88
8	6340	38.38	7320	40.08	7280	38.06	38.84
9	8790	53.21	9830	53.82	10230	53.48	53.50
10	11290	68.34	12530	68.60	13240	69.21	68.72
11	13410	81.17	14820	81.14	15480	80.92	81.08
12	15280	92.49	16945	92.77	17660	92.32	92.53
13	16110	97.52	17845	97.70	18675	97.62	97.61
14	16410	99.33	18165	99.45	19025	99.45	99.41
15	16520	100.00	18265	100.00	19130	100.00	100.00

Figure 8-2

The sales columns show cumulatively the actual amounts sold each week. The percent columns list the cumulative percentages to date. The three-year average column is the average percentage for the three years, by period. For example, week 1 is (1.82 + 1.97 + 1.88) ÷ 3 = 1.89.

Total sales for the season are a function of sales to date and the average sales for the same time frame in previous years. Assume that sales for weeks 1 and 2 of year 4 are 760. Historically, this represents 4.13% of total seasonal sales. Thus, the total sales projection for the season is 760 ÷ .0413 = 18402. How reliable is this estimate? With only two weeks of new sales available and those low booking weeks at that, the forecast is not etched in stone (more like chiseled in marshmallow). As more sales accrue, the forecast will change. What the forecaster does at this point is compare seasonal sales for the past three years, which indicates an increasing level of business each year. Could the same be true this year? The forecaster can review the order book to see if there is continuity with the past three years and also speak with the sales manager. Perhaps, a caveat will be attached to the forecast. In any event the forecaster will advise all consumers that the estimate is preliminary and made available for planning purposes.

As time elapses and more bookings are received, the seasonal estimate will change. If cumulative sales at the end of week 3 are 1250 the forecast is 19084, (1250 ÷ .0655). At week 4 the forecast is 19072 if sales are 1850.

To facilitate planning, the level of bookings may be calculated for each period once total seasonal sales are estimated. With a forecast of 19072, anticipated bookings through week 10 are: 19072 x .6872 = 13106. If only the week's estimate is desired for, say, week 10 subtract week 10's estimate from week 9's estimate.

If this technique is employed to forecast a product group, individual end items within the group may be estimated by assigning a percentage to each item based upon its historical ratio. Generally, forecasts of individual end items will not be as accurate as aggregated forecasts.

Bookings Forecast by Delivery Date, Non-cumulative

Week	Shipments Year 1	% of Total	Shipments Year 2	% of Total	Shipments Year 3	% of Total	Average Percent	Year 4 Forecast
9	400	2.42	395	2.16	390	2.04	2.21	421
10	420	2.54	420	2.30	435	2.27	2.37	452
11	800	4.84	900	4.93	870	4.55	4.77	910
12	1760	10.65	2055	11.25	2230	11.66	11.19	2134
13	6590	39.89	7300	39.97	7510	39.26	39.71	7573
14	6140	37.17	6785	37.15	7355	38.45	37.59	7169
15	410	2.48	410	2.24	340	1.78	2.17	413
Total	16520		18265		19130			19072

Figure 8-3

The bookings forecast described above is anticipated bookings by received date. For planning its manufacture or its import schedule or its buying schedule, the company will want to know when the products are due for delivery. Figure 8-3 translates the bookings history into bookings by requested delivery date. Delivery dates are taken from the orders received.

The three-year average percent from Figure 8-3 is used to determine projected sales by delivery date. This tells the company when goods need to be ready for shipping. At week 4 the forecast for the season was estimated to be 19072 units. Delivery begins week 9. Thus, the shipping forecast for week 9 is 19072 x .0221 = 421, for week 10 it is 19072 x .0237 = 452. Of course, as more data becomes available the total seasonal estimate will change.

Control Group Approach

This procedure necessitates calling upon the same group of customers each year. They are accounts that place their orders early in the season. If orders from other customers are received, they are ignored in the forecasting routine. The customer group is carefully selected in order to secure a fair representation of the company's market. The customer group represents a reasonable sampling of total sales, historically determined. Good company sales records and research are prerequisites.

The group of customers is selected by the Marketing Department based upon the criterion of typicality, that is, how closely the group's purchases reflect the company's market as a whole. This procedure requires that the purchases of each candidate account be examined to see how closely they parallel sales in previous years. The question to be answered is: once a group is selected do their sales have a relational affinity with total seasonal sales?

Once the group is chosen, forecasts for previous seasons are prepared using the technique to see if the group fairly represents the market. If not, new candidates can be tried. The larger the sample the more accurate is the results. However, early results are important, which suggests a small sampling. Is the size of the sample adequate? If the technique works in several past seasons (that is good forecasts result), the sample is valid. Every new season is a call to reevaluate the procedure and the control group.

The example company has 2,000 active accounts. There are 112 accounts in the selected sample. Actual sales for the last comparable season were 96,000 units. The sample group purchased 5000 units. The sample group is 5.6% of total accounts (112 ÷ 2000); average sales are 5.2% of total sales (5000 ÷ 96000).

The company may (and probably will) want to forecast later with another method. The following is a comparison of sales last year and this year for the sample group:

	Units Sold	Accounts Buying	Ave. Units Sold	Success Rate
Last Year	5000	100	50	89.3%
This Year	6006	91	66	81.3%

Average units sold last year is 50 (5000/100). There are 112 sample accounts of which 100 purchased 5000 units; 12 companies did not buy the item. This year the average is 66 units (6006/91). Of the 112 sample companies, 91 bought 6006 units. The other 21 customers did not buy the item. The success rate is 89.3% last year (100/112) and 81.3% this year (91/112). The success rate is the number of customers in the sample that bought the item, expressed as a percentage.

To forecast bookings proceed as follows:

Step 1: Prepare an estimate of last year's bookings and compare with actual bookings.

Average units x total customers x success rate

50 x 2000 x .893 = 89,300

Actual sales ÷ estimated sales

96,000 ÷ 89,300 = 1.075

1.075 is the variation multiplier. Because there is a difference between actual and estimate (about –7%), it may be assumed that the same difference will apply in the current year, thus, the adjustment factor.

Step 2: Substitute current year data in the equation and the multiplier and solve:

1.075 (66 x 2000 x .813) = 115,365, the current year forecast

The primary rationale rests in a representative control group that constitutes the sample and that the same relative conditions will apply in the current year.

A shortcut method is available:

Control group sales last year ÷ total sales last year

5000 ÷ 96000 = .05208

This years sales ÷ the quotient above

6006 ÷ .05208 = 115,323

Time as Control

This is an approach similar to the one above except that time, not a control group, is the controlling factor. In the control group method continuity exists in that the same customers are contacted year to year; time is not a consideration. In this procedure time is the control. The steps are the same as those presented above.

Assume that the sales force calls upon its customers in the sequence and at the times considered most appropriate by each salesman. The technique is based upon sales and the number of customers contacted in a predetermined time frame. Prospective customers, those not contacted previously, are excluded from the statistics.

	Units Sold	Accounts Contacted	Accounts Buying	Average Units Sold	Success Rate
Last Year	5000	112	100	50	89.3%
This Year	6000	180	150	40	83.3%

$$50 \times 2000 \times .893 = 89{,}300$$

$$96000 \div 89300 = 1.075$$

$$1.075(40 \times 2000 \times .833) = 71{,}638$$

The shortcut method described above is not available for this procedure.

This method has intuitive appeal because it is simple to apply. But there is a major shortcoming that may prove dangerous to reliable estimating. Because there is not an established sample group, thus sampling continuity, the results may not be typical of the population (the total customer base). This year may consist of different customers or more or less customers than the previous year. Likely, it is comparing apples and oranges. Unless several years of previous test forecasts indicate otherwise, find another model.

Chapter 9

Forecasting with Demographic Data

Forecasting is a necessary prerequisite to strategic and operational planning. Demographic information is one of the raw materials used in building models capable of describing the future business situation, usually in the form of demand.

A forecasting model may employ a single demographic data series, as in simple regression or time series analysis, or demographic projections may be used in combination with economic and company generated data. Demographic projections by themselves provide trend information, the general direction. In a forecasting format, demand potential may be quantitatively captured utilizing the methods described in this book.

The consumer environment is an ever-changing phenomenon. Those that serve that market may get a false reading of the longer-range future unless demographic material is considered.

Because demographic statistics are people oriented (population, households and families, income), their usefulness to industries that sell directly to consumers is obvious. But the consumer is frequently the ultimate customer in a chain of manufacturers, distributors, importers, and retailers; therefore, the spectrum of benefit derived from demographic data extends to those companies that sell to manufacturers of consumer goods, and beyond, to many other manufacturing and service firms.

Forecasting Environment

Although individual companies have different forecasting needs and service related companies are dissimilar to manufacturing companies, many forecasting requirements are common to all firms. In the short-term, each needs to estimate its sales. In the longer-term, companies are not only interested in demand, but also in demographic trends, technological changes, changes in customer attitudes, and business costs, to mention a few. The business environment is dynamic.

Understanding demographics is one element in estimating the future market.

Although there are a number of individual forecasting needs, each need should be considered in the context of an integrated plan or a strategy. Strategy is concerned with the future, beginning with the near-term and extending to the long-term, with all plans in accord. Because of the uncertainty of the future, strategies are periodically reviewed based upon new forecasts, trends, and other data.

Basic forecasting considerations for strategy formulation include estimating the future business climate (the general direction of business), consumer trends, industry sales expectations, and demand potential for the company.

Other considerations derived from or in support of the strategy include regional, state or other geographical sales forecasts and demographic profiles, future capacity requirements and capital expenditures, location of branch warehouses, location of retail outlets, market positioning, advertising strategies, and identification of key selling areas.

Usage in Industrial Forecasting

Demographic data are one of the ingredients in industrial forecasting that when skillfully employed fill many of the specific needs described above. Theoretically, demographic data may be incorporated into most forecasting methodologies, but in practice, utility is usually limited to applications described in the following paragraphs. Demographic data as a forecasting source have not been extensively applied except in market research, but there are instances in which they are especially pertinent. Because demographic changes are gradual, usage in forecasting is appropriate primarily to the long-term, for instance, annualized estimates for several years in the future.

A demographic series may be the basis for time series forecasting of industry or company sales if there is a demonstrable relationship between the level of sales and the data level in the demographic series. In this context, trend projections are a likely forecasting application, with actual sales historically fitted to the data in the demographic series. These projections then become the base data for estimating future sales, perhaps (and likely) with the inclusion of economic estimates.

In general, the applicability of this approach is limited to those companies that sell to a definable portion of the consumer population or in the supply chain where the final product is a consumer product. Products sold primarily for an age group (children's clothing by sex or age, baby products, or products used mainly by the elderly), products appealing predominantly to an area of the country (climate related items, cowboy hats), or products dependent upon the number of households or upon income levels are examples. Shifting populations (migrations), changing age patterns, and demographic economics may signal the modification of competitive relationships within a market or may be reflective of a market that is changing its character. Time series analysis is one means of examining these anticipations. At some point, almost all products relate to people in one sense or another, but if the relationship is somewhat remote, population with other indicators or other indicators without population may be more applicable.

The technique establishes the sales direction for the longer term, expressed in the specifics of numbers. The demand estimates thus obtained, however, are tenuous because of the inaccuracy of long-term projections and the unrealistic assumption that competitive relationships and market conditions will remain unchanged. If these statistics are presented with an understanding of their limitations, they speak in terms that management comprehends, thus providing guidance for strategic planning.

It is equally apt to examine demographic data in nonspecific terms to determine future direction, that is, without expressly relating demographic data to company sales. A manufacturer of teen oriented products, for instance, may study a projection of age distribution for a number of future years, graphically plot the data for trend, perform a few simple computations, and conclude the general size of the future market.

Demographic forecasts have strategic implications. Assume forecasts of a population segment that is shrinking. A manufacturer dependent upon that market segment would ask questions relating to the future direction of the company. Should the company diversify into other product lines? Are there weak companies that will disappear leaving the competitive posture relatively unchanged? If not, what must the company do to insure financial strength in a shrinking market? How should the firm position itself now to optimize its share of the future market? Conversely, the company may have to contend with a growing market. And new technology that booms forward invites many companies to jump on the train and many of them will later collapse when the train derails. It is an astute executive who can win in that market. This is a little digression from population statistics, per se, but it is surely apropos in today's economy.

In the preceding paragraphs, the look has been at future sales in relation to a single demographic series. Sales may be specified in a model (quantitative analysis) or implied (population data only). Both are necessary: the study of demographic projections as an entity, separate from economic data, because of the ramifications that people oriented changes have upon a market or a company, and demographic data as a component of future buying power.

An alternate to time series analysis is to employ a single demographic series as the independent variable in a simple regression equation. As a means of determining demand this is statistically a more acceptable method than time series analysis. To combine demographic and economic data in the same model requires the adoption of a multiple regression format.

Multiple regression equations are designed to answer questions about the future by abstracting the essential nature of the process being described. One or more demographic series may be used independently or combined with economic data in the same formulation. If economic data are the primary independent variables, adding demographic data may have the advantage of reducing or eliminating (if they exist) the problems of serial correlation, multicollinearity, and heteroskedasticity, as discussed in Chapter 7. Forecasting future buying power, the level of industry sales, and market share are some applications. An especially useful statistic is the level of product or product group demand in each of a number of future years. A multiple regression equation that represents the key economic and demographic influences affecting product demand is an important method of gathering information for use is strategy formulation.

In developing strategy, the longer term is an extension of the near-term future, with both in agreement once the strategy is formulated. Having available different estimates of the future should not be depreciated. It permits examination of tentative goals within a range of probability. In fact, it may be advisable to test goals within a wider range of possibility to evaluate the risk involved. In the near-term and mid-term, it is important to know with some certainty the demand that may be expected. In the long-term, direction and range are the considerations. Demographic data have application in forecasting the general economic and business climate, projecting market potential, and in the empirical analysis of the marketplace.

Unforeseeable events, whether environmental, governmental, technological, or economic, may disrupt long-range forecasts. That is the reason to limit conclusions to range and direction, and to consider these as general conclusions, which are reasonably accurate predictors of the future although the timing may be somewhat different.

A company that sells consumer products nationwide will forecast demand on a national basis, but it will need to subdivide that forecast for the purposes of determining buying power by region or state or by some other population grouping, such as income levels. Demographic data may be used for these purposes if a correlation with demand exists at the level being considered. A market index based upon several market indicators is another method to consider. Probably the most widely known source is "The Survey of Buying Power" published by *Sales and Marketing Management Magazine*. With the help of the Survey the national forecast can be divided into market potential by geographic area.

Sources

If all the demographic materials currently available, and all economic data for that matter, poured from the heavens they would bury anyone standing in a not too small room. Yet, a particular data series may not be available in the detail required for incorporation into a forecasting model. Sometimes, data can be mathematically extended or modified to provide the detail or the data may be obtainable from a different source.

Because of the complexity and variety of existing demographic materials, the first job of the forecaster is to seek familiarity with the types of data that are being produced. Of course, the same advice is applicable to economic data. The forecaster then:

- ❖ Identifies the basic forecasting needs and the types of data that can fulfill those needs. There may be a number of candidates, not all of which will be demographic in nature. When designing and testing models, some series may be discarded as redundant or not advisable because of the cautions outlined in Chapter 7.

- ❖ Determines the purpose that the data will serve and the level of detail required. Only current year projections may be needed (what should be the current distribution of our advertising dollars?) or projections for the intermediate term (what will the market look like two years from now?) or projections may be needed for each of the next five or ten years (a detailed examination of the future by applying formal forecasting methods). Strategic planning without the latter detail is simplistic and dangerous, but all three are likely to be necessary. The caveats expressed previously apply: point estimates for a distant future are also dangerous and should be considered as a point within a range.

- ❖ Acquires data at the level of detail required and formulates a forecasting system and designs the models.

Following are some of the sources for data acquisition. The web is alive with possible sources.

- ❖ Private companies and societies can provide a variety of services and demographic products. They have information that may not be otherwise available, from broad national and international statistics to zip code demographics. *Sales and Marketing Management Magazine* was previously mentioned. *American Demographics Magazine* published by Dow Jones is another source. Universities maintain web sites, such as Mansfield University, for Census and Demographics (www.mnsfld.edu/depts/lib/census.htm/) And the University of Michigan (www.censusscope.org/).

- ❖ Of course, the premier source is the Census Bureau. Census data cover a wide spectrum of the types of information valuable to companies.

- ❖ State data centers may be able to fill-in when other sources fail. The United Nations is a rich source for information pertaining to foreign markets.

Applying Demographics to Forecasting

Demographic information is available in many forms, a few of which are explained in the following paragraphs.

Population pyramids are one way in which population characteristics may be analyzed. Pyramids are graphs that present the age and sex characteristics of a population. The population of interest may be the United States, foreign countries, cities, counties, or other geographic entities. Because pyramids are visual representations, they help in understanding the information being displayed, especially recognizing similarities and differences between years. Another purpose is that of comparability, of identifying geographical areas that have similar characteristics.

Another valuable source that will help executives understand the meaning of demographic statistics is the text material that accompanies the Census Bureau tables. Explanations may include population size and growth and age distribution with information regarding the procedures used to derive the projections.

A few of the series that may be useful and that are found on the Census web site are: several series of household projections that detail the composition of households and families; NP-T1, total resident population by year, for lowest, middle, and highest series; NP-T2, total resident population by quarter, middle series; and NP-T3-A through NP-T3-D total resident population by five year age groups and sex, annual, middle series. The middle series may be considered the most likely values. The Census Bureau prepares a number of data series based upon alternate assumptions about future fertility, mortality, and net migration levels. Lowest, middle, and highest series are the distilled results of these statistical calculations. Population series contain estimates and projections. Estimates are the Bureau's best approximation of the past. Projections are based upon assumptions about future demographic trends.

Series NP-T1, for example, provides projections in all three series, but note the divergence between the different series, a possible forecasting dilemma.

	Projections			High-Low Difference %
Year	Low	Middle	High	
2003	280624	282798	285422	1.7
2005	284000	287716	292339	2.9
2007	287106	292583	299557	4.3
2010	291413	299862	310910	6.7
2015	297977	312268	331636	11.3
2020	303664	324927	354642	16.8

Numbers in thousands

If projections are to be incorporated into a multiple regression equation, a single series is selected, probably the middle series. If the objective is to determine general direction because population of itself has a material impact on industry or company sales, a range is more appropriate, perhaps with the middle series as the point estimate, and high and low series as the parameter limitations. With projections of five years (possibly ten years), the percentage divergence is reasonable, but the percentage difference in longer estimates may cloud the issue. Economic projections can supplement population projections as a separate series or in a regression equation using, say, the middle series. This subject is considered in more detail in later chapters.

The further into the future the forecaster looks the more obscure the landscape, the wider the range of probability, and the larger the error. Both economic and demographic data are subject to these errors. Detailed planning, therefore, should encompass as few years as possible. Longer-term forecasts should be more generalized, primarily to indicate direction, thus the reason for a range.

The multiple regression format allows what-if examinations. By varying one component (independent variable) while holding the others constant, the influence that that variable has upon demand can be evaluated. For instance, economic data can be held constant while the highest or lowest demographic series is substituted for the middle series. Or each of the economic components, one at a time, could be varied. Or more than one variable could be varied simultaneously. A number of possible demands would emerge and the most probable range could then be selected.

Many products are related to one or more age groups rather than to the population as a whole. A company selling these products is interested in population forecasts for those age groups that use its products. Series NP-T3 projects resident population by 5-year age groups and sex and by special age categories. Census tables that show the projected age distributions by regions and states are also available. Knowing future age distributions by state, for example, may be important for determining sales potential by geographical area. Calculating ratios assist in determining if there should be a shifting emphasis and if so the magnitude of the change needed. The growth ratio tells how much growth or decline may be expected in each category. Analyzing the population time series by age and/or sex and the related ratios help management decide if there should be a changed emphasis and to what degree.

To address the relationship between sales and population specifically, time series analysis and regression are suitable methods. Depending upon the circumstances, two approaches are possible.

❖ If industry or company sales are relational with total population, a regression equation incorporating population and economic data may be used to forecast total demand. Demand for each age group is determined by simple regression or time series analysis. The sum of the age group forecasts is compared to the total demand forecast. Likely, the discrepancy between the two will be significant requiring resolution. If total sales are historically expressive, adjustment is made to the individual age group forecasts. If historically age group forecasts are more accurate, total sales are changed.

❖ If the company sells only to certain age groups, total population probably will not be a valid measure of sales. Rather, formulate an equation for each age group. Simple regression may be adequate. Adding economic factors is a possibility. It may be feasible to consolidate all sales into one equation and then divide the resulting demand forecast into age group forecasts by percentage. A series of equations in an econometric format is another, although complex, possibility.

The goodness of forecasts is tested historically by the methods explained in this book. Economic conditions may not affect sales equally in each age group. The impact of recession, for instance, may cause sales to retreat further in some age categories than it does in others. In historical testing the forecasting equations this must be considered. This rationale applies to forecasting not only by age and sex but equally to regional or state forecasting. An economic condition that affects one product group may affect another differently. Children's products may continue stronger than adult products (as in clothing) in an economic downturn. Consumers may move down the price scale in times of uncertainty. Conversely, in boom times there is a tendency to move up the price scale and to spend more freely. Sales levels for big-ticket items frequently depend upon interest rates. But none of this is absolute. Industry and company sales histories in relation to the economy and demographic statistics are better understood when all possibilities are explored.

Chapter 10

Econometrics and Some Related Techniques

Econometrics may be defined as that discipline concerned with formulating economic models that empirically estimate an economy. The economy being studied may be a government, an industry, a business, a segment of these entities, or another economic grouping. For our purposes, the definition is simplified to generally include all quantitative methods employing causal relationships.

An objective of econometrics is to specify a model that abstracts the essence from the economy, thus describing the essential nature of the system being investigated. For businesses, the question concerns how the general movement of the economy affects sales, thus profits. The methodology is applicable to macroeconomics and microeconomics.

Macroeconomics is the examination of economic aggregates such as the gross domestic product (GDP) and its major subdivisions. It deals with the forces and interrelationships that affect large sectors of a national or regional economy. The model that expresses the phenomena is often complex and may consist of several hundred equations. Generally, the complexity and cost of developing macroeconomic models is impractical (really impossible) for most companies. Business is a consumer rather than an initiator. Companies, however, can adopt or develop less complex models to meet specific business requirements, especially as they pertain to forecasting. Macroeconomic outputs are inputs to causal models of the types examined in Chapter 7.

Microeconomics is concerned with the behavior of smaller economic units such as industries and by extension business firms. It is more practical for a company to develop models that describe its internal workings or those that describe its relationship to its industry or to pertinent economic time series (as in a regression model) than it is to develop macro models. In addition to forecasting, the model may be the basis for choosing between alternative policies or strategies.

The output from econometric models may be divided into three categories, each of which may issue from the same model:

❖ Forecasting an element important to the business enterprise. The forecast may be made to determine the level of future sales, expected profits, or any other primary segment of business. At the macro level, forecasts are made of the national economy and its major sectors.

❖ Structural analysis is concerned with the structure of economic relationships. Its purpose is to investigate the system or subsystem to gain an understanding of the essential phenomena. It may be used to test competing theories or as a preliminary study for policy evaluation. In the latter mode, its goal is to appraise the impact of each available alternative or to eliminate invalid alternatives, those not supported by the evidence. At the business level, the analysis may be made to study the relationship between two or more variables. For example, a company may wish to examine the responsiveness of sales to changes in product price; the relationship between cost (as in a quality study), price, and profit; or the level of consumer demand compared with the cost of credit.

❖ Policy evaluation is the use of an econometric model to select a policy from competing alternatives. It may also be used to examine a single alternative in relation to different environments. In macroeconomics, formulating monetary and fiscal policies are representative examples of the choices that affect national policy. In a business firm, several capital investment options may be available. The company may analyze each choice in relation to criteria that determine future value. Policy evaluation at the company level is interpreted to mean evaluating objectives and goals that are quantifications of the general policies.

The econometric process encompasses both the forecasting and decision making functions and is characterized by mutual support. The model may fulfill the three output needs specified above. Econometrics is a quantitative approach in which the model is explicit and unambiguous in the same way as the models in the preceding chapters, however and in general, the econometric methodology is more demanding in specifying the content and parameters of the model.

A common method of solving econometric problems is to develop equations from regression analysis (regression is the first step) that describe the economic segment being studied. For our purposes, we broaden the explanation somewhat to include the examples given in

Chapter 7 as econometric problems. Thus, the examples in this chapter are micro models employable by business firms.

There are several common characteristics:

❖ All business decisions that include the future are made from forecasts or estimates, whether those forecasts are explicit as in econometrics, implicit as in qualitative methods, or nonexistent as when the future is not considered – the future will be the same as the past. Forecasts may be point estimates: one value for each period projected, with the forecast made independently of the decision making process but later influencing it. Or a forecast may be made for each alternative, when alternatives exist, as a measure of the probable results that will occur for each of the circumstances being tested. Point forecasts, although they may be expressed as a range, are the type thus far described. Econometrics assumes the availability of choices and recognizes the influence of managers in the forecasting process.

❖ Choices are usually available in dealing with economic problems. If the alternatives can be quantified, an objective evaluation of the options is possible. Many problems, however, do not require a preliminary forecast. Typically, theses problems are straightforward, often complex, and are solved by other mathematical means. An example internal to an industrial company is investigating the routing of production through alternate work centers to achieve least cost. But many economic problems involve a look into the future and necessitate the estimation that is provided by forecasting.

❖ Often, there is an interdependent relationship between economic problems. To achieve a good in one area of the enterprise may adversely affect another area. These are trade-off situations in which the impact on each affected activity must be assessed.

U.S. Economic Structure

The economy is represented in the National Income and Product Accounts (NIPA). There are nine categories: National product and income; personal income and outlays; government receipts and expenditures; foreign transactions; saving and investment; income, employment, and product by industry; quantity and price indexes; supplementary tables; and seasonally unadjusted estimates. Often, the elements that make-up the NIPA are part of the forecasting equation. Some of these plus other economic indicators have been used in previous chapters' examples. Gross domestic product (GDP), a major measure, may be considered as the sum or market value of goods and services produced by labor and property in the United States. Its sub-elements are personal consumption expenditures which are the goods and services purchased by persons living in the U.S., consisting of durable and nondurable goods and services; gross private domestic investment, representing fixed investment and business inventory changes; net exports, which are exports less imports and indicate a trade surplus (positive number) or a trade deficit (negative number); and government consumption expenditures and gross investment, which is compensation of government employees and government purchases from business. Detail about these accounts can be found in the *Survey of Current Business* published by The Bureau of Economic Analysis.

There are three terms that require definition. Current or nominal dollars are the actual dollars for each period. Constant dollars are benchmarked to a specific year to mitigate the effects of inflation and are now somewhat out of fashion. Chain-weighted dollars replace constant dollars because they increase the accuracy of data adjusted for inflation.

The NIPA and the wealth of other economic data available provide a reservoir of information that may be applicable in forecasting sales and business activity, say, as parts of a regression model or a model of the business climate in longer range projections.

Business Cycles

An important forecasting consideration is the business cycle because the magnitude of economic and business activity that may be expected at a particular point in time is conditional, at least in part, upon the business cycle.

Business Conditions Digest, published by the Commerce Department, defined business cycles as "sequences of expansion and contraction in various economic processes that show up as major fluctuations in aggregate economic activity – that is, in comprehensive measures of production, employment, income, and trade." Business cycles are recurrent but non-periodic, which makes them difficult to predict. Duration and intensity vary.

Cycles are distinguished by phases of expansion and contraction with turning points that divide the two. Not all fluctuations in business activity are attributable to cycles. Seasonal variations and trend are two other factors that influence the level of business activity. In Chapter 3 these terms are defined in conjunction with describing the method for segregating the components of a time series. The business cycle constitutes a variation from the long-term trend. If there is a long-term growth trend, for example, the business cycle involves fluctuations around that trend.

If a turn in economic activity can be presaged – if only in general terms and imprecisely as to timing – an important aspect of forecasting has nevertheless been fulfilled. The company is in a position to plan an expansion or contraction in business activity, to act with caution as the cycle develops or comes into existence, or to take actions that will optimize a coming upturn or minimize a foreshadowed downturn. In other words, it gives the businessman a decision-making edge.

Turning points are those economic data points that signal that a business cycle has reached its trough (the point where the cycle is at its lowest) or its peak (the cycle is at its highest). To say the least, forecasting turning points is difficult. The National Bureau of Economic Research (NBER) establishes the official peak and trough dates for the U. S. economy. The NBER generally does not announce these dates until long after the actual turning points have arrived. These dates are universal reference dates. A business cycle is measured from trough to previous trough or peak to previous peak.

Two other terms of interest are: expansion and contraction. Expansion or recovery is the condition occurring when a cycle rises, measured from trough to peak. Contraction or recession is that phase when national output falls, measured from peak to trough.

Cyclical Indicators and Turning Points

Cyclical indicators are one tool in analyzing economic conditions. They identify economic time series as leading, coincident (coinciding), or lagging indicators, which signifies their relationship to the movement of various economic series. The timing of a leading indicator at turning points tends to occur in advance of the economic activity. Coinciding indicators reach turning points at roughly the same time as the general economy. Lagging indicators reach peaks and troughs of economic activity after the business cycle turns. In forecasting, leading indicators may foretell a change – each leads a different length of time. Combining leading indicators with other data increases the probability of predicting turning points. This subject is examined later in this chapter. Coinciding indicators verify that a change is taking place. Lagging indicators confirm that the change is well underway.

The Conference Board's *Business Cycle Indicators*, which is published monthly, classifies many of the cyclical indicators according to their relationship with the economy. (See their web site at www.globalindicators.org.)

The Conference Board's composite index of leading economic indicators is a weighted average of those series listed below. It is a major source for estimating turning points.

The index of leading indicators changes from time to time, currently they are:

GOM910 Composite leading index (1996 = 100), consisting of:

BCI 1 Average weekly hours, manufacturing

BCI 5 Average weekly initial claims for unemployment insurance (4 wk average, SA)

BCI 8 Mfgs' new orders, consumer goods & materials (millions, chained 1996 $)

BCI 19 Index of stock prices 500 common stocks, NSA (1941-43 =10)

BCI 27 Mfgs' new orders, nondefense capital goods (millions, chained 1996 $)

BCI 29 Building permits for new private housing units (millions)

BCI 32 Vendor performance, slower deliveries diffusion index (percent)

BCI 83 Index of consumer confidence

BCI 106 Money supply, M2 (billions, chained 1996 $)

BCI 129 Interest rate spread, 10-year Treasury bonds less federal funds (rate banks charge each other compared with 10-yr Treasury bond yield)

Coinciding (coincident) indicators are:

GOM 920 Composite index (1996 = 100)

BCI 41 Employees on nonagricultural payrolls (thousands)

BCI 47 Index of industrial production (1922 = 100)

BCI 51 Personal income less transfer payments (AR billions chained 1996 $)

BCI 57 Manufacturing and trade sales (millions chained 1996 $)

Lagging indicators are:

GOM 930 Composite lagging index (1996 = 100)

BCI 91 Average duration of unemployment in weeks

BCI 77 Ratio of manufacturing and trade inventories to sales (chained 1996 $)

BCI 62 Change in labor cost per unit of manufacturing output (6 month % AR)

BCI 109 Average prime rate charged by banks NSA (%)

BCI 101 Outstanding commercial and industrial loans (millions chained 1996 $)

BCI 95 Ratio of consumer installment credit to personal income (%)

BCI 120 Change in consumer price index for services (6 month % AR)

Individual leading indicators can be erratic and generally should be used only in conjunction with composite indices. Composite indices contain a number of individual series that average over time and that makes them trustworthier for forecasting. Leading indicators do not measure the intensity or the duration of the economic change. And they do not always tell the truth. Sometimes, their signal of a turn in economic fortunes may be in error, which explains why economists use many different series in addition to leading indicators in their analysis of the economy. Still, complex and less complicated methods have in common an inability to always be right.

Because leading indicators are not as difficult to understand as more complex methodologies, they have that as an advantage over other econometric models. Comparing individual leading economic indicators to reach a conclusion as to a turning point can be confusing in that one or more may move in an opposite direction from the others. For example, while writing this chapter consumer confidence declined while building permits for new housing were strong. But mortgage rates had been especially low compared to the not so distant past. Could that account for the disparity? A weighted average of economic indicators is one possibility to overcome this difficulty. It should be noted that more complex econometric formulations are subject to the same failures.

The NBER uses monthly measures of industrial production, employment, the volume of sales relating to manufacturing and wholesale-retail, and personal income less transfer payments, in real terms (real terms corrects for inflation), to determine the turning points in the economy. Also, other measures may be considered. In defining a recession, the NBER considers three factors known as the three Ds: it encompasses a considerable length of time (duration), there must be a sizeable reduction in output (depth), and it affects at least several important sectors of the economy (diffusion). Unfortunately for forecasters, the publishing of turning points is usually long after its occurrence. As examples, the dating committee announced the trough that occurred in March 1991 in December 1992 and the peak of March 2001 was declared in November 2001.

What constitutes a turning point? There are various interpretations. The NBER's definition is given above, but there are popular gauges. The most frequently encountered is that a recession can be expected forthwith or has arrived if there are two consecutive quarterly declines in real gross domestic product (GDP). Real GDP is defined as billions of chained 1996 dollars, seasonally adjusted at annual rates. The recession (the beginning of an expansion) ends when there are two consecutive quarters of real GDP gain. GDP does not foretell a turning point, however. Its use as a gage is problematic in that it does not provide monthly data (GDP is reported quarterly). Additionally, there can be serious downturns without two consecutive quarters of negative growth. Another less frequently encountered measure, often considered naïve, is three consecutive months of decline of any magnitude in the Index of Leading Economic Indicators. The Conference Board, however, declares that "a downward movement in the composite index of two percent annual rate or more over six months coupled with declines in the majority of component series is needed before a recession warning can be considered reliable." A decline in the rate of change of one percent over six months may be indicative of an economic contraction when coupled with a diffusion index under 50%, and it is a good but not perfect predictor. When comparing the results from the less rigorous two-quarter rule with NBER results, the former can be considered as a warning sign (but not a prophesy of change). It is best to forego this "rule" completely, however, and develop a methodology better suited to forecasting, as described later in this chapter. By the time the rule shows up, the astute forecaster should have foreseen a probable contraction developing. The NBER rule considers that stagnant or very moderate growth is a continuation of recession, thus their defined recessions may be of longer duration. Remember, NBER pronouncements regarding recession beginning dates occur long after the fact.

Predicting turning points using appropriate leading economic indicators and subsequently estimating the future there from may not give results as good as a complex econometric model (but again, they might), however, it may serve the corporation's purpose by giving direction and warning. Using the methodology suggested later can give even better results. Complexity is not a guarantee of accuracy, far from it. Armstrong in *Long Range Forecasting* (see references) repeatedly indicates that simplicity is better than complexity and that the results are likely to be as good as or better than very complicated formulations. Of course, what is simple to an econometrician and to a practitioner are probably two different things. Nevertheless, it is my belief that the least complexity possible rules (almost). It has been noted by many of the knowledgeable that economists have forecast twelve of the past nine recessions.

So, as a non-professor of economics, is this muddling your understanding of how to forecast the mid- to long-term? Should we be reading the tealeaves? Later in this chapter and in Chapter 12 we will address this subject with practical examples that are applicable and usable. A few conclusions, which may be disheartening, follow, but the clouds will soon dissipate.

The job of the econometrician and any forecaster using economic data is made more difficult by the imperfections of the underlying economic data, both as it pertains to inclusiveness and in the goodness of the relationship between "the data" and actuality, thus reliability and timeliness suffer. Many of the time series data points are not available in final form until several months after the fact.

The more complex the formulations the more likely there will be discrepancies between observed data and the forces influencing behavior. Conversely, simplicity may not adequately describe the behavior. There is a wealth of economic data, much of it inadequate or not timely for forecast purposes, however, that is all there is. It is problematic, but the econometrician and the rest of us have no choice but to accept what is available.

Cyclical impact is pervasive throughout the economy, but different segments of the economy experience the impact in different ways. In bad times, capital goods, consumer durable goods, and construction industries tend to suffer more than the non-durable goods industries. Outlays for durable and capital goods can usually be delayed. In recession, consumers make do. Companies needing less production capacity will wait to modernize their plants. Conversely, people still need basic items, such as food and clothing. Although they may change their buying patterns or reduce the number of their purchases, they continue to need certain items. A person may move down in price point or repair what would otherwise be discarded, but purchases will not be stopped. In some instances, it is possible that business may increase because of the recession; for example, inexpensive clothing sales may increase as people move downward. It is important to know the nature of the impact that turning points and the subsequent change in direction will have on your industry.

Diffusion Indices and Rates of Change

A diffusion index measures the breath of a recession or recovery (how widespread) and whether it is continuing to spread. Indices are usually prepared for composite series such as the Conference Board's leading indicators. Composite indices consist of numerous components. A diffusion index is a summary of how the individual components are moving over a given time span. They express the percentage of components that are rising. Cyclical changes in diffusion indices generally lead those in the corresponding composites. The range of movement is between 100, indicating that all components are rising, to zero, indicating that none are rising. Widespread increases mean rapid growth whereas widespread declines are associated with sharp downturns. During expansionary periods, the indices are generally above 50% and below that during contractions. In evaluating a diffusion index, however, the 50% criterion must be tempered by caution. In recent years, the different components of a composite index sometimes have not moved in consort and may even differ substantially. Ideally, the percentage should be closer to zero percent, say 20%, or 100 percent, say 70%, to confirm a turning point, however, the trend may be revealing of direction. Examination of the individual sectors (components) may reveal important insights that will help to evaluate the economic condition. It is usually impossible to know the precise timing of a turning point before the fact. Discounting certain component series or applying a weighting factor may indicate direction and be the warning that is critical. Because of instability in a series measured over a short time span, it is generally better to use a series measured over the longer term. If the duration of an increase or decrease is of very short duration, it should not be thought of as an expansion or contraction.

It may be useful to follow not only the diffusion index for the composite of leading indicators but also those for coincident and lagging indicators. This provides continuity in decision making and planning for the near-term future.

Another series that helps to identify the economic situation is the rate of change (growth rate). A diffusion index measures direction and scope; rate of change measures degree of change (momentum) as well as direction. The momentum of the series, not the levels of activity, is that which is being computed. Rates of change usually lead the composite indices to which they are related but not always.

Calculating a Diffusion Index

A diffusion index may be computed for any number of periods. For example, in determining the percentage of stocks with positive movement, usually the average of the past ten days or ten weeks is used. For the business applications presented in this book, a diffusion index is usually calculated on the basis of one, three, or six months. The latter is a more reliable signal of a turning point because it is less volatile. If there is positive movement, a value of 1 is assigned. If the data item remains unchanged (stable) between periods, a value of 0.5 is assigned. Negative movements are valued at zero. A question the forecaster must answer is what constitutes a movement? You may decide that any movement, even the smallest amount, comprises a change; thus, if the first period is 2000 and the second period is 2000.1 a value of 1 is assigned. If the change was from 2000 to 1999.9 a value of zero is assigned. Another approach is to define a change as more than a certain small percentage, perhaps 0.05% (as used by the Conference Board). Values that rise or fall at least 0.05% take the value of 1 or zero.

The formula for calculating the index is to assign a value to each component, then sum the values of the components, then divide by the number of components and multiply by 100. Three examples follow. In the first two examples there are ten components, which could be a composite index of leading indicators if the numbers were not made-up for this example.

A one-month diffusion index:

Component	1	2	3	4	5	6	7	8	9	10	Index Level
Month 1	10	50	30	40	60	35	55	60	50	75	
Month 2	15	40	35	40	65	30	50	65	50	80	
Value	1	0	1	.5	1	0	0	1	.5	1	60
3	20	45	35	45	65	25	50	70	55	75	
Value	1	1	.5	1	.5	0	.5	1	1	0	75
4	25	45	40	40	70	25	55	75	55	80	
Value	1	.5	1	0	1	.5	1	1	.5	1	75
5	30	45	45	40	75	30	50	80	60	85	
Value	1	.5	1	.5	1	1	0	1	1	1	80
6	35	50	50	40	80	30	60	85	60	85	
Value	1	1	1	.5	1	.5	1	1	.5	.5	80

For period 1 and 2: the sum of the values is 6; 6/10 = 0.6; 0.6 x 100 = 60, which is the diffusion index.

To compute a six-period diffusion index, the above steps are followed, however, the values are determined from the first and sixth periods. The value for the first component for periods 1 and 6 is 1 because the component increased from 10 to 35. In a multiple period index, the values and index numbers are centered at the middle period. If there is an even number of periods the diffusion index level is placed at the fourth period in a six period index, for example:

Component	1	2	3	4	5	6	7	8	9	10	
Value	1	.5	1	.5	1	0	1	1	1	1	80

The value 80 is placed at the fourth not the sixth month.

Another style of diffusion index can be seen in surveys wherein the respondents answer questions with, say, a positive, neutral, of negative response and an index is computed for each question. For instance, if in question 1 asked of 100 persons, 25% of the answers were positive, 50% neutral, and 25% negative, the index is 50: (25 x 1) + (50 x 0.5) + (25 x 0).

The above does not represent all the ways a diffusion index may be computed. In one business outlook survey the index was determined by subtracting the number of those indicating an increase from those indicating a decrease. "No change" answers were not considered. For our purposes the system described in the first two examples will be applied.

Sometimes an index will be expressed by a direction of change chart. Instead of using 1, 0.5, and 0, the chart uses plus signs (meaning 1) minus signs (meaning 0) and ± (meaning 0.5). The arithmetic is the same, however.

If a series is in percent format, such as the interest rate spread, the arithmetic difference rather than the percentage change is applied. In some instances a positive is actually a decline in the index, an example is the average weekly initial claims for unemployment insurance. Down is good.

Calculating the Rate of Change

Rate of change (ROC) is a concept that finds wide usage in mathematics, science, the financial market (stocks, etc), and in forecasting. There are several ROC formats and more than a few methods available for computing rates of change. The following paragraphs describe several methods as may be applied to forecasting. Because forecasting is generally related to time (as in a time series of observations) in one way or another, our examples are limited to the forecasting arena.

A rate of change is the change of one variable divided by a corresponding change in a related variable. In forecasting, x is the independent variable and is related in time to y. In the examples following, x represent time and y the demand. Figure 10-1 illustrates a time series in which demand is a linear function. This style chart is recognizable from the section in Chapter 3 that explains how to calculate a trend. Recall that a simplified method of determining trend in a regression (least squares) equation is available when x is time, therefore, one technique is to apply least squares, in which case the *slope* of the line is the rate of change (explained below). Another technique is to solve the following linear equation:

$$\text{ROC} = \Delta y \div \Delta x = (y_2 - y_1) \div (x_2 - x_1)$$

The sign Δ is the Greek letter delta, which represents the difference between the most recent value and the earlier (first) value within the range being considered. This definition is applicable to both the y and x series. To solve the equation, substitute the values from Figure 10-1 as follows: $(87 - 50)/(13 - 1) = 3.08$. Note that the x column used in the calculation is *not* the coded value but the period column. The result is the *average* rate of change for the periods specified. An average rate can be computed for any interval of time. This is discussed in more detail below.

Another technique for determining the average rate of change is to find the slope of the line, which is the b value in the regression equation $a + b(x)$. See Chapter 6 for an explanation. The rate of change, therefore, is 3.005. Note that there is a small difference in ROC between the two methods, not an unusual condition. Solving the equation for period 13 results in a forecasted demand of 88, explained as $70 + 3.005(6)$.

A Demand Series

Period	Code (x)	Demand (y)	xy	x^2
1	-6	50	-300	36
2	-5	54	-270	25
3	-4	58	-232	16
4	-3	63	-189	9
5	-2	61	-122	4
6	-1	70	-70	1
7	0	72	0	0
8	1	76	76	1
9	2	74	148	4
10	3	80	240	9
11	4	81	324	16
12	5	84	420	25
13	6	87	522	36
Sum (Σ)		910	547	182

Figure 10-1

An average rate of change is a constant; that is, for each period in the interval (the number of observations) the rate of change is the same.

An average rate of change may also be expressed as a percentage. The formula is:

ROC = 100*(last number – first number)/(first number)

$$100*(87 - 50)/50 = 37/50 = 74\%$$

or

$$(87/50)*(100)-100 = 74\%$$

Two other terms that may be seen on the forecasting playing field are ratios and proportions. Comparisons can be expressed as actual or relative values. If the total is 6000 and it is subdivided into 4000 in one category and 2000 in another category, it is 4000:2000 or relatively as 4:2 or 2:1. Relative values are ratios. Ratios may be written as a fraction indicating division, as 2/1 translates to $2 \div 1 = 2$, which means 2 to 1. In ratios the number after the colon is always 1, for example, 18.6:7.4 is 18.6/7.4, thus 2.514 or 2.514:1. A proportion is equality between two ratios. Thus, a:b = c:d is a proportion saying that the ratios of a:b and c:d are equal. If three terms are known, the fourth can be found by cross multiplication, as ad = bc.

Rate of change is an analytical tool that may be used to compare results for two or more periods. Comparison may be made between last quarter's and this quarter's sales or profits, for instance, or between this year's total and last year's total, or between a month last year and the same month this year. For example, if sales this January are 18% higher than last January, that is a rate of change computed for one month. Although rates of change can be calculated for any number of periods, twelve months and six months are probably the most common, except for stock market calculations. Rate of change, remember, does not measure in dollar terms (nor in any other unit measure). Rather, it measures momentum (growth rate), not the activity level.

As an example, comparing monthly sales this year with last year (a twelve month curve), the rate of change is calculated based upon the sums of January through December, February through the next January, etc. The comparison is between the same twelve-month total this year with the twelve-month total of the previous year. This gives the annual percentage change for each year. Any point above the line of equilibrium (the zero line) indicates that activity has increased when compared with last year, even if there is a month-to-month decline and that decline remains above zero. Points below the zero line indicate that activity decreased in comparison with last year. The rate of change could be a rising curve, but as long as it remained below zero it is still a decrease from last year. The highest data point above zero on the curve identifies when the growth rate peaked. Actual activity, however, may have peaked in some other month. Conversely, the same rationale applies to data below the zero line. The lowest data point is where growth was lowest; however, actual business activity may have reached its trough at a different time.

Any two periods may be compared, for example, current quarter with the comparable quarter last year. An advantage of a twelve-month comparison is that an adjustment for seasonal considerations is unnecessary. Data that are measured in different units (one in dollars, another in pounds, for instance) are comparable when rate of change is the medium.

Figures 10-2 through 10-6 provide an illustration of rate of change and related data. As with most techniques described in this book, they can be programmed in Excel or similar spreadsheets. What conclusions can a forecaster or analyst derive from the data?

There are three time series that have been converted to ROC:

1. End item sales. These are the total sales of a product that is made by more than one manufacturer (likely, all producers or importers of that product) and, say, sold to retailers or consumers. As logically, it could be one brand of a major product line, such as a make of automobile or it could be housing starts if that is the market supplied by our example company. It may also be an economic indicator or a composite index of economic indicators.

2. Total component sales (Figure 10-3). This is total sales of a component or group of components that are sold to the end-item manufacturers by all supplying companies. It is total industry sales. Not all of the end-items contain the component(s), but the proportion of the end-items that contain the components to those that do not is constant.

3. Company sales (Figure 10-3). This is company sales of the above component(s). It is the company's market share.

Total End-Item Sales

Month	End-Item Sales	12 Month Sum	Moving Avg	Month	End-Item Sales	12 Month Sum	Moving Avg
January	380			January	1470	15590	1470.8
February	400			February	1490	15880	1500.8
March	490			March	1490	16400	1526.7
April	450			April	1490	16790	1555.0
May	510			May	1520	17080	1582.5
June	660		656.7	June	1570	17370	1609.2
July	690		708.3	July	1640	17650	1629.2
August	770		775.0	August	1690	18010	1642.5
September	800		815.0	September	1710	18320	1649.2
October	840		869.2	October	1730	18660	1650.0
November	920		929.2	November	1740	18990	1642.5
December	970	7880	980.8	December	1770	19310	1634.2
January	1000	8500	1036.7	January	1710	19550	1622.5
February	1200	9300	1083.3	February	1650	19710	1601.7
March	970	9780	1133.3	March	1570	19790	1573.3
April	1100	10430	1179.2	April	1500	19800	1535.0
May	1230	11150	1220.0	May	1430	19710	1489.2
June	1280	11770	1260.0	June	1470	19610	1440.0
July	1360	12440	1299.2	July	1500	19470	
August	1330	13000	1323.3	August	1440	19220	
September	1400	13600	1366.7	September	1370	18880	
October	1390	14150	1399.2	October	1270	18420	
November	1410	14640	1423.3	November	1190	17870	
December	1450	15120	1447.5	December	1180	17280	

Figure 10-2

Figure 10-2 provides a four-year history of end-item sales of a product manufactured (or imported or both) by all companies. This data is compared with component industry and company sales in the tables that follow. A review of sales tells the story of a three-year rise in sales followed by a twelve-month decline. Based on that data alone, an analyst could conclude a continuance of the decline. As will be illustrated later, this is not necessarily so if a turning point can be estimated.

Twelve-month totals of sales are used to calculate the twelve-month rates of change below. The total of 7880 is the sum of January through December of the first year and 8500 is the sum of February though January. The twelve-month moving average centered is given for informational purposes. Because of the linear nature of sales, the moving average compares rather favorably to actual sales. If the current time was June of the third year and July through December sales had not yet occurred, the series could be used to forecast those unknown months; but see Chapter 4 for methodology and the turning point discussion below before drawing conclusions.

Industry and company sales (Figure 10-3) may be compared with each other and with end-item sales. Industry sales lag end-item sales by two months and are roughly 25% of end item sales; for example, March industry sales are 25% of January end-item sales (380 x .25 = 95). The relationship is seen in Figure 10-5 graph. Company sales, i.e. its market share, fluctuate within a few percentage point as depicted in Figure 10-6, but are more stable when computed on a twelve-month basis.

The ROC's in Figure 10-4 are percentages. Rates of change not as percentages could also be computed, however, the percentage figures work well for our purposes. These twelve month rates of change were calculated as previously described, for example from Figure 10-2: $100*(15120-7880)/7880 = 91.9$. Sales for the second twelve months (January through December) are compared with the like period of the first year. What is being calculated in a rate of change is not the percentage that one number is to another but what percent the difference between the two numbers is relative to the first number, thus a measure of momentum.

In Figure 10-6, the market share by month is the percentage of total industry sales attributable to the company for each of the months in the series. In March the market share is 10%, which is company sales divided by industry sales, then multiplied by 100: $(9.5/95)*100$, see Figure 10.3. Likewise, the market share for twelve months is the percentage of sales on an annual basis. Company share is 9.61: $(190.2/1980)*100$, which relates to February in Figure 10-3.

Component Industry and Company Sales

Month	Industry Sales	Moving Sum	Co Sales	Moving Sum
Jan				
Feb				
Mar	95.0		9.5	
Apr	100.0		10.0	
May	120.0		11.0	
June	115.0		11.5	
July	126.5		13.5	
Aug	167.0		17.1	
Sep	172.5		17.2	
Oct	190.5		19.0	
Nov	202.0		23.0	
Dec	219.0		18.3	
Jan	230.0		20.0	
Feb	242.5	1980.0	20.1	190.2
Mar	253.0	2138.0	21.0	201.7
Apr	304.0	2342.0	23.9	215.6
May	242.5	2464.5	17.9	222.5
June	275.0	2624.5	20.6	231.6
July	307.5	2805.5	24.6	242.7
Aug	316.0	2954.5	31.6	257.2
Sep	330.0	3112.0	33.3	273.3
Oct	338.0	3259.5	33.8	288.1
Nov	350.0	3407.5	34.0	299.1
Dec	347.5	3536.0	34.8	315.6
Jan	352.5	3658.5	35.5	331.1
Feb	366.5	3782.5	37.0	348.0
Mar	367.5	3897.0	36.8	363.8
Apr	372.5	3965.5	37.3	377.1
May	377.0	4100.0	39.8	399.0
June	375.0	4200.0	40.2	418.6
July	390.0	4282.5	39.0	433.0
Aug	392.5	4359.0	31.4	432.8
Sep	416.0	4445.0	29.1	428.6
Oct	422.5	4529.5	21.9	416.7
Nov	429.5	4609.0	25.4	408.1
Dec	432.5	4694.0	32.1	405.4
Jan	435.0	4776.5	45.0	414.9
Feb	439.5	4849.5	44.0	421.9
Mar	423.5	4905.5	44.8	430.0
Apr	412.5	4945.5	43.6	436.3
May	392.5	4961.0	42.0	438.5
June	370.0	4956.0	39.0	437.3
July	354.0	4920.0	38.0	436.3
Aug	362.5	4890.0	35.0	439.9
Sep	375.0	4849.0	35.5	446.3
Oct	360.0	4786.5	32.0	456.4
Nov	342.5	4699.5	33.2	464.2
Dec	317.5	4584.5	28.3	460.4

Figure 10-3

ROC % Comparisons

Month	End-Item ROC	Industry ROC	Company ROC
Dec	91.9		
Jan	83.4		
Feb	70.8	91.0	83.0
Mar	67.7	82.3	80.3
Apr	61.0	69.3	74.9
May	53.2	66.4	79.3
Jun	47.6	60.0	80.7
Jly	41.9	52.6	78.4
Aug	38.5	47.5	68.3
Sep	34.7	42.8	56.8
Oct	31.9	39.0	44.6
Nov	29.7	35.3	36.4
Dec	27.7	32.7	28.5
Jan	25.4	30.6	25.3
Feb	24.1	28.2	21.2
Mar	20.7	25.9	18.2
Apr	17.9	24.7	15.7
May	15.4	21.0	9.9
Jun	12.9	18.0	4.5
Jly	10.3	14.9	0.8
Aug	6.7	12.2	1.6
Sep	3.1	9.1	4.1
Oct	-1.3	5.7	9.5
Nov	-5.9	2.0	13.7
Dec	-10.5	-2.3	13.6

Start date is December, second year

Figure10-4

Rates of Change as Percentages

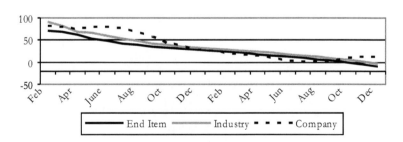

Figure 10-5

Company Market Share as a Percentage of Industry Sales

Month	Market Share Month	Market Share 12 Months	Month	Market Share Month	Market Share 12 Months
March	10.00		February	10.10	9.20
April	10.00		March	10.00	9.33
May	9.17		April	10.00	9.51
June	10.00		May	10.56	9.73
July	10.67		June	10.72	9.97
August	10.24		July	10.00	10.11
September	9.97		August	8.00	9.93
October	9.97		September	7.00	9.64
November	11.39		October	5.18	9.20
December	8.36		November	5.91	8.85
January	8.70		December	7.42	8.64
February	8.29	9.61	January	10.34	8.69
March	8.30	9.43	February	10.01	8.70
April	7.86	9.21	March	10.58	8.76
May	7.38	9.03	April	10.57	8.82
June	7.49	8.82	May	10.70	8.84
July	8.00	8.65	June	10.54	8.82
August	10.00	8.71	July	10.73	8.87
September	10.09	8.78	August	9.66	9.00
October	10.00	8.84	September	9.47	9.20
November	9.71	8.78	October	8.89	9.54
December	10.01	8.93	November	9.69	9.88
January	10.07	9.05	December	8.91	10.04

March is March of first year

Figure 10-6

Another perspective is acquired by looking at the ROC that compares three months of sales, say, this year with sales in the same three months of last year. Figure 10-7 is a table of these comparisons. The calculations are the same as the ROC calculations previously explained, except that only three months are summed, which is the base for computing the ROC. For the end item, as example, January through March in Figure 10-2 sums to 1270 in the first year and twelve months later the three month sum is 3170 (1000 + 1200 + 970), thus 100*(3170 − 1270)/1270 = 149.6%. Note that the lag between end item and industry sales is also apparent in the three-month rate of change. Figure 10-8 is a graphical representation of the three-month ROC.

Figures 10-2 through 10-8 examine a demand series, presenting the material in several formats for comparison and analysis. An interpretation of the data follows. It should be noted that a company might select a time frame of one or more months as a benchmark and calculate rates of change for the current period(s) to compare with the benchmark period(s). For example, a company may compare a quarter last year with the same quarter this year to determine how well the company is performing in relation to the benchmark quarter. In the same manner, an historical quarter can be a benchmark for all future quarters. Deseasonalization is necessary if there is a seasonal aspect in the demand (see Chapter 3).

Three-Month ROC, as Percent

Month	ROC End-Item	ROC Industry	ROC Company
March	149.6		
April	144.0		
May	127.6	153.8	105.9
June	122.8	145.2	92.0
July	108.1	128.2	75.3
August	87.3	120.0	82.4
September	81.0	104.6	87.2
October	71.0	85.7	85.2
November	64.1	80.2	70.8
December	55.7	69.3	70.1
January	49.8	61.3	70.1
February	39.1	54.2	83.7
March	40.4	49.8	78.8
April	36.7	38.4	70.8
May	36.4	39.7	81.2
June	26.9	36.9	87.9
July	22.2	38.4	88.6
August	23.4	28.8	44.0
September	23.2	25.7	11.2
October	24.5	25.1	-16.5
November	23.3	24.6	-24.4
December	23.3	24.0	-22.6
January	20.6	23.5	-1.7
February	16.3	22.6	12.9
March	10.8	19.5	22.5
April	5.6	15.3	19.3
May	0.0	10.0	14.6
June	-3.9	4.5	6.3
July	-7.0	-2.2	0.0
August	-10.0	-6.1	1.3
September	-14.5	-8.9	9.0
October	-20.5	-10.8	24.4
November	-26.1	-15.0	31.8
December	-30.5	-20.6	17.8

March is March of year 2

Figure 10-7

Three-Month Rate of Change % Graph

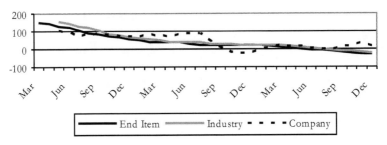

Figure 10-8

Further on, the techniques described in this chapter are discussed in relation to predicting contractions, expansions, and turning points.

Analyzing Company and Industry Sales

Preliminary to analyzing industry and company sales, a look at the end item sales pattern is in order. Figure 10-2 points out the continuous increase in sales for the first three years at which point fortune changes because there is a downturn that continues for the remainder of the series. There are several possible reasons for the contraction; for instance, there may be a change in consumer preference, new technology replacing old, or an economic contraction or recession. Although not a part of this example, examining economic data, when appropriate, and forecasting, there from is normally a part of the process, especially for the longer range. An example is presented later.

How do industry and company patterns relate to the end-item pattern? Essentially, the pattern is the same except that the downturn in industry sales occurs two months later (Figure 10-3). Company and industry sales lag end-item sales by two months. This condition can be observed throughout the series. Company sales are not as clear-cut because there is more fluctuation month-to-month.

An interesting side observation is that because of the lag, end item sales could be used as a leading indicator in forecasting as in a regression model. Also notable is the increase in company sales. It may be a wonderment how the company could keep up with the increasing demand. Although there is a downturn in sales, December of the last year is still much larger than March of the first year. A somewhat different and enlightening picture emerges when we calculate the rate of change.

Before examining ROC, a review of company market share in Figure 10-6 reveals interesting information. The variation when viewed month-to-month shows a high-low difference where the high is more than twice the low at the most extreme. Differences of 20% are not uncommon. This can be a concern to the company depending upon the reasons. A logical objective is to find the reasons as a foundation for developing an improvement strategy. Annually, the variation moves within a much smaller range. It is a better indicator than the monthly figures because radical, short run changes are avoided. This indicates that market share over time remains roughly the same. Still, some of the low sales months can be disturbing.

The twelve-month rates of change are contained in Figure 10-4. A graphical view is presented in Figure 10-5. The graph illustrates the relationship between the three demand series. Note that end item sales and industry sales follow the same path. Company sales, with notable exceptions, roughly follow the industry sales trend. Although actual sales are increasing until the fourth year, the rates of change decline for all four years. On its surface, this is an enigma until we recall that ROC charts measure the rate of growth, that is, momentum, not the actual sales activity. Keep in mind the following when interpreting ROC:

❖ A line above the zero line indicates that sales of the activity being measured have increased during the current twelve months as compared with the previous twelve months. This applies whether the line is going up or down, just as long as it remains above zero. Conversely, a line below zero is indicative that sales are decreasing, whether the line is going up or down. If the ROC is based on six month, three months or any other number of periods, the same rule applies. ROC compares two like periods.

❖ When a line is above another line on the same chart it indicates that the entity represented by that line is growing at the faster pace, therefore, comparatively gaining market share. ROC measures cyclical behavior. Whereas end item and industry sales as measured by ROC appear to be joined at the hip (move together) in Figure 10-5, company sales have a more rocky history, sometimes growing faster than the others, sometimes losing momentum in comparison with them.

What conclusions can be drawn? Two additional charts are added, Figures 10-9 and 10-10.

Graph of Industry Sales
See Figure 10-3

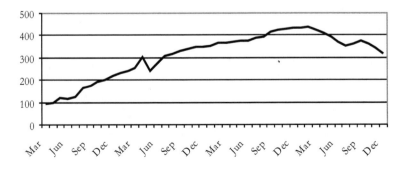

Figure 10-9

Graph of Company Sales
See Figure 10-3

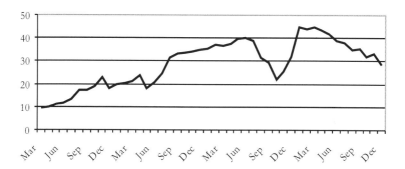

Figure 10-10

Figures 10-2 and 10-3 show that end item, industry, and company sales generally increased throughout the four-year period (but with ups and downs), that is, the later periods are higher than first year sales. Looking at sales only, the company might be pleased with its performance when comparing earlier and later months, even though there are periods of decline. If the review occurs in the fall of the third year, there may be concern; but then sales again picked up.

A study of the rates of change alters the perspective, indicating that although end item, industry, and company sales grew they grew at a continuously declining rate (losing momentum) until end item and industry ROC's passed through zero (see Figures 10-4 and 10-5). At that point, sales began decreasing when compared with the previous twelve months. Although company sales reached near zero they did not go negative. In fact, market share on a twelve-month basis increased thereafter. For a part of the time frame as represented in the ROC charts, the company was gaining market share because its curve was above the industry's curve. When its curve fell below the industry curve, market share was lost. It is important for the company to research the reasons for changes in its market share, an activity vital to planning and forecasting. As essential, is an understanding of why industry sales continuously lost momentum. Knowing may allow the company to influence future sales. If, for example, the component product(s) supplied to industry is becoming obsolescent, planning will be materially affected. Perhaps the economy is in recession, which affects industry sales. These may not be the probable cases, but the reasons for the ROC's is vital planning data.

The highest and lowest points on these curves specifies when the growth rates were at their highest and lowest, not when the actual sales reached their high and low.

Another part of the puzzle is industry and company sales.

A review of the graphs in Figures 10-9 and 10-10 indicates that there is a relationship between industry and company sales, but not in an absolute way. The company knows that its sales are dependent upon industry sales, but that its market share can be influenced by other factors as revealed by the rate of change charts (Figures 10-5 and 10-8). Selecting a forecasting method and frequent review of its applicability are routine functions of a forecaster. Until the downturn in sales, simple regression (least squares with time as the independent variable, Chapter 6) works well as there is an upward trend. Is it applicable after the downturn? Will it continue to forecast reasonably? Probably not. The graph suggests that better results may be obtained if more than one forecasting technique is used as in a simulation model containing several methods in which the system selects the most accurate method or combined forecasting described later in this chapter concerning point forecasting the longer term.

The industry's and company's actual sales increased for about the first three years, then a decline began. However, during the first three years, the ROC points to lost momentum in the rate of growth (growing at a slower pace). In analyzing sales, forecasting sales is not necessarily sufficient. Market share and growth rate are both planning indicators. Although the sales curve may be pleasing, examining the growth rate may indicate lost opportunity, but it may also indicate the opposite, and that calls for scrutiny. At the least, ROC puts sales in perspective.

Forecasting the Longer Term

The longer into the future a company looks the cloudier the atmosphere. Vagaries enter the equation; the unknown lurks in the shadows. Sales, thus revenues and profits, are dependent upon many factors that are difficult to predict. What can be done is to project the future based upon the best knowledge available. Probably the most difficult task is assessing when turning points in the economy will occur and estimating the severity of downturns and the value of upswings. A precise science is not available for this task. Professional economists are also fooled. But there are techniques that can be applied which, if nothing else, act as early warnings to possible turns in the economy. In addition to developing a method to estimate the longer term, a company should read the business press and the Internet to gauge the thinking of economists. Professional services are available to help in the endeavor of estimating the longer term. One such is Micrometrics at www.micrometrics-inc.com. See John Crosby's book *Cycles, Trends, and Turning Points* published by the American Marketing Association, in which he describes several methods for longer term and turning point forecasting, with an emphasis on ARRM's. Can we at this juncture develop a practical methodology that will serve these purposes? One such follows in the next two subsections. There are three tasks:

❖ Forecast major contractions and expansions in the economy. It is assumed that company sales are at least partially dependent upon the state of the economy. The objective is not to pinpoint precisely when a recession will begin, for that is not possible, rather to determine if it is likely that there will be a change in the direction of the economy and to reasonably ascertain its timing and importance.

❖ Project the mid- to long-term economy (or that portion important to the company), beginning with an estimate of real gross domestic product (GDP) as it represents the majority of economic activity. Elements of GDP and other economic indicators may be relevant. Changes in direction (turning points) play a major role in this forecasting. In assessing turning points and forecasting the economy, it should be noted that the National Bureau of Economic Research (NBER) gives little weight to GDP in its determination of recession dates. It defines a recession as "a significant decline in activity spread across the economy, lasting more than a few months, visible in industrial production, employment, real income, and wholesale-retail sales." Other indicators are also considered by the NBER. Although recessions are sometimes identified by two or more quarters of decline in GDP – especially in the popular press -- not all are so inclined, including the recession that began in March 2001. Whereas our methodology for formulating turning points does not include GDP, it is a series not to be ignored. Rather, it acts as a barometer, giving a general direction to the economy overall.

❖ Forecast mid- to long-term company sales in consideration of the above.

Forecasting Turning Points

The integrated approach to predicting turning points employed in the example below contains several distinct parts. Together, they help to overcome the shortfalls found in this type of forecasting. The ones developed for or included in this example are:

❖ The Composite Index of Leading Economic Indicators, developed and published by the Conference Board, is the base. The index was described earlier in this chapter. Their criteria for determining the onset of a recession (and conversely, a recovery) is applied, but modified: a decline in the index of at least one percent over six months as measured by the rate of change, defined as a negative one percent or more, coupled with declines in the majority of the components as measured by a six month diffusion index that is below 50% constitutes a recession warning. How successful has the index been when used by itself and in accordance with the Board's definition? Since 1959 there have been two false signals (no recession). Advanced warning through the 1990 recession occurred in four cases, respectively in months: five, two, three, and nine. For the last two recessions included in this study the warning took place three months and two months after the recession started. The index, however, continues to be a primary source when coupled with the other procedures in our integrated system. Composite indices, one and six-month diffusion indices, individual component series, and many other economic series are available from the Conference Board at www.globalindicators.org.

❖ A composite index consisting of five series, developed specifically for inclusion in this procedure, is added to the mix. Historically, these series have proven to be relevant to forecasting contractions and recoveries. The five series are: the Purchasing Managers Index (PMI), which is a composite index of seasonally adjusted, weighted diffusion indices that consists of new orders, production, employment, supplier deliveries, and inventories; index of stock prices, borrowed from the Conference Board's index; plant and equipment contracts/orders; corporate net cash flow; and corporate profits after tax. The last two are expressed as quarterly data and thus, unfortunately, had to be interpolated to monthly figures. ROC % and diffusion over a period of six month is the basis for a recession warning, providing that both are less than 50%. The equations are explained below.

❖ A decline of three consecutive months in the ROC % of the Conference Board's composite index coupled with a diffusion index of less than 50%. This decline takes place before the minus one percent decline explained above.

❖ The diffusion indices of the two composites are simultaneously less than 50%.

❖ When the spread (yield curve) between the interest rate on the ten-year Treasury note and the three-month Treasury bill at constant maturity is equal to or negatively larger than -0.15%. The spreads before January 1982 are statistical estimates because data did not exist for the three-month bill. Mr. Fred Adams of the Federal Reserve Board kindly developed the mathematics for the estimated spreads. The estimates would be very close to the actuals if actual data had existed. This is not the same curve that is contained in the Conference Board's composite index.

These indicators I term "tip-offs" (or in poker parlance "tells") as they are used as warning signals of a possible change in the economy. During the historical period in which the tip-offs were tested, each, except the spread, gave one or more false signals of a contraction. However, when two or more were examined in combination, there were no false signals.

Another important indicator that should be examined separately is the Purchasing Managers Index, described earlier. In this case, the month-by-month index is used. According to its publisher, the Institute for Supply Management, a PMI reading above 50% indicates that manufacturing is generally expanding whereas below 50% indicates that manufacturing is declining. A PMI over time that is more than 42.7% indicates that the economy (the GDP) is expanding; less than 42.7% indicates a general decline. The distance between 42.7% and 50% is a measure of the strength of the expansion. Normally, the index of itself is not a predictor of a serious downturn but rather a confirmation. It is more nearly a concurrent or lagging indicator than it is a leading indicator. Nonetheless, it is worthy of including in the forecasting agenda as it provides needed insight. A major advantage of the PMI is its real time availability, which is not true of the other data.

Before walking through an example of how the above data are employed in forecasting turning points, an explanation of how the numbers are calculated is in order.

❖ The Conference Board's composite index and the six-month diffusion index were obtained on the Board's data web site at www.globalindicators.org.

❖ The five series composite index: calculate a six-month ROC % for each of the five indicators, as follows (plant and equipment contracts and orders is the example): Step 1: calculating for June 1967, first, sum the individual index numbers for January through June 1967 which gives a six-month sum of activity; the total for January through June is 127,981. Next, subtract the total for the previous six months (July through December 1966), which is 142,483, from the January through June 1967 total, then, divide by the December 1966 sum and multiply by 100 to put it into percentage form. Thus, (127981 − 142483)/142483*100 = -10.18 %. The reader will recognize this as the ROC % equation explained earlier. Step 2: convert the result from Step 1 into a "new" index of 1 or 0 (as in a diffusion index) using as criteria: if the result from Step 1 is less (worse) than −0.9 enter 0; if more (better) than −1.0 enter 1; otherwise enter 0.5. This is done for each of the five series. Step 3: prepare a summary (consolidated) index of the five indicators. The procedure is identical to calculating a diffusion index as previously explained although it is a six-month ROC % summary (sum the 5 indices, divide by 5, multiply by 100). Step 4: prepare a diffusion index of the five series. The original index numbers are used in the calculations. This is a six-month comparison; for example, June 1967 compared with December 1966. For each series solve this formula: if June 1967(for instance) is greater than December 1966 enter 1; if June 1967 is less than December 1966 enter 0; otherwise enter 0.5. Next, sum the five answers, divide by five and multiply by 100. Post at the fourth month. This is the procedure for calculating a diffusion index described earlier in this chapter.

❖ The spread (yield curve) between the ten-year Treasury note and the three-month Treasury bill: first, sum the monthly index percentages of the ten-year note for a period of six months (for instance, January through June 1965) and for the three-month bill, then, divide by six to get an average for each. Subtract the average for the bill from the average for the note; this provides a six month average spread expressed as a percentage, thus, 4.21% - 3.97% = 0.24%. The tip-off criterion for a possible major contraction is whether the result (here as 0.24%) is less that −0.15%. For convenience, the criterion can be translated into 1's and 0's, with zero as the tip-off. The formula, applying 0.24% as example, is: if 0.24% is less (worse) than −0.15% enter 0; if greater than −0.15% enter 1; otherwise enter 0.5. In this instance, the entry is 1.

Some of the calculations may seem unconventional, but they were developed to historically provide good forecasting results. Modification in the future is possible as new data become available. The example following illustrates the general tactical methodology that a forecaster may apply when predicting turning points.

The examples following utilize the data from Figure 10-11 and provide the basis for the forecasting rationale given below. Remember, we have the advantage of actual month-end data, which may not be the case in the real world.

Extracted Data for Forecasting Turning Points

Period	Index	ROC %	Diffusion	ROC %	Diffusion	Spread %	Summary
	Conference Board Composite			5-Series Composite		Spread (Yield Curve)	
68Nov	74.1	1.15	90	80	80	0.10	1
Dec	74.1	1.47	60	80	80	0.07	1
69 Jan	74.4	1.61	60	100	60	0.02	1
Feb	74.4	2.07	40	100	40	-0.03	1
Mar	74.3	2.18	45	100	20	-0.04	1
Apr	74.5	1.90	20	100	0	-0.07	1
May	73.8	1.41	30	100	0	-0.07	1
Jun	73.5	0.91	30	60	20	-0.06	1
Jly	73.2	0.32	20	60	0	-0.10	1
Aug	73.2	-0.38	10	60	0	-0.17	0
Sep	73.4	-0.81	10	20	0	-0.21	0
Oct	72.8	-1.32	20	0	20	-0.21	0
Nov	72.5	-1.55	10	0	0	-0.28	0
Dec	72.1	-1.73	10	0	0	-0.35	0
70 Jan	71.5	-1.85	20	0	0	-0.32	0
Feb	70.8	-2.12	30	0	0	-0.26	0
Mar	70.5	-2.58	20	0	0	-0.19	0
Apr	69.8	-2.89	20	0	20	-0.06	1
May	70.3	-3.10	40	0	0	0.14	1
Jun	70.5	-3.16	40	0	40	0.37	1
Jly	70.4	-3.03	50	0	20	0.57	1
Aug	70.7	-2.52	50	0	20	0.74	1
Sep	70.6	-1.84	60	0	40	0.88	1
Oct	70.4	-1.01	70	0	60	0.98	1
Nov	70.5	-0.45	80	0	100	1.07	1
Dec	71.7	0.21	90	20	100	1.15	1
71 Jan	72.4	0.95	100	40	100	1.29	1
Feb	73.0	1.52	100	80	100	1.53	1
Mar	73.5	2.18	90	80	100	1.72	1

Figure 10-11

The time is month ending, January 1969. First, the forecaster looks at the Conference Board's composite index. The index has been holding steady for the past several months and ROC has been increasing. The diffusion index remains above 50%. ROC measures momentum (rate of growth). Because ROC is above the zero-line it illustrates that activity has been increasing compared with six months earlier. Additionally, ROC is actually gaining momentum. Thus, the composite index portrays a positive economic outlook. The five-series composite's ROC and diffusion index are both positive. The yield curve is declining but the summary measure remains positive. Examining the other two tip-off criteria does not reveal any reason to be concerned. (Criteria are given above.) The forecaster's conclusion is that the economy is continuing to be strong. Note, that this does not take into account any specifics that may be gleamed from the economic press. Its review is also a part of forecasting.

The time is month ending, February 1969. ROC for the Conference Board's composite index shows a significant increase in the rate of growth, but the diffusion index falls below 50%. The five-series composite remains strong except for the diffusion index. These are mixed signals. The spread is declining and is negative (a cause for concern), but the summary remains 1. Note that there is a tip-off in that both diffusion indices have fallen below 50. A caution flag is raised because of the tip-off but it indicates watchfulness not a red flag. A red flag is run-up once another negative joins this tip-off. The forecaster has reason to be concerned when the spread continues to decline and passes into a negative position, even though this is not an "official" tip-off. Is a contraction or recession on its way? The forecaster is not ready to commit to that possibility. More evidence is needed.

The time is month ending, June 1969. Between February and June the forecaster has become increasing concerned that a contraction is coming. A preliminary warning could be issued based upon the continuous decline in the spread and in the diffusion indices tip-off plus the Conference Board's falling ROC after April. At the end of June there has been a three-month decline in the Conference Board's composite, dropping from 2.18% in March to 0.91% in June. This is the second tip-off. Combined with the continuing fall in the spread, the forecaster will issue a contraction or recession watch. When will a significant contraction come into being? That is the unknown, but it is reasonable to suggest that a major downturn (contraction) or recession is probable and likely within six months or thereabouts. The forecaster hedges this statement with the caveat that as time passes more data will provide a better time estimate. The following summarizes the status of the five indicators (see Figure 10-11):

- ❖ Conference Board's index: decline in ROC at –1% or more (no), diffusion index under 50% (yes), ∴ not a tip-off.

- ❖ Five series composite index: ROC under 50% (no), diffusion index under 50% (yes), ∴ not a tip-off.

- ❖ Conference Board's index: three-month decline in ROC (yes), diffusion index under 50% (yes), ∴ a tip-off.

- ❖ Both indices: both diffusion indices less than 50% (yes), ∴ a tip-off.

- ❖ Yield curve: at 0 (no), ∴ not a tip-off.

By August, the yield curve summary is at zero, another tip-off indicator. In September, the five-series composite meets the contraction requirement. By October end, the Conference Board's composite has met our recession requirement. By August or September it is virtually assured that a recession is forthcoming. October tips the scale to 100%. Although the official dates of the recession will not be known until some future time, the "bad" is upon the economy by October latest. Not being a timid soul, the forecaster committed to a major downturn in the economy by September (perhaps before considering that the Conference Board's ROC is in a continuous downward spiral). By reading economists and reviewing specific series shown in the past to be pertinent to the company or industry, the forecaster would have further information upon which to base a decision.

The forecaster cannot say that a recession has begun or will begin on a specific date. What is being predicted is that a serious economic condition is developing and likely will turn into a recession in the near-term, with emphasis directed to the effect that such conditions will have upon the company. Using one or more of the techniques described in this book, a short- to mid-term company forecast is prepared and updated monthly. Part of procedure is to examine other economic series that are pertinent to the company's business including a review of GDP. (A recession did occur from December 1969 through November 1970.)

What does the PMI tell the forecaster? It is reviewed at the end of each month and plays its role in forecasting. Figure 10-12 shows a partial history. Before December 1969 the index was consistently above 50%. In February 1971 the index reached 54.8 and remained above 50.

PMI Index

Month	Index	Month	Index
December 1969	52.0	July	49.5
January 1970	48.7	August	47.3
February	47.4	September	44.1
March	46.9	October	42.4
April	45.0	November	39.7
May	47.2	December	45.4
June	51.1	January 1971	47.9

Figure 10-12

Because the PMI is not a leading indicator, the forecaster uses it as a gauge of current condition. By definition, manufacturing remains strong (expanding) until January end at which point it drops below 50. At 48.7, manufacturing is losing ground. The forecaster follows the progress month-by-month and notes that the index continues to show weakness until June and thereafter falling again. As far as the economy overall is concerned, by definition, the economy continues to expand until October end. Because a recession is in progress or, in the mind of the forecaster, at least in a serious downturn, special attention is given to economic series not included in the leading indicators, those that are pertinent to company forecasting.

In fact, the NBER declared that a recession had begun in December 1969, although it was not announced until later. The forecaster now has the task of predicting when the economy will recover. The process is reversed.

The time is month ending, December 1969. It is evident that the economy continues to head down a rough trail. The Conference Board's composite index is decreasing steadily as is the five series composite. The first hopeful sign does not occur until April 1970 when the spread summary becomes a 1. A positive change in the spread is frequently, but not always, a very early indicator. The forecaster now waits for a second tip-off. In forecasting company sales or profits, etc., one or more of the techniques described in this book is used, relating such to a forecast of the economy. Explanation of long-term forecasting as it relates to the economy, turning points, and the company follows in the next section.

The time is month ending, July 1970. A positive sign of an improving economy exist in the Conference Board's diffusion index as it illustrates increased economic activity. However, this is not enough to suggest that the economy is turning upwards (coming out of the recession).

The time is month ending, October 1970. In September, there is an increase in the Conference Board's ROC for three months, from -3.16 in June to −1.84 in September. This is the second positive indicator. Coupled with the general improvement in all indicators except the five series ROC during the past several months, the forecaster issues a preliminary report in September that the economy is improving and that a continuance will indicate an end to the recession in the near future. In October, both diffusion indices are above 50%, which leads to a definite report of a forthcoming upturn in the economy. November continues with positive news in the Conference Board's composite. Now, only the five series ROC is in negative territory, which is often (but not always) "late" in seeing a turn around. Perhaps, the forecaster will examine each indicator in the five series composite, especially if any are pertinent to the business level of the company or industry.

The PMI reacted positively in February and remained above 50% thereafter. In the manufacturing environment, a company may find the PMI a most useful barometer of recovery.

Officially, the recession ended in November 1970.

Point Forecasting the Longer Term

Management wants to see point forecasts – numbers for evaluation. There are three problems: knowing when turning points will occur, the depth of contractions and the trend of the recoveries, and the uncertainty of the longer term future. Economic conditions change in ways that are unknown at the time estimates of the future are developed. Nevertheless, the systems described below forecast with numbers, optimistically if not with total confidence, but with the caveat that things change with government intervention or in accordance with changing economic conditions or the rules of anti-physics, the first law of which is: that which can not be will be.

Three subjects are discussed: longer term economic forecasting, estimating the economy during contractions and recoveries, and longer term company forecasting.

The most extensive measure of the overall economy is gross domestic product (GDP), which is the starting point for economic forecasting. GDP comes in two flavors: nominal GDP and real GDP. Nominal (current) GDP is the total market value of all goods and services produced in the United States. It is measured in current dollars, the prices actually paid. Real GDP transforms nominal GDP into constant dollars, by adjusting out inflation; the measure is billions of 1996-chained dollars. Because real GDP rules out inflation, it is a truer measure of the health of the economy. It expresses quantity in constant dollars. Unfortunately, the series are quarterly, not monthly, and the GDP numbers are published three times: the advance GDP announced at the end of the quarter, the preliminary revision (second month) and the final at the third month, which may not be final. Using other than final numbers is a clumsy dance routine as revisions may be significant, but the forecaster cannot wait forever.

The basis for the following forecasting model is real GDP. Nominal GDP may have forecasting applicability if there is a relationship (as in regression) with company sales.

Real GDP is in a continual state of increase, declining only during major downturns, however, the growth rate varies between a fairly rapid pace and a slow pace as measured by ROC. The forecaster considers this reality when developing a forecasting technique. The charts in Figure 10-13 and 10-14 illustrate GDP behavior.

Figure 10-13 represents real GDP for the period 1976 through 1993. It illustrates the generally increasing economy, but one that is not growing at a steady rate. GDP is in a continual state of growth but momentum varies. Figures 10-14a and 10-14b cover the period that is used in the forecasting example that follows. The four-quarter ROC (annual growth rate) expressed as a percentage is depicted in Figure 10-14a. It is a comparison of current year and previous year. It is interesting to note the periods of recession: December 1969 to November 1970 and November 1973 to March 1975.

Real Gross Domestic Product

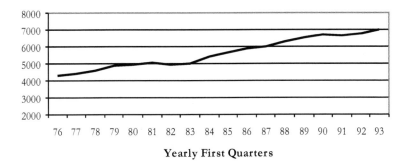

Yearly First Quarters

Figure 10-13

Growth Rate of Gross Domestic Product as Percent

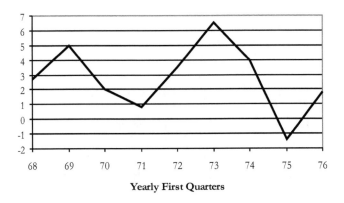

Yearly First Quarters

Figure 10-14a

Real Gross Domestic Product

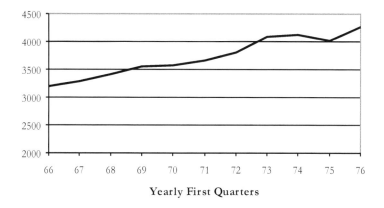

Yearly First Quarters

Figure 10-14b

Figure 10-14b charts real GDP. Growth is continuous but momentum varies. This is important and is discussed as part of the forecasting example.

Before getting to the forecasting example, there is another concept to explain: **combined forecasting.** It is forecasting the same data independently with several models and then averaging (combining) the forecasts; for example, with independent forecasts of 100, 220, 180, the combined forecast is 166.7. Often, gains in accuracy are achieved as measured by error variance. Extrapolation methods, for example, may be combined with qualitative and causal models. Each of the independent forecasts may (or may not) be weighted. In theory, gains are greatest when each technique is different (independent) from the others, but this may not always be true. Our example contains extrapolation techniques and includes several exponential equations. The principle of simplicity is remembered: avoid complexity whenever feasible. Usually, it is said, best results are obtained when applied to a longer forecast horizon.

The data below give the MAPE for each of the forecasting methods and for the combined forecasts as a means of determining the best forecasting scheme. The test (development) period – 1965 through 1971 – was chosen arbitrarily, but should be fairly typical of long-term real GDP, although the momentum may differ from this example. MAPE's indicate the average percentage variations that may be expected. Mostly, GDP fluctuates very little quarter to quarter, which means the MAPE should be very small.

METHOD	MAPE
1. Exponential smoothing α0.3	1.12
2. Exponential smoothing α0.5	0.83
3. Exponential smoothing α0.7	0.75
4. Least squares (regression)	1.51
5. Parabola	0.78
a. Combined (1, 2, and 3)	0.81
b. New combined (1, 2, and 3)	0.79
c. Combined (1, 2, 3, and 4)	0.59
d. New combined (1, 2, 3, and 4)	0.71
e. Combined (all five)	0.56
f. New combined (all five)	0.69

Each of the combined forecasting methods represented by c through f has a lower MAPE than any single technique, thus they are better choices. The combined forecasts are the sum of the individual forecasts divided by the number of forecasts to get a new (average) forecast. Once these calculations are completed for each quarter, a new MAPE is computed. The new combined forecasts are derived from the errors between demands and the combined forecasts, for example: sum the errors (with signs) for periods 1through 3, divide by 3 to get an average, and add that average to the combined forecast in period 4. The procedure is designed to "correct" for short-term error and to overcome lag experienced with exponential smoothing. Sometimes the procedure helps substantially, sometimes not, depending upon the overall pattern of the time series. As seen here, it is not advantageous. The individual techniques within the combined methods are weighted the same, that is no weights are assigned. Weighting is a possibility, however. Of course, this is neither exhaustive nor definitive of the methods that may be tried in combined forecasting.

Other interesting statistics are the range of errors (given below) and the distribution of the errors within the series. Distribution can be determined by a histogram; however, a scan of the series shows that radical up and down fluctuations between periods are not common. The high-low differences for each method are reasonably close to each other. The errors calculated by period for the "e" model, for instance, exceed 0.9% only 5 times and only once is the error larger than 1.2% and that is during the recession (recessionary periods). Other recessionary percentages are less than 1%.

| | Range of Error as Percent | | | |
| | Combined Methods | | New Combined Methods | |
	Non-Recessionary	Recesionary	Non-Recessionary	Recesionary
a and b	0.0 to 2.0	0.4 to 2.3	0.1 to 2.2	0.1 to 2.7
c and d	0.0 to 1.5	0.1 to 1.8	0.0 to 1.6	0.0 to 2.2
e and f	0.0 to 1.6	0.1 to 1.9	0.1 to 1.4	0.2 to 2.1

Which forecasting method should the forecaster adopt? One of the three combined methods appears to be the most logical. The range of error is not helpful as the distance that each is from the others is not significant. Because of the uncertainty of the long-range future, the method should be flexible as the nature of the GDP series may change over time. Either c or e is a logical choice because of their low MAPE. At first, the formulation that employs all five techniques seems best. The least squares method assumes a straight line increasing trend, the parabola accounts for curvature, and the exponential smoothing formulae adjust forecasts more quickly (each at a different rate). On second thought, the forecaster wonders whether there will be curvature (the reason for including a second degree parabolic curve equation). In looking at a graph of the real GDP history, a linear relationship appears to be more reasonable. Reluctantly, the parabola is discarded. Note that any one of the individual techniques may be the most accurate at a point in time but not at a later time and not over the long-term.

Before finalizing the choice, the forecaster has decided to try two other combinations: 2, 3, and 5 combined because of their lower MAPE's and 2, 3, 4, and 5. The results follow.

METHOD	MAPE
Combined (2, 3, and 5)	0.59
New combined (2, 3, and 5)	0.65
Combined (2, 3, 4, and 5)	0.55
New combined (2, 3, 4, and 5)	0.65

Either of the two combined forecasts can be in the running. Overall, they do not appear to add anything; therefore, the decision above remains the choice.

Can the forecasts be improved during recession? Perhaps. The forecaster can anticipate major downturns by the procedure described earlier, but cannot know exactly when the downturn will begin, nor its depth or length. The forecast errors during the December 1969-November 1970 recession are larger, but not by much. It may seem unwise to adjust the point forecasts based upon this knowledge, but this reasoning frequently leads to a stroll down the garden path. Although there is some by guess and by golly involved, adjustment, as explained below, appears reasonable when the signs dictate.

The front end of the long-range economic forecast is a short-term forecast because the base data incorporated are real data and not forecasts (well, real and preliminary, unfortunately). This indicates that other series that are pertinent to the company should be included. These may be financial, for instance, sub-series from GDP (PCE, etc.), individual indices from the composite index of leading economic indicators, or other series. More on this subject when long-range company forecasting is discussed.

Four subjects follow: forecasting using real GDP, forecasting using ROC, modifying forecasts to account for recession, and modifying forecasts with independent economic forecasting data.

Forecasting GDP

The time is month ending, December 1971 (the end of the fourth quarter). Figure 10-15 gives the data for the example. The forecaster, of course, only has available the information listed through the fourth quarter of 1971, the current date. The forecasting method selected is combined forecasting, a composite of the four individual estimates. Thirty quarters of history were used to develop the technique (only eight are shown in Figure 10-15). For the fourth quarter 1971, for instance, the combined estimate is the sum of the individual estimates divided by 4: (3723.87 + 3741.8 + 3746.83 + 3783.87) ÷ 4 = 3749.1. The error as a percentage in absolute terms is 0.68%: [(3749.1 − 3723.8) ÷ 3723.8] x 100. The error percentages for the past three quarters of 1971 are very low as they generally have been throughout the forecasting development period. The higher error rates in the fourth quarter 1970 and the first quarter of 1971 occur at the ending of a recession (the trough was in the fourth quarter of 1970). After the recession, the growth rate (ROC) compared with a year earlier has rebounded nicely. The average annual growth rate for the eight quarters prior to the recession was 3.8%. During the same period, actual GDP increased 7.5% or 0.94% on average per quarter. Looking farther back, the average increase is 0.8%. The annual growth rate of the last three quarters of 1971 grew steadily to 3.34%. Will the growth continue? Considering these facts, it is conceivable that the forecast will be underestimating future GDP. The forecasting method looks valid historically when viewing the predominantly small error rate percentages during the thirty-quarter test period and the MAPE. The forecaster feels confident that the method works. Thus, a forecast for the next five years is prepared. Of course, uncertainty is the monster in the closet. Five years is a long time and the economy is not really predictable that far in the future. The forecast works if the historical growth rate is representative of the future rate. The forecaster, however, reviews and possibly revises the forecasts each month even though GDP is reported quarterly. It is expected that the estimates will change as time progresses. If we peek into the future (we can do this, the forecaster cannot) as revealed in Figure 10-15, we see that the growth rate steadily increases to more than 6% until the next recession (November 1973 through March 1975).

Forecasts and Forecasting Data

Quarter	Real GDP	Annual Growth Rate	Quarterly Growth Rate	Quarterly Rate Annualized	Original Forecast	Error as Percent	Forecast (Upper End)	Error as Percent
1970 1	3566.5	1.98	-0.14	-0.55	3597.2	0.86	3616.1	1.39
2	3573.9	1.28	0.21	0.83	3594.4	0.57	3613.2	1.10
3	3605.2	0.70	0.88	3.50	3602.6	0.07	3621.4	0.45
4	3566.5	0.19	-1.07	-4.29	3631.3	1.82	3650.3	2.35
1971 1	3666.1	0.82	2.79	11.17	3611.3	1.50	3630.2	0.98
2	3686.2	1.57	0.55	2.19	3686.4	0.00	3705.7	0.53
3	3714.5	2.21	0.77	3.07	3719.2	0.13	3738.6	0.65
4	3723.8	3.34	0.25	1.00	3749.1	0.68	3768.7	1.21
1972 1	3796.9	3.54	1.96	7.85	3764.1	0.86	3783.8	0.35
2	3883.8	4.10	2.29	9.15	3787.7	2.48	3807.5	1.97
3	3922.3	4.74	0.99	3.97	3811.3	2.83	3831.2	2.32
4	3990.5	5.43	1.74	6.96	3834.9	3.90	3854.9	3.40
1973 1	4092.3	6.48	2.55	10.20	3858.5	5.71	3878.7	5.22
2	4133.3	6.74	1.00	4.01	3882.1	6.08	3902.4	5.59
3	4117.0	6.57	-0.40	-1.58	3905.7	5.13	3926.1	4.64
4	4151.1	5.77	0.83	3.31	3929.3	5.34	3949.8	4.85
1974 1	4119.3	3.98	-0.77	-3.06	3952.9	4.04	3973.6	3.54
2	4130.4	2.35	0.27	1.08	3976.5	3.73	3997.3	3.22
3	4084.5	0.93	-1.11	-4.45	4000.1	2.07	4021.0	1.55
4	4062.0	-0.59	-0.55	-2.20	4023.7	0.94	4044.7	0.43
1975 1	4010.0	-1.42	-1.28	-5.12	4047.3	0.93	4068.5	1.46
2	4045.2	-1.91	0.88	3.51	4070.9	0.64	4092.2	1.16
3	4115.4	-1.53	1.74	6.94	4094.5	0.51	4115.9	0.01
4	4167.2	-0.36	1.26	5.03	4118.1	1.18	4139.6	0.66
1976 1	4266.1	1.88	2.37	9.49	4141.7	2.92	4163.4	2.41
2	4301.5	4.00	0.83	3.32	4165.3	3.17	4187.1	2.66
3	4321.9	5.08	0.48	1.90	4188.9	3.08	4210.8	2.57
4	4357.4	5.56	0.82	3.29	4212.5	3.33	4234.5	2.82

Time is end of the 4th quarter, 1971. GDP for 1972 through 1976 is unknown to the forecaster.
Some rounding; some calculations before rounding.

Figure 10-15

The forecaster believes a forecast range should be developed. Alternate means of computing a forecast range are explained in Chapters 3 and 5. Perhaps, the most preferable procedure -- because it is more mathematically exacting -- is standard deviation as the basis for establishing a range. Normally, two additional forecasts are prepared, low- and high-end forecasts, which define the probable range of error. A standard deviation of 95% is selected. The computed factors for adjusting the original forecast to get new low and high forecasts are 0% and +0.523%; for example, (3764.1*0.00523)+3764.1 = 3783.8 or 3764.1*1.00523 for the first quarter 1972. There is not a low-end forecast because the low-end error was negative, which is interpreted as zero.

The annual (four quarter) growth rate is calculated as a rate of change (four quarters summed); quarterly growth rate is current GDP minus previous quarter GDP divided by previous quarter GDP times 100 to put it in percentage form; quarterly growth rate annualized is the quarterly growth rate multiplied by 4 (for four quarters per year), it may also be calculated directly by applying the above equation but times 400 instead of 100; error as a percent is GDP minus the original forecast divided by GDP times 100 to put it in percentage form (the difference between GDP and forecast is in absolute terms); new error is calculated identically except the upper-end forecast is the base; and the method for calculating the two forecasts is explained above. Quarterly rate annualized is a measure frequently seen in the press and often used by economists. It is a dangerous number for non-economists because it can give a false impression (as a predictor) of how fast (or slow) the economy is progressing.

How accurate are the estimates for the five year forecast period? The original forecast's error as percent during the test period most frequently remained very small except for two quarters at the end of the recession, but recovered thereafter. The upper-end forecast did not do as well during 1971 as the original forecast, however, that could be anticipated considering the small error rate of the original forecast. Comparing error statistics during the forecast period illustrates that the upper-end forecast was the better choice, but the forecasting objective was met by presenting both as the probable range. Sadly, however, the forecasts slid further from actual as time progressed, a condition that the forecaster could not anticipate. Yet, the forecasts for five years in the future must be viewed as highly acceptable, with MAPE's of 2.9 for the original forecast and 2.5 for the upper end forecast. Figure 10-14b illustrates the slide. For a substantial part of the test period, growth was much slower than during the forecasted period (with the exception of the recession that began in November 1973). Selection of the development period, especially as it pertains to its length, is critical, but it should be close to the current date and sufficiently long to be representative. The unknown future puts a lot of guess into the process.

Management needs to recognize the limitations of foretelling the future. Uncertainty is reality. Long-term forecasting is guidance for long-range planning. The best solution is a point forecast plus a range of probability. One method of determining range is described above. Another is selecting periods of various lengths as the development (test) period so that several forecasts are generated. As we have seen, the growth rate is not a constant, thus incorporating different time periods within a reasonable distance of the current date will give different results. If, for example, the economy is coming off a recession, the technique could use only the time before the recession in the extrapolation. A series using a large number of periods and one using a smaller number of periods are possibilities, or one for the nearer term and one for the longer term. The possibilities are almost limitless, but logic is critical. This idea is fraught with danger and care is required not to be capricious. At the time that forecasts are developed, opinions about the economy should be gleamed from professional economists as guidance – the press and the Internet are resources. Judgment is key and simplicity (in as far as possible) in selecting the time frames is important. Keep in mind that standard deviation is an excellent forecasting devise. These ideas worked together could be the root for what-if long range planning.

Remember also, forecast revisions will slowly improve forecasts. Adopting the rationale above will help even more.

Extrapolation is the core of the forecasting technique explained above. Could more complex formulations or methodologies be employed? Of course, but because GDP is an ever-increasing trend over the long-term, extrapolation is appropriate. Concentration has been directed to GDP, which is the barometer of the economy and is therefore important to the company. It may or may not have a causal relationship with company sales. Because the economy affects business, however, it is important to predict GDP and relate it to sales. As important is finding direct relationships between the economy and company sales. Perhaps that link is through GDP to other economic indicators then to sales.

The **annual growth rate** (ROC %) is also a basis for viable forecasting models. The starting point is the fourth quarter of 1971, the last quarter of known data. The forecast begins with the next quarter. Note that in Figure 10-15 the annual growth rate is 3.34%, having grown nicely since the end of the recession. The assumption is that the current growth rate percentage is representative of the future. The average annual growth rate for the eight quarters prior to the recession was 3.8%; therefore, the forecaster has good reason to believe that

3.34% is a "good" expectation. Figure 10-16 illustrates the results of applying the following methods.

ROC Forecasts & Forecast Comparisons

Quarter	Real GDP	Original Forecast, GDP	Upper Forecast, GDP	ROC Fcst Method 1	Absolute Error as Percent	ROC Fcst Method 2	Absolute Error as Percent
1972 Qtr 1	3796.9	3764.1	3783.8	3788.5	0.22	3754.9	1.11
Qtr 2	3883.8	3787.7	3807.5	3820.2	1.64	3786.3	2.51
Qtr 3	3922.3	3811.3	3831.2	3852.1	1.79	3818.0	2.66
Qtr 4	3990.5	3834.9	3854.9	3884.3	2.66	3849.9	3.52
1973 Qtr 1	4092.3	3858.5	3878.7	3916.8	4.29	3882.0	5.14
Qtr 2	4133.3	3882.1	3902.4	3949.5	4.45	3914.5	5.29
Qtr 3	4117.0	3905.7	3926.1	3982.6	3.27	3947.2	4.12
Qtr 4	4151.1	3929.3	3949.8	4015.8	3.26	3980.2	4.12
1974 Qtr 1	4119.3	3952.9	3973.6	4049.4	1.70	4013.5	2.57
Qtr 2	4130.4	3976.5	3997.3	4083.2	1.14	4047.0	2.02
Qtr 3	4084.5	4000.1	4021.0	4117.4	0.80	4080.8	0.09
Qtr 4	4062.0	4023.7	4044.7	4151.8	2.21	4114.9	1.30
1975 Qtr 1	4010.0	4047.3	4068.5	4186.5	4.40	4149.3	3.47
Qtr 2	4045.2	4070.9	4092.2	4221.5	4.36	4184.0	3.43
Qtr 3	4115.4	4094.5	4115.9	4256.8	3.43	4219.0	2.52
Qtr 4	4167.2	4118.1	4139.6	4292.3	3.00	4254.2	2.09
1976 Qtr 1	4266.1	4141.7	4163.4	4328.2	1.46	4289.8	0.56
Qtr 2	4301.5	4165.3	4187.1	4364.4	1.46	4325.7	0.56
Qtr 3	4321.9	4188.9	4210.8	4400.9	1.83	4361.8	0.92
Qtr 4	4357.4	4212.5	4234.5	4437.6	1.84	4398.3	0.94
MAPE:		2.9	2.5		2.50		2.40

Figure 10-16

There are (at least) two ways to begin the process.

Method 1: multiply the rate by GDP four quarters previously because it is an annual rate. With this method we begin with the first quarter 1971 (see Figure 10-15). First, convert the percentage for multiplication, with 3.34 becoming 0.0334 and add 1; thus 3666.1*1.0334 = 3788.5. (Some answers in Figure 10-16 will vary slightly because of rounding.) Each period that follows uses one-fourth of 3.34 for quarterly forecasting; that number is then multiplied by the last forecast; thus 1.00835*3788.5 = 3820.2.

Method 2: multiply GDP for the fourth quarter 1971 by the one-fourth rate; thus the first quarter 1972 forecast is 1.00835*3723.8 = 3754.9 and 3754.9*1.00835 = 3786.3 for the second quarter. The difference in forecast quantities between the two methods may appear to be significant, however, calculating the MAPE's indicates a reasonable difference during the forecast horizon (forecast as compared with actual GDP). Because the forecaster cannot see into the future, there is no awareness of which will be the best. The uncertainty monster always resides under the bed.

Which of the forecasts yielded the most accurate results? Comparing the error percentages (as MAPE's) indicates near equality over the forecast horizon. However, this is not always the case as will be seen shortly. Another possibility not considered here is to continue the trend as seen in 1971 (Figure 10-15) for a reasonable length of time, the number of quarters determined from the historical time series, then reverting to methods 1 or 2. Note that there is considerable judgment involved in these processes.

Can further improvement in accuracy be achieved? There are two possibilities: adjust for nearer term economic changes and incorporate economists' predictions.

Forecasting is not complete without predicting turning points when tip-offs occur. November 1973 was the beginning of a recession. The first tip-off arrived in May, a three month serious decline in the Conference Board's index. August revealed two additional tip-offs: the spread and the Conference Board's index meeting the basic recession warning criteria. Will the forecaster change the estimates? Forecasts *may* slowly adjust to change. There is uncertainty as to the beginning, end, and depth of the downturn. The forecaster routinely reviews and revises the estimates. Note that the forecasts *without revision* have fairly represented the future. A review of the annual growth rates and errors as percent indicate why. But the forecaster is about to get into deep water.

Forecasting Revisions

Time Period	Real GDP	Annual Growth Rate % (ROC)	Original Forecast	Error as %	Revised Forecast	Error as %
1973 Qtr 1	4092.3	6.48				
Qtr 2	4133.3	6.74				
Qtr 3	4117.0	6.57	4202.9	2.09		
Qtr 4	4151.1	5.77	4273.8	2.96	4191.1	0.97
1974 Qtr 1	4119.3	3.98	4345.8	5.50	4179.4	1.46
Qtr 2	4130.4	2.35	4419.0	6.99	4167.7	0.90
Qtr 3	4084.5	0.93	4493.5	10.01	4156.1	1.75
Qtr 4	4062.0	-0.59	4569.2	12.49	4144.4	2.03
1975 Qtr 1	4010.0	-1.42	4646.2	15.86	4132.8	3.06
Qtr 2	4045.2	-1.91	4724.5	16.79	4121.3	1.88
Qtr 3	4115.4	-1.53	4804.1	16.73	4109.7	0.14
Qtr 4	4167.2	-0.36	4885.0	17.23	4098.2	1.66
1976 Qtr 1	4266.1	1.88	4967.3	16.44	4167.3	2.32
Qtr 2	4301.5	4.00	5051.0	17.42	4237.5	1.49
Qtr 3	4321.9	5.08	5136.1	18.84	4308.9	0.30
Qtr 4	4357.4	5.56	5222.7	19.86	4381.5	0.55
			MAPE	13.62		1.42

Recession 4th Qtr 1973-1st Qtr 1975; some rounding

Figure 10-17

By August 1973 there were three tip-offs. At the end of the second quarter, a forecast of GDP was made beginning with the third quarter and without considering the possibility of a major downturn because there was only one tip-off. Figure 10-17 gives the estimates through

1976. The procedure illustrated is forecasting with annual growth rates. The forecaster accepts 6.74% as reasonable (the last known rate), thus the quarterly multiplier is 1.01685 (6.74/4). The third quarter estimate is 4202.9 (4133.3*1.01685). The fourth quarter estimate is 4273.8 (4202.9*1.01685). As can be seen in Figure 10-17, there is no accounting for a possible recession because there have not been three tip-offs, the criterion that the forecaster has chosen. However, allowance, at least, should be made to the probability of a serious downturn after two tip-offs appear. Of course, the forecaster does not know the future, but we can see that the forecast is way off base. The annual growth rate column tells why. Instead of using 6.74%, it would, in this instance, have been appropriate to use an average of previous growth rates. Because of the long-term increasing trend, however, the decision was not illogical. So, whatever the choice, it may not be the best course of action.

With three tip-offs, the forecaster decides that a major downturn, probably a recession, is immanent. These are the criteria used (my eyeball averages based upon five of the example recessions): recession or major downturn in the economy after three tip-offs probable in the next two quarters, total decline will average 2.5%, recession lasts five or six quarters (use six), and recovery after the recession to a reasonable level will take three quarters. Figure 10-17 shows the forecasting results. The decline per quarter is 2.5%/9, which is 0.0028. Division by 9 represents average recession plus average recovery times. The equations for the forecast revisions are:

First period revision: (original forecast*-0.0028)+original forecast

(4202.9*-0.0028)+4202.9 = 4191.1

Subsequent revisions: (last revised forecast*-0.0028)+last revised

(4191.1*-0.0028)+4191.1 = 4179.4

This procedure continues through nine quarters. Thereafter, the last revised forecast and all following are multiplied by the original multiplier; thus, the revised forecast for the first quarter, 1976 is 4098.2*1.01685 = 4167.3.

The necessity for reviving forecasts when the indicators point to a major downturn is clearly apparent from Figure 10-17. The difference in the errors as percent is not always this dramatic. Nonetheless, modifying forecasts for downturns is most always a major improvement devise.

Since each recession is unique with regard to its length, starting date, and depth, averages of some kind become the rule. Determining an average, for this purpose, is both mathematical and judgmental. The question is: what appears to be the most typical for the future? It is not very scientific, but about the best we can do. The method described above was tested on five of the recessions with the following results.

MAPE

Recession	Original Forecast	Revised Forecast
1969	5.0	3.8
1973	13.6	1.4
1980	11.9	2.2
1981	11.6	3.6
1990	3.8	2.4

Economists will have varying opinions regarding the near-term future, but a consensus of sorts can often be gleamed from their writings. As example, say that the economy is basically flat, just a slight increase period to period, approximately a 1% gain each quarter. The Federal Reserve announces that the economy is primed for a comeback. Economists predict that the economy (real GDP) will grow by 3.5% by the end of the calendar year. It is February. That figure can be assumed to mean a 3.5% annual growth rate for the current year and can be incorporated as the first year's growth in the long-range forecast. One caveat when reading the popular press: you will see statements like "the economy expanded at a 1.2% annual rate during the last quarter." Is the writer talking nominal or real GDP? Likely, this is not the annual growth rate (ROC) defined above. Probably, it is a comparison between the last two quarters annualized; thus, it is not a good barometer of the future. Figure 10-15 gives quarterly rates annualized. It is not a pretty picture.

One last remembrance: the economy does not live by GDP alone. Tie GDP to other economic indicators and to company or industry sales.

Long-Range Company Forecasting

Read this section in conjunction with Chapter 12.

The final version of the long-range company forecast is the foundation for long-range planning but may be supplemented by other forecasts to give a set of possibilities. The forecaster begins by forecasting sales, most likely at the product family level. That forecast is expanded into profit planning, facilities expansion planning, technology research, marketing strategies, etc. The forecast horizon is dependent upon the unique properties of the product line and the time it takes to implement a strategy that could, for example, include construction of a new factory. Forecast accuracy in relation to strategy is an important issue. Because of the uncertainty of the long-term future, a forecasting range is calculated. Probably, it is appropriate to prepare several forecasts based upon different scenarios of the future. These are the forerunner to the what-if scenario in strategic and contingency planning. In one approach, a mathematical model is developed based upon the historical record and the economic forecasts. For convenience, this can be called the final version. The same idea is used to develop the other models; however, different assumptions constitute the base number. For example, if the final version of the forecast assumes a long-term five percent annual growth rate in its mathematics, two additional forecasts -- one at three percent, one at six percent -- could be developed. Doing so enhances the what-if analyses. At this point, it is well to remember that it is of first importance to know the general objectives of long-range planning before embarking upon the long-range forecasting journey.

The first effort by the forecaster in mounting the attack on the long-range future is to develop a sales forecast based upon the company's historical time series and the economic forecasts prepared in preparation for company forecasting, adopting an applicable model from those described in this book. Combined forecasts as well as individual forecasts are built. Both time series models and causal models are considered. The length of the back-horizon (the development period) is determined by what in the long run is thought to be typical of the future. The types of economic series that are examined are those pertaining to production, employment, and retail sales, to mention a few. These help to define the economy at the time that the forecast is being prepared. They may not be directly applicable to company sales and may be candidates for inclusion in the forecasting agenda only for the shorter term and in a general way to see the immediate situation (perhaps through this year and next). The studies prepared by economists are pertinent and helpful. Other series that have a direct bearing on company sales should be sought and forecasted. It would be surprising if the forecaster were not initially baffled by this wealth of data. In the process some reconciliation will occur and with the help of economists' analyses a foundation for actual forecasting is laid.

In the examples, periodic forecasts were prepared. It may be that that level of detail is unnecessary to the needs of the company. Perhaps only an annual forecast is required expressed as a rate of growth or in an ending number for the economic indicator or for company sales. Another possibility is a periodic forecast for the first year followed by an annual forecast for the remaining years in the forecast horizon.

Other Business Models

There are many important econometric models that describe parts of the business environment. Most frequently they are complex and require the services of experts to relate them to a company. Following, however, are several models that may be feasible for implementation at the company level as examples of the possible. The most severe limitation in utilizing these models is collecting the raw data (the measurement of the activities that constitute the variables). Data may be unavailable or available in unusable form. If the price level is recognized as a major determinant in the level of demand, for instance, the relationship may be difficult or impossible to isolate. Price elasticity is fairly well known in many industries, but in others it is obscure. At times having a few data points in the price/demand ratio available for extrapolation may be a start. Judgment can also play a role.

Example 1

The law of demand is an ancient concept universally recognized by economists. The measurement of consumer sensitivity to changes in price is the keystone of microeconomics. **Price elasticity of demand** is a commonly used technique. Elasticity is defined as the ratio of the relative change in quantity demanded to the relative change in price. It is a measure of responsiveness or the sensitivity of consumers to prices changes. Stated a different way it is the proportionate change in demand divided by the proportionate change in price. Nonessential goods and those that have many substitutes have higher elasticity than those that are essential to daily life (such as staple food products) or those that have few substitutes. Elasticity may be substantially different at different points on the curve. The demand curve can be estimated with simple linear regression. A nonlinear curve may be transformed with logarithms.

Price elasticity is found by solving the equation:

$$E_d = \Delta q/q \div \Delta p/p$$

E_d = price elasticity of demand

q/q = change in quantity demanded ÷ original quantity demanded

p/p = change in price ÷ original price

Δ signifies a ratio between two specified values

Figure 10-18 illustrates a generalized chart of elasticity with three data points shown. The dots represent price/quantity ratios (there could be many different quantities at a price point). Any point on the solid line is an average of all quantities at that price. At a price of $2.00, for example, the *average* of all quantities sold is 70. How much of the curve is historically tested and how much is speculative? It varies by industry, of course, and by the amount of test marketing done by the company. In our example, the three price-quantity ratios are known plus a few others. The remaining ratios are extrapolated points on the curve. Assume for this example that the curve is basically linear within the pertinent data points.

Price Elasticity of Demand

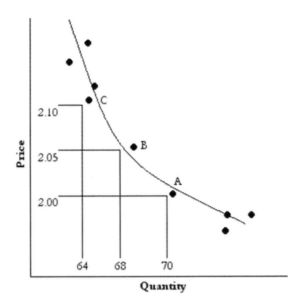

Price is the independent variable
Quantity is the dependent variable
Dots are actual data
Solid line is the estimated demand curve
Figure 10-18

The regular price is $2.00 and the average quantity sold in a given time is 70. (The actual quantity could be 70,000 or 700,000.) The manager begins by comparing the current ratio with two other knowns.

$$(68 - 70)/70 \div (2.05 - 2.00)/2.00 = (-2/70) \div (.05/2) = -1.14$$

$$(64 - 70)/70 \div (2.10 - 2.00)/2.00 = (-6/70) \div (.10/2) = -1.71$$

Characteristically, elasticity measurements have a negative sign since the slope of the demand curve is normally declining. If $E_d = -1$, unity exists as a 1% drop in price causes a 1% increase in demand. If E_d is less than -1 (closer to zero), it indicates a condition of inelasticity, meaning that price changes result in modest changes in purchasing decisions. If E_d is negatively greater than -1 (further from zero), elasticity exists, meaning that changes in price result in substantial changes in the amount purchased. Generally, economists ignore the minus sign to avoid ambiguity, as is done for this example.

Demand at these price points is elastic because the values (elasticity coefficients) 1.14 and 1.17 are larger than 1, thus there is sensitivity to price change. The difference in revenue can now be calculated for the three price levels. The formula is base price times sales per period equals revenue per period, which can be extended to annual revenue by multiplying per period revenue by the number of periods in a year (assume 52 weeks).

$$\$2.00 \times 70 = \$140.00 \times 52 = \$7280$$
$$2.05 \times 68 = \quad 139.40 \times 52 = \quad 7249$$
$$2.10 \times 64 = \quad 134.40 \times 52 = \quad 6989$$

Annual revenue is a tenuous measure as many factors may play a part in the longer term. However, for comparison purposes, annual calculations are used. The series is extended to other price points that are known or can be estimated. Probably, most came from the curve as calculated from known data or as estimated. As the distance from the regular price increases, the results become more questionable, but are available for planning purposes.

Price	Sales	Revenue	Elasticity
1.65	82	7036	0.98
1.70	81	7160	1.05
1.75	80	7280	1.14
1.80	78	7301	1.14
1.85	77	7407	1.33
1.90	76	7509	1.71
1.95	74	7504	2.29
2.00	70	7280	Base
2.05	68	7249	1.14
2.10	64	6989	1.71
2.15	62	6932	1.52
2.20	59	6750	1.57
2.25	57	6669	1.49

The dynamics of elasticity are illustrated by these calculations. Price is a major determinant, a somewhat volatile factor that balances price and demand. Consumer reaction to price changes is expressed by the changes in demand. Revenue maximizes in the $1.90 to $1.95 range. As will be seen shortly, profit also maximizes at this range. Note the difference in elasticity at the different price points. Elasticity tells us how responsive consumers are to a change in price. If a certain percentage change in price results in a bigger change in quantity, demand is elastic, that is, the more elasticity the more sensitive consumers are to a price change.

Because marketing does not live in a vacuum, the affect that increased sales has upon manufacturing (or the ability to increase buys, say, for a distribution company), cost, and profit are appraised.

With regard to manufacturing, the availability of capacity to produce the new level of demand is determined. Will capacity be available at the needed time? Will additional capacity be needed (how much)? If so, what is the additional cost? Will these costs be absorbed before the competition reacts and retrieves lost business (if applicable)? Will there be enough time to procure the materials and manufacture the product by the date needed? What is the relationship between cost, revenue, and profit?

The bottom line is profit (but don't forget return on investment). However, if the firm's strategy includes increasing its market share, price concessions or price reductions may be an important aspect to that strategy. The company may willingly forego a present good (optimum profit now) for a future good. The company may also adopt a short-range tactic that includes pricing either as a marketing test or to introduce a new product or to gain an immediate advantage. Regardless of the specific purpose, the probable influence upon profit is evaluated by considering the trade-off between revenue and fixed and variable costs.

Profit is the difference between revenue and the sum of fixed and variable costs. Accounting practices, for example allocation of revenue and costs to different periods of time is not considered, as the objective is to determine the overall goodness of a pricing strategy.

Fixed or indirect costs are those that remain constant, or essentially constant, regardless of the level of operational activity. Executive salaries, insurance, depreciation, rent, and property taxes are examples of fixed costs. Fixed costs may change with the level of output as in the case of adding machines or facilities to increase production. The new cost may become the fixed cost at those price points, but that depends upon how the company wishes to conduct the evaluation.

Variable or direct costs are those that vary proportionally with the level of output. Raw materials, purchased components or end-items, direct labor, and scrap are examples of variable costs.

Total cost is found by multiplying sales per period by the number of periods per year, then multiplying that product by the variable cost per unit, and then adding the fixed cost. If variable cost is 0.485 per unit and fixed cost is $5262 total cost for 57 units of production per week is $6700, computed as 57x52x0.485+5262. Figure 10-19 completes the calculations to determine the profit at the various sales levels. Total costs and revenues are calculated as explained above; profit is revenue minus total cost; and profit margin is profit divided by revenue, which in this case is sales dollars, then multiplied by 100 to put it in percentage form. These calculations are projected as annual figures. A per period rendering gives an identical profit margin.

Profitability

Sales per Period	Revenue	Total Cost	Profit	Profit Margin
57	6669	6700	-31	-0.5
59	6750	6750	0	0.0
62	6932	6826	106	1.5
64	6989	6876	113	1.6
68	7249	6977	272	3.8
70	7280	7027	253	3.5
74	7504	7128	376	5.0
76	7509	7179	330	4.4
77	7407	7204	203	2.7
78	7301	7229	72	1.0
80	7280	7280	0	0.0
81	7160	7305	-145	-2.0
82	7036	7330	-294	-4.2

Figure 10-19

The relationship between cost, revenue, and profit is depicted graphically in Figure 10-20. This is a breakeven analysis. Breakeven charts may be linear or nonlinear. The technique is extremely useful in evaluating alternatives and is employable in many decision-making situations. The method is thoroughly documented in the literature.

Breakeven Analysis

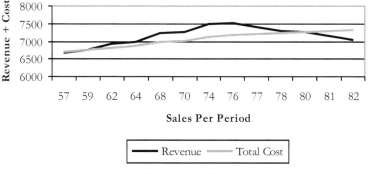

Figure 10-20

The points at which the revenue and total cost lines intersect are the breakeven points. The profit zone is the area between revenue and total cost.

What conclusions can be gleaned from Figures 10-19 and 10-20?

- ❖ The middle part of the demand curve displays the most elasticity; toward the extremities elasticity decreases and will become inelastic. Change in price relative to the market significantly changes the demand at the current price level. A pricing policy could be formulated that recognized this fact thus allowing the company to maintain a competitive advantage. The elasticity statistic is also important in times of slack demand when increasing sales become especially important.

- ❖ Revenue increases as price decreases until it reaches it plateau at about $1.90 (at 76 sales units), indicating that to maximize revenue, a price of $1.90 is appropriate. The point of maximum revenue is not necessarily the point of maximum profitability. The only justification for maximizing revenue is to grow sales by stimulating the market. A policy to permanently increase market share includes more than pricing. Advertising, sales effort, and promotions are some of the concurrent means to be employed. Market share is not measured by sales volume, *per se*; its proper measurement is sales volume in relation to the competition's sales volume.

- ❖ As expected, demand increases as price decreases. It may be justified to reduce price specifically for the purpose of increasing demand while sacrificing profit if the circumstances are unusual. This paragraph implies operating at minimum or zero profit. Unusual circumstances are defined as short-range benefits in which a factor other than revenue or profit is paramount. Examples are retention of a trained workforce during a slow manufacturing period and the capture of new customers.

- ❖ Profit measured as return on sales, peaks at an item price of $1.95 (74 sales units). The current price is $2.00. The company could increase its profit immediately by reducing price. Profit is an important objective but it cannot be considered independently of two other objectives: cash flow and market share. Regardless of the pricing policy adopted, there must be a flow of cash to maintain the operation, pay debt, and expand. At times a compromise position may be necessary. Profit has been defined as the difference between revenue and cost. In determining whether adequate profit is being realized, it may be more suitable to measure profit as return on investment or return on equity or another financial measure of a similar nature.

❖ The profit zone encompasses the area that falls between the two breakeven points. As such, it offers a range within which price points may be established. Profit, however, is not exclusively a function of price compared with cost. Profit may be improved by lowering unit cost or fixed costs or by convincing the consumer to buy more of the product at the established price.

❖ If the level of industry sales overall changes, say, because of a change in the economic picture, that will alter the elasticity picture.

In establishing a pricing policy, the relationship between supply and demand needs to be understood. Each product has an equilibrium price, which is the intersection of the demand and supply curves (Figure 10-21). Price disruptions are usually temporary as a competitive market rejects other price levels as unstable. The shortages that occur when a condition of below equilibrium exists prompt buyers to bid up the price, and firms then allocate more resources to production. The surpluses that result at the above equilibrium price induce lower prices and a reduction in the resources allocated to manufacture.

Generalized Supply and Demand Curve

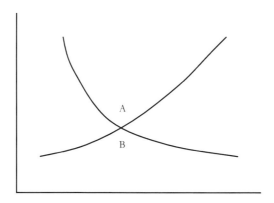

Price equilibrium occurs at the intersection of the two curves. In zone A there is a surplus. In zone B there is a shortage.
Figure 10-21

Thus, the shifts between supply levels tend to equalize the price. The curve may also shift because of changing economic conditions, buyer tastes and expectations, or inflation. A new equilibrium price is established when any of these conditions apply.

The influence that a company's pricing policy has upon the market and price equilibrium is dependent upon the dominance of the company, the stability of the market for that product, and the degree of necessity for the product as perceived by the consumer.

In analyzing the structure of the market – a study that is preliminary to establishing or evaluating policy – it is necessary to forecast demand, revenue, and profit. However, it is just as important to know how the market reacts to price changes, advertising, and the economy. Regression, qualitative methodology, and combined forecasting could be relevant to the analysis. Different formulations may be required for the various parts of the analysis.

A problem exists when employing the elasticity formula. Usually, the base (reference) price is the price that the company normally charges for the product, and calculations proceed from there. In some cases, a choice between two or more prices must be made. Therein lies the problem. The choice will influence the outcome. For illustration, say, the choice is between 200 units at $2.00 and 100 units at $3.00. The elasticity coefficients are 1 and 3, an important difference. The compromise solution is to average the two prices and the two quantities. The compromise is $2.50 and 150 units. A good way in which to eliminate the problem is to modify the formula to read:

(change in quantity)/(sum of quantities/2)÷(change in price)/(sum of prices/2)

Example 2

A company has studied its sales patterns in relation to its market, its internal structure, and the national economy. From this study it determined that sales were partly explained by three economic indicators but that the magnitude of the existing gap between actual and forecast was too large to be attributed to random fluctuation. When the regression equation was tested for significance, serial correlation was discovered. The continuing investigation revealed a correlation to sales in the ratio of prices charged by the competition and by the company. The size of the firm's advertising budget was also discovered to be a significant demand determinant. There appeared to be a correlation between the company's advertising budget and the competition's expenditures for advertising relative to the level of sales, but the ratio did not improve the regression results; therefore, it was dropped in favor of the company-advertising budget. In the final analysis, three independent variables were selected: personal consumption expenditures (the selected economic indicator), the company-advertising budget, and the ratio between the company's price and the competitors' prices (the composite price of major competitors). If one of the price ratios is 10.75:10.50, it reduces to 1.024:1 and becomes the independent variable in a multiple regression equation, as described in Chapter 7.

Two cautions need to be noted. It may be unlikely that the price relationship of the company to each of its individual competitors can be determined, but comparability may be modeled to the competition overall or to the dominant company, as may occur in an oligopoly. Secondly, an important consideration in using the company's advertising budget as an independent variable is the means by which the budget is established. If the advertising budget is a percentage of the sales budget, the relationship is suspect. It is unlikely that it is an indicator of what results may be obtained at different levels of advertising expenditure. If different levels of advertising are employed for similar sales levels, validity is more likely. In most circumstances a ratio of company to industry may be more appropriate. In any event, there must be independence between sales and advertising, not the latter depending upon the former.

The model can be the basis in a what-if scenario that estimates the level of sales (the dependent variable) that will be attained if either the price ratio or the advertising budget is varied. Assume that the company's goal is sales expansion. By holding all of the independent variables constant except one, the influence that varying the value of that explanatory variable has upon sales may be estimated. Because the price ratio (until the competition reacts) and the advertising budget are both under company control, each of these variables may be included in the what-if scenario. By examining independently the effect that each of these variables has upon sales, the forecaster gains an understanding of the structure of the elements of the economy in relation to the company.

The scenario may be expanded to include varying the value of both variables simultaneously to determine the combination that best supports the goal. In this case, the end result is to be able to establish a sales target for the coming year. The sales forecast may be expanded into forecasts of revenue and profit. Sequential targets for a series of future years may also be estimated.

It should be noted that there are limits of validity within which prices and advertising expenditures operate. With regard to prices, the dynamic area is that part of the demand curve that displays elasticity. Advertising also has a dynamic effect. Outside the upper limit, the additional sales do not justify the expenditure. Below the lower limit, advertising is ineffective.

In the longer term, uncertainty becomes more uncertain both from the standpoint of the economy and the competition. The competition is not standing still. They may be changing policy or reacting to your strategy. Longer-range plans, therefore, are subject to periodic review and revision.

Current objectives and anticipated objectives are analyzed assuming different tactics and strategies. An option for each case (the different probabilities assumed when varying the values of the independent variables) is developed. Probabilities are assigned to each option to measure the risk of failure. Qualitative techniques (Chapter 11) can play a role in the analysis.

Company goals are generally multisided or express a constraint, for example: increase market share without profit falling below a predetermined level. Profit, revenue, cash flow, earnings per share of stock, cost, inventory, and customer service objectives, to mention a few, interact and are considered in establishing goals. Most of theses elements are derived through the budgeting process from the original forecasts.

Example 3

Assume a situation in which a company understands that it must improve quality (or update its product to be competitive) and boost its sales effort if it is to grow. (In fact, the company realizes that without product change it will lose market position.) The firm wishes to objectively evaluate the impact that these factors have upon demand, revenue, cost, and profit for the next three years. Realistically, qualitative techniques play a large part in defining the parameters of the study.

To increase demand for its products, the company will target markets in which it currently has little strength. It will specifically identify and pursue potential customers. Initially, the size of the sales force remains unchanged, but may be augmented based upon a demographic study being independently prepared. To gain entry to new customers, a promotional policy is being adopted.

The company recognizes the necessity for quality improvement. A plan was implemented five months earlier that is now beginning to be effective. An aggressive advertising campaign will announce the quality program.

Evaluating the impact that increased sales effort and quality improvement will have upon cost, revenue, and profit logically appears to be qualitative because of the lack of hard fact and parallel history. The analysis, however, may be objective once assumptions are quantified. Research to find roughly similar situations combined with the Delphi method and decision trees (Chapter 11) created an atmosphere in which the formation of logical assumptions was possible. The assumptions are:

❖ Economic conditions remain unchanged. Indicators are being held constant arbitrarily to assess the impact of the other variables.

❖ Sales effort will result in modest gains in bookings the first year (about 1%), primarily from promotional sales. Because of sales effort, total demand the second year increases 3%, the third year another 2%. The importance of quality improvement and advertising are considered separately for the convenience of study, however, the actual sales improvements that will occur cannot be categorized.

❖ Promotional items are sold at cost, therefore revenue is increased but not profit. Cost and revenue are equal. The promotion is applicable to the first year only.

❖ Cost of sales because of sales effort increases insignificantly. The present marketing force will achieve the results.

❖ Based upon a cost study of the results being obtained, the additional cost of the quality improvement and control program has been incidental (added quality inspectors and new computer programs) but these costs are more than offset by the savings generated because of the reduction in scrap and rework. The net effect is a reduction in variable cost because the unit cost of manufacture is lower, by a small but nevertheless significant amount.

❖ The additional cost of advertising in support of the quality program is equal to 10% of revenue for the first year only, thereafter, the advertising budget returns to normal.

❖ Additional sales that will be generated because of quality improvement and advertising are estimated at 4% the first year, 2% the second year, and 1% the third year. Additional sales improve revenue and profit.

❖ Fixed costs do not increase. Capacity and indirect staff are adequate to manufacture at the new level of demand.

The first step is to calculate cost, revenue, and profit before considering the effect that the new strategy will have upon the financial situation. This is a control devise used later for comparison. Economic variables are being held constant. All amounts are in thousands except variable cost and unit price.

Ttl Sales x Avg Variable Unit Cost = Ttl Variable Cost + Fixed Cost = Ttl Cost

320	$78.00	$24960	$18720	$43680

Ttl Sales x Avg Unit Price = Revenue - Ttl Cost = Profit   As % of revenue

320	$145	$46400	$43680	$2720	5.9

Incorporating the assumptions above gives these results:

Increased sales through sales effort (rounded):

First year $320(.01) = 3 + 320 = 323$

Second year $323(.03) = 10 + 323 = 333$

Third year $333(.02) = 7 + 333 = 340$

Increased sales through quality improvement and advertising. These elements of the strategy are also considered as selling points for increasing sales through sales effort.

First year $320(.04) = 13 + 320 = 333$

Second year $333(.02) = 7 + 333 = 340$

Third year $340(.01) = 3 + 340 = 343$

Total estimated increase in sales is: first year 3 + 13 = 16; second year 10 + 7 = 17; third year 7 + 3 = 10. The increased cost of sales is incidental, therefore, not considered. Increased cost and increased revenue for promotions: because they are mutually offsetting, profit results are unchanged, therefore, not considered. Variable cost decreased because of quality programs, specifically, the direct labor and material costs, the total of which is estimated at $1.50 per unit (based upon sampling and cost analysis the past two months). New variable cost is $76.50. The increased cost of advertising is 10% of the first year's revenue before additional bookings (46400*0.10 = 4640). It is added to fixed cost the first year. Although it was initially looked at as a percentage, that percentage was translated to dollars and thus became a fixed amount.

Successful implementation of the strategy results in increased revenue.

Starting Sales + Add'l Sales = Ttl Sales x Unit Price = Revenue

1st year	320	16	336	145	$48720
2nd year	320	33	353	145	$51185
3rd year	320	43	363	145	$52635

Year 2: 16 + 17 = 33; year 3: 33 + 10 = 43

Note that sales increases are cumulative in each succeeding year, each building on the success of the previous year, very ambitious.

New total costs are:

Ttl Sales x Variable Cost = Ttl Variable Cost + Fixed Cost = Ttl ost

1st year	336	76.50		25704	23360	$49064
2nd year	353	76.50		27005	18720	$45725
3rd year	363	76.50		27770	18720	$46490

New profit levels are:

Revenue - Ttl Cost = Profit (As a % of revenue)

1st year	48720	49064	$ -344	-0.7
2nd year	51185	45725	$5460	10.7
3rd year	52635	46490	$6145	11.7

Comparison between current and projected cost, revenue, and profit:

	Cost	Revenue	Profit	Net improvement
Current year	43680	46400	$2720	Base profit
New strategy				
1st year	49064	48720	$-344	-3064 (from 2720 to −344)
2nd year	45725	51185	$5460	2740 (from 2720 to 5460)
3rd year	46490	52635	$6145	3425 (from 2720 to 6145)

The new strategy is ambitious. It requires that the firm retreat from its profit position and sustain a loss the first year. The loss is $344,000 the first year, which is the net difference between $3,064,000 and $2,720,000. A one-year loss, however, helps to put the company in position to maintain a higher profit level in future years. But there are questions. How realistic is the plan? Is the company willing to invest the necessary resources? Is the cumulative improvement strategy *too* ambitious?

There is a dynamic relationship between cost and revenue: revenue grows faster than cost when the expenditure for advertising the first year is discounted. Profit potential advances from 5.9% to 9.8%.

Before approving the strategy, top management insists upon detailed plans that specify how each phase of the strategy is to be implemented. Risk must be mitigated by reward thoughtfully conceived. Marketing, manufacturing, production and material control, and finance are involved. In the marketing plan, for instance, each potential customer is identified with background information, target dates for calling on these potentials are established, responsible executives and salesman are identified, and selling points are developed. An important consideration is to conservatively estimate the number of positive responses that can be anticipated.

Cash flow, debt service, and financing the new level of business are subjects that are addressed by the financial officer. Preliminary budgets are prepared, especially to detail the additional costs, including those costs related to inventory levels and purchasing.

Assuming that the strategy proves feasible and top management approves its implementation, senior executives will be acting in an enlightened manner because of the detailed planning and a willingness to forego current profit to achieve larger profits in the future. They are willing to take a risk. Too often, management maximizes the short-term because the value of the company's stock and management's performance evaluation and personal income are frequently determined by short-term results.

In this analysis, constant economic conditions are assumed in order that the other variables can be evaluated and the risks and rewards assessed. Although the results can be used in a stand-alone analysis, before committing resources it is valuable to expand the analysis by econometrically evaluating the strategy. (Note, a less rigorous alternative is suggested below.) A series of equations is formulated to mathematically express the environment. A separate equation for each significant factor is appropriate: economy, revenue, cost, and profit. Two sets of inputs are used, one representing the worst economic case and the other the most likely case. This is not disaster planning. The worst case for the economy assumes sluggish growth and the other optimistic, but realistic, growth. The two sets of equations are identical except that the data plugged in represents the range between the two economic projections. The range is relatively narrow. If the spread were substantial, the risk would not justify the strategy. The only factors that change are economic indicators and from that revenue and variable cost. This is a complex undertaking requiring matrix algebra or simultaneous equations (or other esoteric mathematics) to process the model.

The point forecasting models described earlier in this chapter and the techniques discussed in Chapter 7 are alternative methods of evaluating the strategy. The objective is to develop a model that describes the economy employing economic indicators that correlate with industry or company sales. A GDP forecast (assuming it does not directly correlate with sales) should also be developed. If it does correlate, it can be one element in a multiple regression or other model.

A range is part of the forecast. The model ties to company sales, thus a company sales range is projected and the analysis can therefore be modified. It is suggested that the analysis be done first, then the economic forecast and modification to company sales and to the analysis. In this manner, it gives a better perspective (at least in my mind) and a more logical approach because the first look is at familiar data.

Example 4

Not infrequently the relationship between the dependent and independent variables is offset in time. An example of this lag is seen earlier in this Chapter. The discussion that follows describes two somewhat similar conditions: the so-called ripple effect and the acceleration principle.

The **ripple effect** describes a relationship in which the demand being forecast occurs at a later time than that of the correlating independent variable(s). Applicable situations include supply chain forecasting, not exactly the same but related (discussed in Chapter 13) and when economic impact is first felt at a somewhat distant level, say, when economic change is first felt at retail. The impact caused by a change in consumer purchases trickles down through the various manufacturing levels, affecting sales at progressively later times. If there is a correlation between retail and company or industry sales and the change occurs first at retail, retail is a leading indicator. The relationship may also be between your company or industry and a level of manufacture closer to retail. Retail sales may directly correlate in a time offset to your sales. That could be the basis for a simple regression model for the short-term. For further out projections, the economy will probably be relevant.

In historically checking to see if a relationship exists, test different period offsets to discover the optimum time differential. Have available broad measures of the economy as represented by GDP and other pertinent time series. Some may correlate with your sales while others may not, but they give the forecaster a look at the economy overall and the possible direction of movement in the short-term. It may come about that the lead time between your sales and the variables will not be the same at every historical turning point, in which case, an average offset may work.

Say, the company makes or imports an end item that is sold at retail or produces a component that is used in end items manufactured for retail. Retail sales overall (and its forecast) or some part of the retail market is probably an early warning of a change in company sales. Series such as personal consumption expenditures and surveys of consumer expectations and the buying intentions of customers or retail leaders are probable independent variables.

If there is consistency in the relationship described by the ripple effect, the forecaster can construct a regression equation that gives reliable forecasts, but to be reliable; the relationship must exist during all phases of a business cycle, not just during cyclical change.

If the relationship is more general, the leading indicator of retail may act as an early warning that alerts the company to impending change. It may also be a judgmental modifier to the results from the existing forecasting procedure.

If the relationship exists only at the time of economic change at the consumer level, for instance, it may still be applied to the regression model. One-way to accomplish this is to add a binary (dummy) variable. A binary variable is an independent variable that equals zero when the condition does not apply and 1 when it does. Dummy variables are explained in Chapter 7.

The capability to apply the ripple effect presupposes that the economic change can be recognized and that there is some historical consistency. If an exacting relationship cannot be determined, the effect can still perform an early warning mission.

Another important consideration applicable to many firms is the **acceleration principle.** Generally, it is thought to apply to capital goods (plant and equipment), but it also applies to other types of investment such as inventory. The principle functions internally to a company or externally as a contributor in the movement of business cycles. Many manufacturers attempt to maintain a fixed ratio between the level of goods that they produce and the capital goods or inventory required to meet that production. In times of stability, companies replace their investment in equipment on a relatively constant basis. When demand increases, however, firms make a net investment in new machinery. New investment of equipment (or inventory, for that matter) is a fairly constant multiple of the increased demand and is in addition to replacement cost. Monetary outlay, because of the multiplier effect, may soar. When the demand levels on a higher plateau, net investment stops and only replacement investment continues. During depressed economic conditions, replacement may be severely curtailed. These conditions represent a substantial swing in sales for the capital goods producer. Swings of small magnitude in the general industrial economy cause major swings in the capital goods market and by extension to other market segments. The same generalization of postponability applies, perhaps to a lesser degree, to durable goods and even non-durable goods sales.

The principle can be illustrated by example. Suppose a manufacturer is at full capacity with 25 machines each valued at $1000. Each machine produces $500 per year, a total of $12500. Thus, the ratio of capital investment to sales is 2:1 ($25000 machinery and plant to $12500 of sales). Each year one machine is replaced. The first year investment is $1000 for a replacement machine, which is the gross investment (no net investment in new machinery). The following year sales increase to $15000 (20%). Five new machines are needed, a net investment of $5000. Additionally, one machine is replaced. The gross investment is $6000, a $5000 increase over the first year. This is a 500% increase (6000-1000/1000). Sales grew 20% whereas investment expanded by 500%.

Will the effect always be this dramatic? No, because the ratio depends upon the changes in sales. If gross investment is to remains constant, the rate of sales increase must also remain constant. In fact, gross investment falls when sales increase at a declining rate (a loss of momentum). But generally a change in the level of sales multiplies the growth rate. If sales decline the effect can be as dramatic as that illustrated. Investment in inventory follows the same rule; however, business firms may adopt a flexible acceleration concept in which only a partial adjustment of stocks is made during varying production periods. Also, in modern materials management practice, the reduction of inventory to its lowest practical level is a primary goal.

Along with many other considerations, the acceleration principle is important when planning the future based upon a mid- or long-range forecast. What is the feasibility of investing in new equipment, for example, when the origin of the investment is a forecast of increased sales? This is particularly pertinent, for instance, if there is a long lead-time for capital goods.

The principle not only applies to internal decision making as described above but also to the forecasting process itself.

The principle stated above also applies to the economy. If sales throughout industry were increasing as illustrated above, investment spending would boom. If consumption does not continue to increase, investment remains still. A leveling of sales causes zero net investment; therefore, gross investment is just replacement cost. Bad times can happen even if stability occurs at a high level, and the consequence can ripple throughout the economy in the form of curtailed income. Thus, the multiplier effect is intensified and the effect is felt on consumption throughout the economy. The acceleration principle and the multiplier interact as an inflationary or deflationary cause of an economic spiral.

How can the complexity of this principle be applied to economic forecasting? Certain economic series may provide insight, series such as new orders for capital goods, machinery and durable goods, and inventory change. Chances are they are leading indicators only in the sense that changes in those series predate changes in your sales. The time offset can be important in forecasting. In time series models such as exponential smoothing there is a definite lag that means that changes are not accounted for adequately until after the economic event occurs. In causal models that include indicators that "predict" these changes, the forecast is materially improved. If it is not possible to incorporate these time series directly into the model, a separate model may be possible to act as an early warning or a modifier.

Chapter 11

Qualitative Techniques

The qualitative approach consists of that group of forecasting methods that depend upon judgment. Qualitative and quantitative methods may interface in the forecasting process, especially when management is aware of pertinent data not available in the forecasting system. Both internally and externally, conditions, policies, and tactics change that materially alter the historical perspective. An example of the proper application of judgment is to assess the actions of competitors in pricing, promotions, and the like and to determine the impact that internal business decisions have upon sales. A question to ask is: what is happening or will be happening in the marketplace and how will that influence sales?

Notwithstanding the necessity for qualitative forecasts and forecast modifications and because of their subjective nature, they should be considered appropriate when quantitative techniques cannot give adequate results. Properly, executive judgment is exercised in the interpretation of information and in the planning and decision-making phases of executive activity. Forecasts are raw data for planning and decision-making. As such, they must be as objective as possible.

If judgment is the only possibility, those making the forecast prepare by obtaining as much information as possible pertaining both to the specifics of the situation and the general economic and business conditions that are expected to prevail during the forecasted time period. Approach forecasting systematically: gather data internal to the company and to your company's market segments, examine business conditions as they have been and are expected to be, and find comparable historical analogies, if possible.

Most frequently, qualitative methods are applicable in the following circumstances:

❖ In non-typical situations; for instance, sudden economic change typified by war or recession that negates historical sales patterns, but see Chapter 10 for determining the timing of recessions and their application to forecasting. Judgment may take the form of modifying the quantitative forecast.

❖ When information in the system may distort the forecast, such as an unusually large (firm) order, especially a one-time order. The order is added to the forecast for the period to arrive at total sales but is not a part of the forecasting process. A comparable circumstance is the removal of data because it distorts the results; for example, a successful one-time promotional effort. It is part of total sales, but not part of the forecast. These, and others, are unusual events, thus modifications are legitimate providing opinion is not the modifier. Opinion implies bias. Changes are grounded in fact. The computer can be programmed to consider these type situations in the form of demand filters. See the section describing dummy variables in Chapter 7; they are an excellent method for handling unusual conditions. This paragraph does not imply discarding the quantitative procedure, only modifying forecasts based on factual information.

❖ To forecast sporadic demand. Some items are sold only on an occasional basis with sales occurring at unspecified times. Because sales are pattern-less, judgment may be the most suitable method, but see Erratic Demand in Chapter 6.

❖ To forecast new product sales. Because comprehensive historical data are not available, qualitative methods may be the only option. However, the forecaster may be able to link the sales of the new product to some other product or event. A parallel situation may exist in which the performance of the new product will be similar to the experience of a product previously introduced to the market. The techniques described in Chapter 8 are often applicable. Or sales may relate to economic events in a causal relationship. Caution is recommended to insure that the marketing situation is comparable when connecting two products (sales emphasis, advertising expenditures, economic conditions, etc). See also the section on growth curves, described later in this chapter.

❖ To forecast the development of new technology that may affect the firm's product structure. The forecast determines when the technological advance will begin to influence the market, what products will be phased out, what new products will be needed, and the timing and magnitude of demand (often implying growth curve concepts). In some industries technological change is the norm.

❖ As a preliminary to long- and mid-range planning. The purpose of strategic planning is to chart a course for the company beyond the immediate future. Strategic planning is a process of systematic analysis to identify viable options and select the alternative that will most nearly fulfill the goals of the corporation. Although the long-term future cannot be anticipated with certainty because of the many unforeseeable influences – political, economic, environmental, governmental, and social – the planner's only choice is to proceed from logical assumptions, which assumptions are derived from the forecast. Before embarking upon the qualitative route, it is best to consider model building of the types described in Chapter 10. Several independent forecasts incorporating different economic assumptions and a forecast range (the historical magnitude of error) are excellent starting points. Chapter 12 discusses strategic planning and forecasting in more detail.

The primary orientation in this book has been directed toward – but not exclusively so -- estimating demand (sales), which is the beginning point for all other internal forecasts. As suggested above, forecasts consider the impact of changes in the business and economic environments. Anticipated out of character changes are logically included in the forecasting agenda, whether based in quantitative or qualitative assumptions. The keyword is objectivity. The remainder of this chapter is devoted to a discussion of the major qualitative techniques.

Executive Judgment

Executive judgment is a forecast made by an individual, usually in the form of a management decision. Although judgment is intuitively appealing, it is subject to the bias of the forecaster and may be made without adequate preparation. It is best applied when the manager is experienced in the industry and has received information from other sources such as an industry trade association. It is most pertinent when used as a modifier.

If a company is small with a simple product line and stable demand experience, executive judgment can be satisfactory in the short-run; however, some of the quantitative models presented in this book can probably be incorporated into the forecasting procedure.

Panel Consensus

Forecasts are made by a selected group of individuals who through interaction arrive at consensus. The purpose of this technique is to mitigate the one-person judgment, the assumption being that several heads are better than one. A dominant personality or an individual by the nature of his position may unduly influence the outcome, or there may be a bandwagon effect that negates independent thinking.

A variation is to have each in the panel estimate the future independently with review by an executive higher in the chain of command. This executive attaches weights to the various estimates to account for the biases and prior batting averages of the forecasters. The forecasts are then averaged.

An appropriate panel consists of selected sales people (or all of them) and/or the sales managers. Sales personnel are closest to the customer and the market; however, the panel can be expanded to include product managers, and the finance, purchasing, production control, and manufacturing managers depending upon their specific job responsibilities and how they tie to the marketplace. The problem with sales personnel's estimates is that they may purposely or unconsciously over or under estimate sales. Over estimates occur because of natural enthusiasm, a necessity for sales professionals. Under estimates result when sales performance is judged by sales quotas, invariably set from the sales forecasts, therefore, sales personnel tend to low-ball the forecast. A broad based panel is an advantage providing that it is market knowledgeable. And do not forget customers, especially those important to the sales of the company. Not only can they supply their sales estimates; they may also have a good ear to the market.

Panel consensus works best with short-range forecasting. Longer range has so many variables that it requires a knowledgeable forecaster to orchestrate the process.

Delphi Method

A panel of experts is formed to consider a question. They do not meet nor are they allowed to discuss the matter with each other. The method insures the purity of their answers, that their judgments remain uninfluenced by other panel members. A set of questions is formulated, usually in writing, and answers solicited from each participant. Anonymity is guaranteed. The second (and any succeeding) set of questions is formulated from the responses received to the last questions. Once tabulated, the responses are distributed to the participants who may modify their original answers. The method is not only applicable to estimating sales but is broadly extendable to other business problems. The Delphi technique is an iterative process in which succeeding questions depend upon the answers to the preceding questions. In addition to answering the question, the participants are normally required to give their reasons for their answers.

The process does not imply consensus although that may occur. Rather than one answer there often remains a spread of opinion after the last in a series of questions is answered. The process, however, has compressed the range of opinion. In suitable cases, a range of probabilities can be assigned. A range is often a useful tool, especially in a what-if scenario. Another solution is to find the median value, say, in a sales forecast as representative, with the range as the upper and lower quartiles.

Design of the questions is critical. Ambiguity may mislead the respondents. Questions, especially those following the initial question, must be carefully designed to avoid leading the experts. Poorly designed questions may incorporate implied answers.

Some types of questions that may be examined through the Delphi technique are: what will be the sales level for product X next year? What future technological breakthroughs will govern our business in the next three years and when will they become relevant? When will process Y be commercially feasible? What production processes will be needed when technology Z replaces current technology? What will be the social and business impact of (a certain process or product) and when will the impact occur?

An initial sales forecasting question could be: when will sales of product A reach (a specified $ level)? Give three dates and the probability of each occurring on the specified dates.

Market Research

Several market research methods are available that are based upon statistical probability. These sample surveys study a small portion of the population and project the results to the full population. Market potential of a product, expectations by firms or individuals of intent to buy a product or product type, product acceptance by the public, and number of persons who intend to buy a replacement for a product type they own are a few of the market research possibilities that may be satisfied by sample surveys.

A small sampling may represent accurately the characteristics of the population being studied, whether that population is a group of consumers or a group of companies. In addition to collecting information useful as a forecast, the survey may gather product and consumer data simultaneously. If there is a gap between the time that data are collected and reported, it may negate the validity of the conclusions. Survey data are usually valid only in the short-term.

Sample surveys are powerful tools requiring careful design and execution, which implies the services of experts because of the complexity of the method. However, a survey of the buying intentions of its customers is a type of survey that a company can conduct.

A survey of consumer buying intentions is a good purveyor of consumer sentiment. The University of Michigan and the Conference Board publish this information, as does the Census Bureau. Surveys of intended plant and equipment expenditures are reported in the *Survey of Current Business* and by the Conference Board.

Probability Trees and Bayesian Revisions

The probability (decision) tree model allows competing alternatives to be evaluated by assigning probabilities to each choice. It is a means of analyzing the possibilities and selecting that alternative that best fulfills the predetermined objective. Bayesian analysis is a concept for revising original probability estimates when new data are incorporated into the process.

Probabilities can be determined statistically by applying probability theory when data supports this approach, judgmentally when information cannot be quantified or managerial or expert experience is the only availability, or by a combination of statistics and judgment.

Subjective probability estimates are opinions of those knowledgeable in the area under consideration. Sometimes these judgment calls are expressed in general terms, such as: unlikely, a good chance, highly probable. Greatest effectiveness, especially in forecasting, attends when probabilities are quantified. Normally, the consensus of several is better than an individual's judgment.

The examples that follow illustrate a means of assigning values to generalized probability terms.

The forecaster asks several (or more) knowledgeable managers questions in writing or through email and values are averaged to arrive at consensus. Probabilities always sum to 1 (100%). In examining the possibility that one of two events is the most likely to take place, the question may be: what is the probability of Event A occurring; what is the probability of event B occurring? A set of questions can also be developed.

1. What is the maximum number of product A that we will sell next year? This is the highest possible number and unlikely to be achieved.
2. What is the least number that we will sell next year? This is the absolute lowest that is possible.
3. Considering the answers to questions 1 and 2, what is the most likely possibility between the two extremes? Assuming that the

percentage in question 3 is the mid-point of sales, what are the low and high practical sales range?

The participants answer questions 1 and 2 before they see question 3.

One-on-one with each participant takes the general form of the following:

Forecaster asks, "Of the two events which do you think is the most likely to occur? (The events are mutually exclusive. Only one of the two can happen.)

Participant replies, "Event A."

Forecaster, "Then, Event B is the least likely. With the understanding that Event A's probability of happening is greater than 50%, would you say that Event A is twice as likely to occur, or three times as likely, or only slightly more likely?"

Participant, "That's difficult to say."

Forecaster, "Would it be between slightly and two times more likely or would it be more than two times?"

Participant, "Probably between slightly and two times more likely."

Forecaster, "If Event A is slightly more likely, the ratio would be somewhere in the ball park of a 55% chance of Event A taking place rather than Event B. But Event B still has a 45% chance. On the other hand, if Event A were twice as likely to happen, the ratio would be roughly 65:35 in favor of Event A. Which is the *least* likely: 55:45 or 65:35?"

Participant, "I'd say 55:45."

Forecaster, "OK. That leaves an approximate ratio of 65:35 in favor of Event A. Let's try two other ratios in that ballpark: 70:30 and 60:40. Which of the three is least likely?"

Participant, "This is tougher. It's getting too fine, but I'd say that the last two are both equally unlikely, but I can't really tell."

Forecaster, "Even under the best circumstances there will be some variance, so 65:35 in favor of Event A appears to be our best estimate."

The process of assigning probabilities and analysis by the **Bayesian** method is illustrated in this example.

A manufacturing company is considering building a new factory, a major capital investment. Economic projections made in the manner suggested in Chapter 10 indicate a growing economy. The decision to build or not build will be decided after considering three factors: estimated industry sales, the estimated growth of the economy, and the anticipated actions of the competition (all companies in direct competition collectively), all of whom are assumed to have economic projections of some sort although they may not be the same as those produced by the company. It takes three years to build and bring a new plant on-line. Current industry capacity fulfills the present sales level with a small amount of capacity unused. Total capacity is inadequate to meet the company's market share of projected industry sales several years hence.

If the decision is to build, the size of the new plant will be: either building to anticipated market share or to market share plus X.

The first question is whether future industry sales will support expansion of industry capacity. A multiple regression equation was formulated to project industry sales for five years in the future and to provide data regarding the direction of the economy in the longer term. The previous forecast of GDP began the process. Forecasts of other economic indicators that correlate with industry sales were prepared and used as independent variables in the regression model. Historically, the company has a 12% market share. The regression model predicts substantial but not unreasonable growth, however, reservations remain, which account for some of the conditions below. As time progresses, the future will become more clear, but the initial planning decision needs to be made now and the "to go forward" decision is due in the near future.

Knowing the uncertainty of the future, a panel reviewed the results. Consensus provided the percentages for the four representative conditions that were identified as probable and appropriate to the build, no build decision. Of course, the reasoning is subjective, however, in addition to the internally generated figures, the company reviewed economists' evaluations of the future and contacted major customers for their evaluations.

> A = Industry sales within a range of ±20% of the sales projection a 50% chance.
>
> B = Industry sales greater than projected by at least 21%: a 7% chance.
>
> C = Industry sales less than projected by at least 21% but no more than 30% less: a 35% chance.
>
> D = Industry sales less than projected by at least 31%: an 8% chance.

The probability tree is illustrated in Figure 11-1. Considering the projected economic future as represented by estimated industry sales, the tentative decision is to build a new plant. The probability that industry sales will increase at least to the forecasted growth level (within a reasonable range) and possibly more is 57% (50+7). There is a 35% chance that sales will under-perform between 21% and 30% and another 8% chance that sales will be less than that. The ratio is 57:43 or 1.33:1, not a stunning endorsement but favorable.

Probability Tree

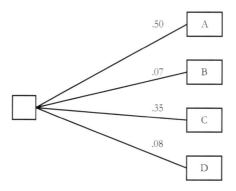

Figure 11-1

The company does not live in a vacuum. The reaction of the competition must be considered. The same raw data is available to all and it is assumed that the competition will make long-range projections. Four possibilities are identified.

E = competition assumes the same growth as the company and expands to its anticipated market share within a range of ±20%.

F = competition builds to a level greater than anticipated market share by a minimum of 21%.

G = competition builds to a level below anticipated market share by a minimum of 21%.

H = competition does not build, builds only to a minor degree, or builds late.

How each competitor reacts is dependent upon how it perceives the future. Individual companies react differently in their decisions because they interpret future opportunities differently. For these reasons each of the four possibilities (E through H) are applicable to each of the possible economic conditions (A through D).

The results of management's study of the competition are depicted in Figure 11-2. Probabilities A and B were combined into one percentage. As a prelude to this part of the study, each major competitor was studied relative to past decisions in the marketplace, management style and philosophy, and their financial situation. Although the study is sketchy in many of its parts, the company got a feeling for the industry. Management realizes, of course, that the probabilities assigned are subjective, especially about the decision-making process in the major competitors' executive offices.

Each of the possibilities (E through H) was assigned to each of the three economic conditions and new probabilities were calculated. Note that the sum of the probabilities in each economic group is 1.00.

The way in which to read the decision tree is to begin at start (S). Reading the uppermost lines, for example, there is a 57% chance that future industry sales will happen as projected within the range indicated in the original A and B. Of the competing companies, 60% will expand to anticipated market share within the range ±20%.

Once the tree is completed, probabilities are revised by multiplication: multiply the two probabilities, thus the product of A and E is 34% (.57 x .60). The probability that more than one independent event will occur at the same time or in succession is the product of all the individual probabilities. In making its building decision, the company wants to know how many companies will react to each of the four specified conditions (E through H). To make this determination, regroup the data and sum. The conclusions are that:

> 41% will build to anticipated market share within a range of ±20%, condition E.
>
> 15% will build to a level at least 21% greater than anticipated share, condition F.
>
> 30% will build to a level below anticipated market share, condition G.
>
> 14% will not expand, expand only to a minor degree, or build late, condition H.

These figures indicate that 56% (41 + 15) of the competition will build facilities that either match or exceed the projected market while 44% will under-build or not build at all. Intuitively, the result suggests capacity expansion, however, the probability that the market will follow the forecast is 57%.

Analysis of Economic & Competitive Position

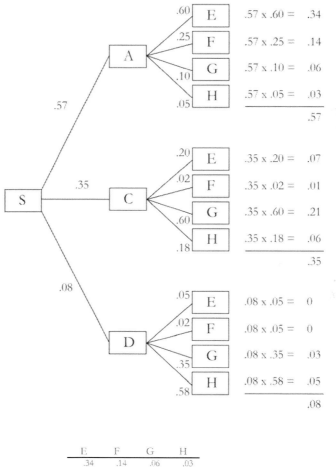

Figure 11-2

Before the company makes its decision it will quantify the outcome data to see if it can get a better insight into the future. Figure 11-3 shows the findings of their study. Arbitrarily, future industry sales is set at 10,000, which is the increase over total current sales, and the number of competitor companies is set at 10 because these values simplify calculation. The numbers assigned do not matter, only the final ratio.

Anticipated Capacity Increase

Company	Capacity Increase		Company	Capacity Increase
1	1000		6	650 + 350
2	1000		7	700
3	1000		8	700
4	1000		9	350 + 100
5	1300		10	200
				Total = 8350

Depicts total capacity increase, not what each numbered company may do

Figure 11-3

From Figure 11-2 we learn that 41% (round to 40%) of the competition will expand to anticipated market share, ±20% (perhaps to a bit more). Assuming a normal distribution, the plus and minus quantities cancel (equal distribution around the mid-point). Therefore, distribution around the center may be ignored. Increased capacity is 1,000 for four companies (the first four quantities in Figure 11-3):

$$10,000 \div 10 = 1,000$$

$$10 \times .40 = 4 \text{ plants}$$

Fifteen percent of the companies will build to a level greater than anticipation (condition F). A range of 21% to 40% seems logical, which is an approximate mid-point of 30%.

$$.15 \times 10 = 1.5 \text{ companies}$$

$$1,000 \times 1.30 = 1,300 \text{ capacity increase}$$

$$.5 \times 1,300 = 650 \text{ representing the half company}$$

Thirty percent will build to a level below anticipation (condition G), estimated as 70% of share.

$$.30 \times 10 = 3$$

$$1,000 \times .70 = 700 \text{ (2 entries)}$$

$$.5 \times 700 = 350 \text{ (2 entries)}$$

Fourteen percent will, at best, expand to a minor degree or expand late. Judgmentally, new capacity is set at 300 for 1.5 plants (entered as 200 + 100).

Total expansion in Figure 11-3 is 8,350, which is 1,650 less than the total projected increase of 10,000. This is a 16.5% under-build for the ten companies in the study. The company concludes that it should not only expand its physical plant but that it should build more than its anticipated share. Recall that company market share is 12%. The subjective nature of the study demands caution. The final decision of how large a factory to build depends upon the faith that the executives place in the probabilities they assigned, a belief that industry sales will expand as estimated, and the degree of risk they are willing to take. A possible solution is to build to a certain capacity with plant design such that factory size can be increased later, a two-phase solution.

The Bayesian method has the advantage that judgmental, empirical, and statistical data can be combined into a formula for forecasting. Normally, the Bayesian decision rule is applied, which states the event with the highest expected value is chosen because it represents the best solution.

The effectiveness of qualitative methods depends upon the sagaciousness of the forecasters and participants in the procedures. Because judgment is colored by personality and the ambitions that executives have for the firm, objectivity suffers. To mitigate this undesirable forecasting condition, obtain as much data and outside information as possible, select carefully the procedure, bring in as many managers or experts as feasible, and conduct the exercise in a way that the outcome can not be predetermined. It is not uncommon that judgmental forecasting is conducted (usually informally) as a means of justifying an implicit decision. This is another of the limitations of qualitative techniques.

Technological Forecasting

Business constantly improves or changes the products offered and develops new products on a regular basis. New technology is common, especially in hi-tech industries producing electronic goods for industry or the consumer market. But change is not exclusive to these industries. To remain dynamic and entice customers to buy their products, companies modify and create new products, even when this does not involve new technology. This applies equally to products ranging from automobiles to soft drinks. Change for products incorporating new technology frequently occurs over a period of several years or more, when both research and introduction of the product to market and the phase-out of the old product are considered. And in many cases new is a supplement to an existing product. Knowing what technology will be developed in the long-term is difficult but cannot be ignored, even if conclusions can only be made in general terms. Technological forecasting asks several questions:

What changes in technology will occur in the next several years; what impact will these changes have upon our industry; and what should be the firm's role?

How will the new products we are developing impact our current product offering? As the product grows in popularity what will be the replacement factor for the old product?

Once introduced, what will be the rate of growth as pertains to quantity and time?

The method or form that the forecast takes is dependent upon the questions. Quantitative methods that relate a new product to a like or similar product(s) can be used to forecast. A comparison is made employing techniques such as regression, or more likely growth curves (see the next section). The comparison is made with other company product introductions or products introduced by other companies or the industry in general. In this procedure, it is assumed that factors such as advertising expenditures will be equal and that the economy will be approximately the same. In the general sense, if a technology change has been continuing over time, a time series technique can be applied to extend that change into the future. A qualitative technique like the ones described in this chapter (a panel of experts, etc.) may be able to estimate or at least give insight into the technological future. Market research may be applicable to answer questions as: what changes would you like to see in this product and what technology do you think would replace current technology in this product category (asked of experts)? Estimating the probabilities of different possibilities also enters into the picture, thus decision trees are a possible technique.

Studies have been made as to which provides the best technological projections: objective or subjective forecasts, with results on both sides of the ledger. However, it is generally concluded that objective methods are best whenever they can be used. As will be seen, however, judgment enters the picture at an early stage.

Growth Curves

Growth curves of the type explained in Chapter 6 (Non-Linear Trend Analysis) are available for technological forecasting and for estimating sales of new product introductions. Usually, these are long-term forecasts; however, growth curves are equally applicable to items that have a short life cycle. Chapter 8 describes techniques that are relevant to sales cycle analysis.

Growth curves frequently take an S-shaped form. Although these curves are not restricted to estimating sales, the following example uses sales to illustrate the procedure. There are three distinct phases in the S-shape or logistic curve. At first, sales are small and increase slowly. In the second stage, there is rapid acceleration in sales. Stage three is the plateau, the point at which sales level out. For items with a short life cycle, however, the third stage is the terminal stage (almost all orders have been booked). The exact shape of a growth curve varies with the product and outside influences such as the economy and the actions of the competition. The length of time to reach the plateau may be short as when there is an abbreviated selling season or stretch over a period of years as is sometimes the case with new technology.

Chapters 6 and 8 describe non-linear curves that are applicable for forecasting new product introductions and estimating the acceptance level of new technology. It may occur that those procedures do not describe the situation. In that case, the following technique can be useful.

New product introductions may be items that the company has developed and is bringing to market. These are products that are new, something that will replace or greatly improve an existing product. In the same sense, the introduction may be industry-wide and the company wants to know how sales of its products will be affected. With regard to new technology, typical inquiries are estimating when new products incorporating this technology can be brought to market and projecting industry sales when the product is already developed and several companies are ready to initiate sales.

Judgment enters the picture in several ways, for example: the initial forecast through stage two, determining the pattern of the curve to be applied (picking an historical curve), how the competition will react, and when a technology in development will be ready.

Initially, one of the non-linear curves previously described should be tried if one can be found that fits. Because the forecaster will probably be forecasting a new item or technology with which there has been zero experience, finding a curve from previous introductions or technology development that is representative is a matter of judgment. The curve selected is a surrogate (control) for the new product or technology. The forecaster assumes that the new S-type curve will be in sync with the surrogate curve. There may be several S-type curves that are logical candidates. If so, averaging them to arrive at a new curve may be the best solution.

Suppose that the forecaster is estimating sales for a new product. The initial forecast assumes that the new curve will imitate the surrogate in pattern and time. A qualitative approach is used to estimate total sales through the first two stages of product introduction. It is projected that sales will be 15,000. Surrogate sales were 10,000; therefore, "new" sales are 1.5 times "old" sales. If sales in the first three periods, say, were a total of 1% or 100, new product sales should be 150. By using the percentages for each period, the curve can be completed.

Once sales data begins to accumulate, the curve can be modified.

As an example, say, a company wants to forecast sales for a new product it will soon bring to market. A panel has examined previous introductions and determined that a particular curve is most representative of the new product. Economic conditions are roughly the same and marketing expenditures will be in the same ballpark. Looking at the market for this type of product and considering what is available reinforces the view that the new product will follow the same pattern as the previous product. The panel estimates that total sales through stage two will be 380,000 units. Sales for the control product were 282,050 units. Stages one and two lasted forty periods.

Sales per period of the surrogate product are given in Figure 11-4, both by period and cumulatively. The original forecast column gives the anticipated sales for a forecast of 380,000 units. At period 4, for instance, estimated sales are 472 units (0.001241*380,000). Regardless of actual sales at period 4, the company will not change its total projection because the percentage is very small, approximately 0.1241%, and there is insufficient sales this early in the procedure. At period 10, sales are 4100 units cumulatively, which represents a little over 1% of projected sales, that is, 3450/282050 = .012232. Note that the 4100 units are actual sales, not forecast. Numbers in period 11 forward are cumulative forecasts. If the company decides to change the forecast, the new estimate would be about 335,190 units (4100/0.012232) at period 40. The forecast at period 11, for example, is 335190*(1.7904/100) = 6001. Should the company change its forecast and its manufacturing plan? The side-step answer is: that depends upon a number of factors unique to individual companies.

At period 15 sales are 17,444 units (actual sales), which projected through period 40 is 300,000 units. Nearly 6% of sales occur through period 15 if the surrogate pattern is an accurate reflection of new product sales. Before considering modification of the company's marketing and manufacturing plans, the pattern of sales of the new product in relation to sales of the surrogate product is examined. Although not shown in Figure 11-4, sales were recorded for each known period. At period 15 the percentage that each previous period was to the whole assuming sales of 300,000 units was calculated. Those percentages were compared with the percentages in the surrogate sales curve to see if the pattern of the new product was similar to the surrogate. As there is compatibility, the panel reviewed the estimates and concluded that a projection of 380,000 through phase two is too high but that actual sales will be at least 300,000 and possibly more. Remember that the product will continue to sell after period 40 and likely at a brisk pace. Mistakes on the high side will not be a manufacturing disaster. The forecaster continues to collect data and forecast sales and the panel continues to review those forecasts together with other data and information it gathers from its research.

Growth Curve Sales Forecast

Period	Surrogate Sales (non-cum)	Surrogate Sales (cum)	% Of Total Sales	Original Forecast	Forecast at Period 10	Forecast at Period 15
1	50					
2	75					
3	100					
4	125	350	0.1241	472		
5	150	500	0.1773	674		
6	200	700	0.2482	943		
7	300	1000	0.3545	1347		
8	500	1500	0.5318	2021		
9	850	2350	0.8332	3166		
10	1100	3450	1.2232	4648	4100	
11	1600	5050	1.7904	6804	6001	
12	2000	7050	2.5000	9498	8378	
13	2600	9650	3.4214	13001	11468	
14	3100	12750	4.5205	17178	15152	
15	3650	16400	5.8146	22095	19490	17444
16	4150	20550	7.2859	27687	24422	21858
17	4600	25150	8.9169	33884	29888	26751
18	5200	30350	10.7605	40890	36068	32282
19	5700	36050	12.7814	48569	42842	38344
20	6250	42300	14.9973	56990	50270	44992
21	6800	49100	17.4083	66151	58351	52225
22	7300	56400	19.9965	75987	67026	59989
23	7900	64300	22.7974	86630	76414	68392
24	8550	72850	25.8288	98149	86575	77486
25	9000	81850	29.0197	110275	97271	87059
26	9500	91350	32.3879	123074	108561	97164
27	10000	101350	35.9333	136547	120445	107800
28	10600	111950	39.6915	150828	133042	119075
29	11200	123150	43.6625	165917	146352	130987
30	11700	134850	47.8107	181681	160257	143432
31	12350	147200	52.1893	198319	174933	156568
32	12900	160100	56.7629	215699	190264	170289
33	13500	173600	61.5494	233888	206307	184648
34	14100	187700	66.5485	252884	223064	196645
35	14700	202400	71.7603	272689	240533	215281
36	15300	217700	77.1849	293302	258716	231555
37	15800	233500	82.7867	314590	277493	248360
38	16100	249600	88.4949	336281	296626	265485
39	16200	265800	94.2386	358107	315878	282716
40	16250	282050	100.0000	380000	335190	300000

Figure 11-4

Chapter 12

Strategic and Long-Range Planning and Forecasting

Strategy formation is an organized way to appraise the future and establish goals in furtherance of the welfare of the organization. The planning process assesses the current situation and direction in consideration of a changing environment and establishes future goals and the means to achieve those goals. The strategic plan provides direction and focuses attention so that managers and executives work together to achieve the organization's future objectives. For our purposes, strategy is defined as what will be done and basically how it will be done. The long-range plan is the implementing document, laying-out the intermediate objectives by time-line. The long-range plan logically takes the form of a business plan, expanding objectives into financial data.

Strategy can be divided into two parts: grand (master) strategy and functional strategy. The master strategy states the overall mission of the company and the means of accomplishment. It is the outgrowth of top management's conceptualization of the future as it relates to the firm. Functional strategies deal with marketing, finance, diversification and growth, product structure, and research and development. From the master strategy functional strategies are developed.

Although different formats can be utilized effectively to develop a strategic plan, the following elements are indicative of a comprehensive plan.

The first task in developing a strategic plan is to do a **SWOT analysis**: strengths, weaknesses, opportunities and threats, an approach often seen. In addition to forming a basis for charting the future, the analysis helps to evaluate the plan as it evolves.

The **mission statement** formalizes the purpose of the business. It clearly defines the company's business and how that business fits into the industry overall. It may reference its relationship to the market and its place in the competitive environment. The mission seems obvious to those working in the firm. By formalizing the mission, however, the company articulates its understanding of its business in the present and the future. And in so doing, the executives may find that the obvious was not quite so obvious after all.

Closely related to the mission statement is the **vision statement**, which looks at the future. It starts with a conceptualization by the CEO or the executive committee (or board of directors). The statement answers questions such as where will the industry be in X number of years and what will be the role of our company? It is a guiding light. Together with the goals, this purpose statement conveys what the firm hopes to accomplish. It envisions the future in light of the mission.

Once the above steps are completed, the company is in position to establish its **major goals**. Goals are targets to be accomplished within a given time frame. They are specific and include, as appropriate, sales and market share growth, designing a new sales and marketing division, research and development direction, improvement of profit and return on investment, facilities expansion, reorganization to increase efficiency, adding new products, developing partnerships with customers and suppliers, diversification, etc. Goals guide strategy; strategy guides action.

The key strategies paragraph states in broad terms what actions will be taken to secure the success of the goals. Strategies are the source material and the guide for formulating the action plan (the long-range plan). Although strategy is not limited in its scope by definition, it should be restricted to those actions needed to accomplish the goals, thus they fundamentally impact the future success of the company.

Many individuals may participate in strategic planning, but do so at various levels. The process begins with the board of directors' and top management's direction to planning committees or teams and it continues to influence the development of the plan through its reviews of progress. Top management also insures that the strategic and the long-range plans are executed. Planning committees consist of the executives that will be responsible for implementation. The number of members should be limited to avoid too many cooks in the kitchen. However, these executives may task others to develop specific parts of the strategic plan.

Before the process begins but after initial direction is given there are preliminary tasks to be accomplished. The first is to determine that the company is ready for strategic planning. Are there any major issues that will interfere with the strategic plan? They must first be resolved. There are other considerations as may be appropriate. Are resources available or can they be secured, both financial and physical? Has intelligence been collected regarding the competition and the market? Sources are competitors' records as may be public, customers' evaluations of the future market, the past history of competitor actions with regard to the manner in which they react to changing markets, competitors' research and development programs if such can be determined legally, including their past history in introducing new products, and trade association information. Financial data such as projected cash flow may also be useful.

The first part of Chapter 11 provides a definition of strategic planning and should be reviewed in conjunction with this chapter.

The **long-range (business) plan** is the time phased implementing document for the strategic plan. The long-range forecast, presented as a range of probabilities, indicates the possible long-range economic future and the future as it pertains to the company before strategic changes are made. Knowing that the long term is uncertain and may be different than any of the projections does not negate the necessity for forecasting. Predicting the future gives a basis for planning actions and may be coupled with what-if scenarios and contingency planning. If the future is different than anticipated, there is a good chance that plans can be modified as to action or timing. Without an implementing plan based on an estimate of the future, a company is sloshing through the mud barefoot.

Before going to example a few general comments is befitting consideration.

Short- and long-range goals should be in balance. Specifically, they should not be counterproductive nor should one negate the other.

A decision to plan strategically implies risk, however, risk must be rational, that is, within the capabilities of the firm. This indicates the need for available resources or for resources that can be secured and implies that less than sterling success will not greatly harm the company. If a strategy is to acquire another company, for instance, determine the ramifications of that purchase financially considering several possible economic scenarios, perhaps a decision tree approach will be appropriate. The same reasoning applies to new product development and introduction. Strategic planning is an analytical process in which decision involves the commitment of resources. It is also a learning process in that the planners learn new things about the industry, market, competitors, and the strengths and weaknesses of the company.

In addition to the questions posed above, in dealing with the future, pertinent questions are: what changes can be expected in the future marketplace, in products, and customers; how will our business change; how do we prepare for the future; and what changes in today's product and market commitments need to be made and when?

Strategy must be compatible with size, but not to say that commitment of considerable resources is less than desirable. The question is: what are the ramifications if that strategy fails? Perhaps more pertinent: is the strategy realistic? Consider a goal that requires borrowing to a level that could seriously impact the company if accomplishment is less than brilliant.

The above is an explanation of the essential fundamentals. It is introduction for further study. Following is an example, simplified, of course.

The example company is mid-size for the industry. There are two large companies that lead the industry in the product lines that the example company manufactures. There are a half dozen others that manufacture the same products and are roughly the same size as the example company. The market is of a size that it can support all of these companies. The two largest companies command approximately sixty percent of the business. The example company's market share is on average seven percent. In the past, product innovations have come from the two largest companies, but these innovations are more nearly aligned to improvements (modifications) in existing products. The smaller companies are able to follow the lead, but lose sales until they catch-up. Radically new or different products are not a consideration.

As the economy grows so grows the sales of the industry's products. Generally, industry sales are reflective of GDP. The forecasting methodology for estimating industry sales, however, should be based upon a study of economic and other indicators. Any of the techniques described in this book are candidates for forecasting: time series, regression, combined forecasts, etc. Several forecasts may be made and reconciled by judgment, if necessary. For an additional view of long-range planning, see that section in Chapter 10.

The company has prepared a long-range forecast of the economy and industry sales. (The forecasts are shown in Figure 12-1.) An industry forecast may be independent of the economic forecast but reconciled with it or may be directly derived from it. Three forecasts of industry sales were prepared: mid-, low-, and high-range. The company forecast (based upon market share) was projected from the mid-range industry forecast. Forecasting methodology was selected from those described in this book.

Time is January 2004. Actual industry sales for the fourth quarter 2003 are 475,900 units and company sales are 33,300 units. Quantities are in thousands.

If company sales follow the industry sales forecast as they have done historically, sales will increase from 33,300 units to 38,800 units in

the next five years, an increase of 16.5%. The company has two major
objectives: sales growth and profit growth. A strategic plan time phased
to accomplish these objectives is the course chosen by the company.
The final plans follow. Note, that the possibility of a recession is not
considered, but it cannot be ignored in the process.

Industry and Company Forecasts

Period	Industry Forecast	Company Forecast
2004 Qtr 1	481.0	33.7
Qtr 2	487.9	34.2
Qtr 3	493.0	34.5
Qtr 4	496.4	34.7
2005 Qtr 1	503.8	35.3
Qtr 2	506.6	35.5
Qtr 3	511.7	35.8
Qtr 4	520.1	36.4
2006 Qtr 1	524.0	36.7
Qtr 2	526.5	36.9
Qtr 3	533.2	37.3
Qtr 4	542.4	38.0
2007 Qtr 1	545.8	38.2
Qtr 2	552.3	38.7
Qtr 3	553.1	38.7
Qtr 4	554.6	38.8
2008 Qtr 1	553.8	38.8
Qtr 2	551.6	38.6
Qtr 3	551.2	38.6
Qtr 4	554.9	38.8

Figure 12-1

The strategic plan

Company strengths

1. Company has a secure place in the market. Customer base has
   been steady through the years.
2. Product line has excellent reception.
3. Executive and management staff is dedicated to the business.
4. Customer service is among the best in the industry.
5. Board of directors provides good support and allows flexibility
   to the executive staff.

Company weaknesses

1. Sales and Marketing are focused on current customers because
   of a lack of staff to expand.
2. Research and development not staffed to lead in product
   design/modification.
3. Production systems and materials management although good
   do not encompass the latest methods and technology.
4. Executives and managers are satisfied with the level of business
   and the business methods employed (although they disagree).

Threats to the company
1. Major competitors could aggressively seek to increase their market share.
2. Companies not currently producing the industry's product line could enter the market.

Opportunities for the company
1. Ability to expand market share by assertive market penetration is possible (but to a degree limited by the total market and the actions of competitors).
2. The number of product modifications can be increased with an expanded R & D function. Company can expand into related fields through R & D research and product marketing follow-on.
3. Products can be marketed overseas.

Mission statement
The company manufactures and markets a line of components that is sold directly to manufacturers for incorporation into their products. These components are flexible in that they are used in a wide-range of current end items. New end items generally replace older end items; therefore, the market only expands slowly. Because these components are basic to the end item manufacturer's products, changes in the components are such as to be improvements to existing products. Sales are made directly to the end item manufacturers. What has not been considered is the feasibility of developing new products related to the current line, thus expanding sales into other markets.

Vision statement
Based upon a long-term growing economy as represented by GDP and other economic indicators it may be expected that the sale of our products will continue to increase in proportion to the market for those end items that use our products. It is not assured, however, that we will continue to command the same market share unless actions are taken to fix our place in the industry. This is a continuing endeavor. The company, however, cannot be satisfied with its current market share in light of our objective to grow the business in sales and profit. Therefore, actions are required that insure future growth. A continuing need for our industry's products is anticipated with our market share continuing through aggressive marketing, but new programs are needed to increase our share of the existing market. But this is not sufficient. We will seek out new markets overseas. We will design new products for different markets. We will increase productivity through better control systems and engineering. It is anticipated that our plan of action

will be fully implemented in five years. This is a two-fold effort: to optimize the current sales of our products and to expand into new markets with new products.

Major goals

1. Increase our domestic market share for our current line by 3% (to 10%) in the next two years.
2. Develop an overseas market for our current products; concentrating on certain researched geographical areas. Achieve sales of 20,000 units quarterly in five years.
3. Develop a line of products related in manufacture to those now produced and sell to the domestic market. Achieve sales of 20,000 units quarterly in five years.
4. Reduce inventory levels, reduce throughput time, and increase productivity and efficiency in our factory to improve profit and return on investment, to be accomplished in eighteen months.
5. As dollars, increase profit by 50%. During the sales expansion period it is expected that the profit margin will decline slightly until sales programs are in place. Profit goal to be realized by the end of the fifth year.
6. Build a new factory(s) to manufacture the increased product load. The initial timing is for reference only. Timing will be determined as goals 1 through 3 develop.

Note that building a new factory does not imply that it will be built in the U.S. A facility could be opened overseas (buy or build) to take advantage of lower costs or proximity to foreign markets. Rather than own its factory, the company could contract with an overseas firm or enter a limited partnership, which possibly ties-in with the second goal.

Key Strategies

1. VP Marketing: prepare a plan to increase our domestic market share of current products (goal 1) and research the overseas markets (goal 2).
2. VP Marketing, VP Manufacturing, and Director R & D: conduct a study and develop a plan for the manufacture and marketing of new products (goal 3).
3. VP Manufacturing, VP Engineering, and Director Material Management: research and study production control and engineering systems to achieve goal 4. Recommend a course of action.
4. CFO: after plans for the above goals have been initially formulated, prepare a financial statement for evaluating the plans and meeting the profit and ROI objectives (goal 5).

5. VP Manufacturing, VP Engineering, and CFO: provide an initial plan for increasing our physical production capability in support of the above objectives including cost estimates. It is anticipated that several alternatives will be provided.
6. CEO and Executive Committee: review and evaluate the plans, have plans modified as needed, and present to the Board for approval.
7. Each department head: prepare time phased implementing plans under the direction of the appropriate executives.

The strategy is not ready until the above actions have been completed and approved. It is also necessary to review the plans in consideration of the low and high industry forecasts. If one of those occurs, what is the impact on the strategic plan?

Once the strategy has been approved, an implementing plan of action is formulated. It lays out in reasonable detail what will be accomplished during each implementing phase and includes benchmarks. The long-range forecast was instrumental in starting the process as it predicted company sales. Financial estimates, the anticipated normal growth pattern, the need for an additional production facility, etc. is formulated from the forecast. The forecast is updated frequently; plans are reviewed periodically.

The process can be formalized in a business plan. The business plan extends the strategy financially, defining revenue, cost, and profit objectives. Projections expressed as budgets, balance sheets, and other financial instruments are constructed.

Logically, a what-if scenario is a reasonable approach. Once the implementing plan is inaugurated, the question (again) is asked: what if the low-range forecast more nearly resembles the future? Remember, our example company chose the mid-range forecast on which to base the timing of its goals completions. How will this change our strategy? How should we account for the differences? The same approach is applicable to the high-range forecast. The decision to take action on each interim goal – to commit resources -- can be pegged to the forecast and situation at the time that the decision must be made.

Pitfalls in strategic planning abound. Chief among them is the unwillingness of executives and managers to objectively eyeball the business, especially when it comes to their own areas of responsibility. The wagons are likely to circle. To overcome this tendency, the CEO makes clear that faultfinding is not in the mix (if executives were not doing an excellent job they would not be employed). The focus is on the future: an organized approach to decision-making and commitment. Success lies in being responsive to a dynamic, changing environment.

Changed planning action, when the future proves to be different than anticipated is the watchword.

Because of the uncertainty of the long-term future, reluctance to commit to the long-term is a possible pitfall. The purpose of the long-range plan is to establish interim goals, which serves two purposes: benchmarks to insure that progress is being made toward the major goals in an organized and timely manner and that goals remain viable in light of changing economic conditions (a changed long-range forecast). In this sense strategic planning is an adaptive approach. Understanding the review process should negate the reluctance to commit.

Recall that the company prepared three forecasts: low, middle, and high. It selected the middle forecast but did not neglect the others, which raises a question: was the possibility (or probability) of a recession occurring within the next five years considered? Trying to pinpoint an if-and-when is an exercise in futility. It is better to estimate the impact that a recession could have on the strategy, as a readiness measure should the bad happen. Of course, the depth and length of a recession are illusive ghosts, but considering the possibility that a recession will raise its ugly head is a necessity.

Chapter 13

Operational Forecasting

Operations for the purpose of this chapter include all departments that are consumers of forecasts and involved in the day-to-day running of the business: the here and now; specifically, manufacturing, materials management, purchasing, sales and marketing, merchandising, and finance. Whereas strategy is concerned with the long-term, operational forecasting deals with the short-term (usually six months), perhaps through the mid-term (normally six months to a year). Typically, forecasts are prelude to determining what materials and products will be needed and when they will be required. It is instrumental in establishing inventory and safety levels, estimating sales and planning marketing programs, projecting cash flow and financing requirements, planning capacity and manning levels, planning distribution and transportation requirements, etc. Forecasting and planning are part of the same business endeavor. Manufacturing, distribution, retail, and all those businesses in between share many of the same needs.

Each department within a business has its own objectives. Often, they conflict. For example, Sales is intent upon maximizing the number of orders taken and with customer service, manufacturing wants to minimize cost by maximizing throughput (minimum change over, long production runs), which may not serve on-time delivery of customer orders or may result in unacceptable inventory levels, and materials and inventory managers desire small inventory levels. Each activity may have its own estimates or its own criteria and may not understand the impact that its decisions have upon other departments. There needs to be one forecast only. It triggers company and departmental planning. To overcome the typical shortfalls, an integrated approach to forecasting and planning is essential. Later in this chapter we will examine how integration can be achieved.

All of the forecasting techniques and methods described in this book are potential candidates for operational forecasting. The front end of the long-range forecast may act as the operational forecast or a separate forecast may be prepared. To quote an old saw: it all depends upon the situation. As simple as possible is a good catchphrase, however, consistency and accuracy are the two most important criteria.

A top-down or a bottom-up approach to forecasting individual end items is possible. Selection depends upon what works best. Both bottom-up and top-down forecasts can be prepared then reconciled. A big difference in the results of the two approaches signals a serious problem necessitating scrutiny of the process.

In top-down, product families are forecast and individual item estimates are derived from the aggregate forecast. Disaggregating may be accomplished through a historical ratio or percentage that each item bears to the whole. Individual end items are stock-keeping units. Requirements for raw materials and components that are processed to make a selling unit are derived from actual sales or forecasted sales. Component and material needs are not forecasted.

In bottom-up, each end item is forecast and then the separate items aggregated to arrive at a product family forecast. What constitutes an aggregate forecast? It can take several forms. For instance, combine by product family (group), by sales region, by major customers individually plus a total for minor customers, and by dollar value. One forecasting model may suit all the items sold by the company or it may be that different items require different models. Some items may exhibit seasonality while others do not. Or some may have a short life cycle or have erratic demand while others are stable. A product may serve more than one market requiring separate forecasts for each market. This occurs when the different markets react to different economic or sales stimuli. Individual forecasts are combined into one projection. Once the methodology is selected and programmed, the forecasts can be sorted to meet the applicable needs outlined above.

If aggregate forecasts are made and then disaggregated, sales of all the individual items (probably) must move in the same direction (not is opposite directions). If there are two products where an increase in the sales of one offsets sales in the other, for instance, care must be taken to insure the model(s) reflects that condition.

Chapters 1 and 2 discusses issues that are important to operational forecasting including potential problems, and they should be reviewed in conjunction with this chapter. At the close of Chapter 1, a listing of significant factors that affect sales, thus forecast modeling, are given. As explained in Chapter 2, two forecasts are normally required: one for bookings and one detailing the amount that will be sold by requested delivery or promise date. The bookings forecast is the estimated amount that will be sold in each sales time bucket. It is anticipated orders by received dates. The forecast by requested delivery date is either the date that the customers have requested delivery or the promise dates assigned by the company and agreed to by the customers.

The bookings and delivery forecasts agree in total quantity, only the dates differ. It may be necessary to factor in a percentage for cancellations. If so, the number is an offset to the forecast. However, demand history is assumed to be net of cancellations, as it should be. Statistics regarding cancellations is also a collectable item. Additionally, statistics are collected regarding the number of orders and quantities shipped as promised, which by default indicates those shipped early or late. Shipments, however, are not demand.

There are other conditions that can cause problems.

The company can overbook orders (who wants to turn down an order?). From a customer service standpoint this is a bad practice. When the company accepts an order, the order is entered into the bookings time bucket and into the requested delivery date or promised time bucket. If the order results in an overbooking in the delivery time bucket, the system should activate a warning that an overbooking has occurred. A better practice is to find the next available unfilled time period for order entry. Note that the forecasting system collects actual order data as well as estimating sales.

The requested delivery date of an order may be changed by the customer to a later or earlier time period or customers may order more than they really need. Although there are several logical reasons for changing the size or timing of an order, it is particularly insidious during a time when customers feel there will be a shortage of your products. They increase the order quantity to an amount higher than actually required or they request an earlier delivery date. The logic of the customer is that if an allocation comes into play, the allocated percentage may equal or be close to the amount really needed. Similarly, delivery slippage may see the order shipped when actually needed. Should the supplying company not allocate, the customer can cancel a part of his order. Customers may also order less or the same amount during a period of anticipated shortage while simultaneously placing orders with several companies to hedge their bets. Again, cancellation is a possible customer tactic.

If the customer or the company changes the timing of an order, care must be taken to insure that those orders appear only in one time bucket (one for bookings and one for requested/promised delivery date). It can occur that the order will appear in the original and the changed time period disguised as part of overall demand, which would overstate demand, thus having serious ramifications on sales, production, purchasing, and finance. That part of the system that deals with order change should automatically debit and credit orders in the applicable time periods. A report of order change by the customer (quantity and timing) will aid the Sales Department. The report should provide the reasons for the change. Additionally, if requested delivery dates by customers overbook a time bucket, the system notes the overbooking. It may be that the bookings forecast should also have a pegging capability that reflects when the customers wanted the products, not when delivery was promised. Remember, each individual sale is entered in the period when it was booked (when the orders was taken) and this is not changed except when there is a change in the order size.

It stands to reason that orders should not be taken for delivery time periods that are booked to capacity. A new promise date that is feasible should be cleared with the customer. An open to sell report can be programmed as part of the demand management system. It is important to keep order purity to preserve the integrity of the system. Note that there are capacity management techniques that can actually increase capacity without adding people or equipment. Coordination between production and sales can solve problems.

Company history or history of pertinent independent variables are the raw data for forecasting. Not unlikely in the short- to mid-range the company in forecasting its sales or industry sales will develop a time series model. But any of the models described in this book are candidates. The forecaster should not forget combined and simulation models in the testing process. The company forecast could also be -- in whole or in part – the customer's forecast, as when the business is servicing one or more large customers. In the latter case, it is advisable that the company forecasts independently and reconciles its projection with the forecast prepared by the customer. This is especially pertinent with regard to periodic forecast revisions. Later in this chapter forecasting in relation to supply chains will be discussed.

Data accuracy has been discussed. Without reasonably accurate sales data, forecasts can be skewed in unknowable directions. As previously noted, shipments do not equate to demand. In many companies the most reliable sales information is contained in the financial records. If accuracy is a problem, translating the financial records to a forecasting format may be the solution. Such a solution requires that data become available before the financial book is closed, which can mean some special programming. If an integrated system is in place, real time sales data should be available.

A manufacturing company may produce to order or to anticipation. In the former environment, the production cycle begins with the order, and delivery is based upon manufacturing and perhaps raw materials lead-times and the orders already in the system. Forecasting is especially important in identifying capacity requirements, triggering the marketing and sales endeavor, and establishing materials buying plans. Manufacturing to anticipation depends upon forecasting not only for determining capacity and sales activity but also as a base for establishing production schedules and all the supporting actions. Manufacturing schedules need to have constancy. Forecast revisions for a company that builds to anticipation within the manufacturing lead-time can be disruptive. The watchword is "avoid", or at least leave the schedule alone.

The short-run forecast at an absolute minimum is equal to the lead-time for purchasing parts and components plus production cycle time in a manufacturing environment and the procurement lead-time for end items sold by, say, an importer. Because forecasts serve many masters, it is a good idea to forecast at least through the mid-range. Although the forecast may change within the lead-time window, plans can be frozen in the short run to avoid operational disruption.

The sales, operations, and other dependent activities in a company are like separate parts of the same body in that each of the several parts has a different function, but with each dependent upon the others for the well being of the whole. One way in which to insure that the process works, that is, that all plans are in sync is through **Sales and Operations Planning.**

The APICS (Association for Operations Management) dictionary, eleventh edition, defines sales and operations planning as:

A process to develop tactical plans that provide management the ability to strategically direct its business to achieve competitive advantage on a continuous basis by integrating customer-focused marketing plans for new and existing products with the management of the supply chain. The process brings together all the plans for the business (sales, marketing, development, manufacturing, sourcing, and financial) into one integrated set of plans. It is performed at least once a month and is reviewed by management at an aggregate (product family) level. The process must reconcile all supply, demand, and new product plans at both the detail and aggregate levels and tie to the business plan. It is the definitive statement of the company's plans for the near to intermediate term, covering a horizon sufficient to plan for resources and to support the annual business planning process. Executed properly, the sales and operation planning process links the strategic plans for the business with its execution and reviews performance measurements for continuous improvement.

A primary activity of the S&OP process is the development and modification of demand (sales) and supply plans. Meetings are held periodically, usually monthly, to discuss these and other issues. The participants are those tasked with making supply and demand decisions for the firm, thus participants are decision-making representatives from sales and marketing, manufacturing, and materials management and purchasing as these represent the supply and demand sides of the business. Finance is included as well as a high-ranking general level executive, who may be the chairperson, because these executives can interpret plans in relation to financial restraints, profits, and the strategic goals of the business. Other activities, such as R&D and Engineering, may be appropriately included.

The top-level plan in a company is the strategic plan, often labeled the business plan, but in my mind the business plan is a quantification of the strategy. Together, these plans form a statement of the long-range strategy. Revenue, cost, and profit objectives are defined. Projected budgets and other financial instruments are generated. The business plan is the long-range master plan that guides sales and operations planning.

The process begins with aggregated, operational (product family) forecasts, expressed in units and dollars. At the meeting, these forecasts are discussed in relation to each department's knowledge of the way in which the forecasts impact their activities. Rough-cut supply and demand plans are brought to the meeting by the appropriate members and are shared with the other participants. These plans are reconciled with the forecasts. Shortcomings are identified. Second-cut demand and supply plans are developed. This planning may be done after the meeting and presented at the next meeting, which in this initial process follows quickly. Plans are compatible with company goals. Forecasts are reviewed in light of the second-cut plans to determine compatibility. Operating plans are then finalized. A business plan is developed. Once approved, these plans are the marching orders for the company. They focus each department on a single set of realistic objectives. Subsequent meetings review and evaluate forecasts and plans in consideration of what has actually happened (deviations from forecasts and plans), current and expected changes in the market, and internal problems. Modification or adjustments may be necessary.

It may occur that the S&OP will not be precisely in tune with the forecasts. Marketing, for example, may have a program that anticipates a major increase in sales. In such cases, the forecasts (time phased) may be revised to be compatible with the S&OP. The original forecasts are not discarded as they play an important role in the revision process. The new and old forecasts are projected forward at each revision period to see if the demand plan is on-course.

S&OP also serves the purpose of insuring that unusual situations are properly addressed. Assume a sudden influx of orders above the capability of the company to service. A meeting of the S&OP team can address the situation and determine appropriate action. Can capacity be increased? If so, when? What promises can be made and kept? What is the impact upon customer service? How will the decision affect future business and the company's reputation? Equally, situations can arise with purchasing and manufacturing. A coordinated examination by the team leads to the best solution.

S&OP balances sales, manufacturing, inventory management, materials management, purchasing, and finance, thus precluding arbitrary or one-person decisions. It logically organizes the business and manages change effectively. And in its feedback mechanism S&OP measures performance in relation to plan. The entire scope of the business is conducted in an organized, coordinated manner.

A word about forecasting dollars at the aggregate level: it may be possible to derive dollars directly from the aggregate units forecasts in a way that is close enough for planning purposes. But if there are wide price variations between individual products, the forecasts may need to be disaggregated, perhaps by assigning percentages to each of the several items, then summing the individual amounts. When manufacturing is building detailed plans, it may be necessary to translate units to standard hours.

The process as described appears to be one that every manager in the company can embrace. But this is not necessarily so. Getting real cooperation and communication may be difficult. People work to their own agendas, which may not be aimed – although inadvertently – at the best overall interest of the company. Two words come to mind: parochialism and fiefdom. People tend to be caught up in their own activities, not understanding the way in which their functions interact with and affect other departments. It is not unknown that managers protect their own areas of responsibility as something personally owned. The solution is to impart a thorough understanding of S&OP and how it materially influences the well-being of the firm, how the cooperative effort is expected, and that team-work is the order of the day. Previously it was suggested that a high-ranking general level executive could logically be the chairperson. The advantage is that the other managers will be more apt to cooperate willingly. The disadvantage is that these managers will try to anticipate "what the big fellow wants" and react accordingly. Properly, the chairperson develops the agenda for meetings with the help of the managers and during the meetings moderates, listens, and guides. The best solution is education prior to implementing the process. S&OP does not mean relinquishing managerial responsibility; rather it is a cooperative process that benefits everyone.

A primary characteristic of business is change. A company reacts to the dynamics of the marketplace, the economy, and the competition. Because business is not static, a company must have a coordinated planning base, the capability to monitor progress, the ability to interpret results, and the skill to correct the course of the business. The planning base includes measuring the near- and mid-term future continually, both externally and internally, and developing tactics for success. To do these things effectively, it may be said that the right hand must know what the left hand is doing, but this is insufficient. The actions taken by a department need to be in concert with all other departments. Sales and operations planning fosters interdepartmental cooperation. Team members, from the departments mentioned previously, are assigned by name and are required to attend meetings. Delegation is not an option. The team is a decision-making body with those decisions reached, generally, through consensus, with subsequent approval from the high command for those decisions having significant financial implications.

In a coordinated and organized manner, S&OP allows the company to:

- ❖ React to changes in the marketplace.
- ❖ Adjust production to avoid excess inventory or backlog.
- ❖ Increase production to meet future sales opportunities.
- ❖ Change plans to adjust for changes in the product mix.
- ❖ Determine shortfalls in the business plan and take corrective actions.
- ❖ Insure that everyone in the boat paddles in the same direction.

The process begins with the operational forecasts, which are the basis for the demand and supply plans. The end result is one master plan for the company. Some companies may view S&OP as a reporting function, which is only partially true. It is a process of systematically evaluating the business considering the economy, the competition, the marketplace, and internal strengths and weaknesses. The business plan through S&OP formalizes and integrates all departmental activities. It is compatible with the strategic plan.

Another subject that demands our attention is the **supply chain.** Companies do not act in a vacuum. They rely upon customers and suppliers. Integrating the total supply chain into one coordinated effort can be a profitable endeavor for each of the partners. The supply chain goals are to increase profit and reduce cost across the chain. It works best when there is trust and partnership. It can fail when companies are unwilling to share information and refuse to fully coordinate their activities. The APICS dictionary defines the supply chain as:

> The global network used to deliver products and services from raw materials to end customers through an engineered flow of information, physical distribution, and cash.

Supply chain management implies a collaborative effort by all companies within a supply chain, say, from the companies that furnish raw materials to component manufacturers who then supply components to the end-item producer who in turns sells finished products to a retailer. It is a direct line, but one that is often fuzzy and complex in that at any level there can be many branches (companies) on the tree. Bills of material may be complex, more than one supplier may provide the same items, and a number of products may be involved. Coordinated forecasting is a fundamental part in the collaborative process and is discussed below. At its best, real-time data is funneled into the supplier network.

Supply chain management is both strategic and operational in nature. In the strategic sense, supply chain management includes the location and size of factories to facilitate service to the customer, allocation of production resources, and inventory policy associated with customer service (what buffers are needed where, for example). In the context of strategy, the assumption is a long-term, mutual commitment between supplier and customer. At the operational level, the process concerns the short-term, with the focus directed to the effective flow of product, which includes cost and timely delivery in its several ramifications. There are many computer generated models, some designed to integrate the entire supply chain with the objective of optimizing or minimizing cost and time. The purchase price associated with a complex, "totally" integrated system may only be feasible to larger corporations. Other operational type systems approach the supply chain as a multiple level inventory problem. They, too, may be complex and may not take account of the production or demand sides of the equation.

Smaller companies cannot ignore supply chain management and forecasting, however, because these are competitive necessities, nor can they operate without a computer network that joins together each link in the chain. Solving this dilemma involves research by the partnership as prelude to developing the best approach for the company and its network of suppliers. The major hurdle once everyone agrees to participate is finding common operating systems. It is likely that the systems internal to the companies will not be in sync with the systems of the other partners or appropriate to the new way of operating.

Supply chain management is partnership and commitment between all companies within the chain. Getting the employees of all companies to participate fully is a serious problem. Equally difficult is integrating the functions, both as pertains to changing the way employees work (changing the culture) and integrating the various companies' operating systems. Besides being very expensive to buy and successfully install, software packages may require changes to the internal operating systems of the companies. If the corporation insisting on the implementation is a mega-corporation cost may not be the problem if it understands the time and frustration elements. But it is not unheard of that suppliers will be scared at radical change they are not equipped to handle. One possible change is that the mega-corporation will want to shift much of its inventory to the suppliers, that is, increase buffers at the lower level, but see the next paragraph. Unless the mega-corporation commits to a supplier advantage, such as increasing its level of business, there can be much gnashing of teeth. Smaller supply chains (no mega or big, big companies) have a problem in finding ways to integrate while holding the expense within reason. At the beginning of the implementation process, there is much preliminary study to be done. For smaller companies, bypassing total integration for a middle ground may be the answer, that is, developing systems with in-house managerial and computer people or with computer savvy consultants that can be extended throughout the chain. If high quality, but not perfection, results, a better profit picture will surface.

Fully implemented, the supply chain system reduces cost and inventories and improves the service level because of the coordinated managerial and planning approach. What occurs is an on-time flow of goods throughout the chain, a smooth, predictable flow. Less uncertainty increases the good and decreases the bad.

In theory, a supply chain may be internal to a corporation, for instance, when there are a number of distribution centers, end item and component manufacturing facilities, and support systems within the corporation. The more expected case is a chain consisting of some internal and many external suppliers and customers. The highest level may be the end item manufacturer or importer, his customers, or the ultimate consumer.

How does forecasting enter the supply chain management picture?

In a supply chain, forecasting is a cooperative (collaborative) effort. The objective is to have one set of forecasts for all partners in the chain. Forecasts are estimates of the ultimate end items (the products of the top tier in the chain) and should be thought of as demand or operational forecasts. Thus, the chain operates under one umbrella with one driving forecast(s). In a supply chain, each link is dependent upon both the next higher and next lower links. With a forecast of the ultimate product, each lower level can determine its requirements through master planning, which includes production and resource planning and master scheduling. In a manufacturing environment, for example, the master plan consists of capacity, production, and material requirements planning (MRP), or upon a more "advanced" system than MRP. The forecast is the independent vehicle, the forerunner for planning, and the planning system is the dependent tool. The operational forecasts and orders, therefore, are the basis for master planning.

Feedback loops monitor performance throughout the supply chain. They answer questions such as: what is our customer service rate (percent of orders delivered on-time) and did our company meet its obligations to the next higher link? If there was a failure, the chain examines the situation to determine the cause with the objective of initiating corrective action. There are a number of reasons for failure: a breakdown in master planning at one or more levels, the forecast within the procurement/manufacturing lead time was understated, an unusual influx of orders at the highest level, transportation problems, etc. Of course, the opposite is possible, leading to a downturn in inventory turnover and the like.

Forecasts are dynamic, not static, under periodic review and revision. All partners are involved.

If each link forecasts independently (temping because each link may have customers not in the supply chain), forecast error within the chain accumulates at each of the lower levels. Whereas each level may have an error rate of, say, five percent, forecasting in isolation creates an error rate equal to the error sum of each independently prepared forecast. Cooperative forecasting results in one forecast for the entire chain. Lower links use that forecast(s) as input to their master planning system. Of course, this does not preclude other forecasts for customers not in the supply chain.

Cooperative forecasting helps to dispel uncertainty. In one way or another, each link participates in the process, with an end result being a forecast signed onto by the partners. Forecasting at its best is not simply statistical. It incorporates market research: information obtained from the sales force, customers, and trade associations, for instance. If there are a number of large company customers globally or spread throughout the United States, their input is critical. They know their customers best. But see the caveats at the end of this chapter.

In a complex environment, one in which there are a large number of items, stocking levels for each link can be established using an ABC categorization and safety stock levels based upon standard deviation. "A" items receive the most attention, the most investment in inventory. Categorization can be based on one of a number of factors such as most profitable, highest volume sellers, or how rapidly shortages can be replenished. The service level for "A" items, for example could be set at 95% or 98%, considering the financial and customer service ramifications. Most important: inventory levels are not established independently of the other partners. They are established across the chain. The generally accepted 80/20 rule may be applicable in designing a forecasting model. The rule states that 20% of the items will produce 80% of the business. Because of their high volume, modeling can be effective. With the remaining, modeling is more difficult but can be accomplished, see Chapter 6. In this scenario, the 20% are the "A" items. A best way to minimize buffer stock is through the implementation of just-in-time procedures, discussed later, throughout the supply chain. Buffer stock in this context refers to work-in-process and safety stock.

Before presenting several illustrative examples, one additional forecasting method is appropriate to define: **simulation forecasting**. In simulation forecasting several (or more) forecasts are prepared using different models with each forecast independently derived, then the most effective model is selected and it becomes the estimate. The process begins anew at each forecasting period, usually each month.

The forecasting techniques that comprise the simulation may be any that are described in this book. In some cases, the use of a number of simple techniques may be sufficient, such as comparing the next several months to a comparable period last year or the past several months with the next several months. Unless sales are relatively stable or easily predictable, simple techniques, if applicable at all, should be supplemented with appropriate methods as described herein. If they exist, seasonal, cyclical, and trend factors are considered in the design of the model. Design of a simulation system is individualistic; unlike men's socks one size does not fit all. The model selected for the current forecast period does not apply to the next forecast period. The computer again projects sales and selects the most accurate method. Usually, the method works best in companies that have a large number of end items with large sales of the individual end items. Originally, the method was developed by Bernard T. Smith of American Hardware and given the name "Focus Forecasting."

Holding the last several periods of known sales aside tests the effectiveness of the various estimates. Projections are prepared of the known past excluding the set aside periods. The estimates of the set asides are compared with the actual data of the set aside periods to determine which estimate is the most accurate. That one becomes the model for that forecasting period. The methods described previously can be used to determine accuracy and reliability. Alternately, the technique with the least difference between the set aside quantity and the forecast quantity may be sufficient for selecting the forecasting method.

A clarifying word about two forecasting methodologies. Combined forecasting was explained in Chapter 10. It is forecasting the same data using different models and then averaging the forecasts. Simulation forecasting forecasts with different (simple) techniques then selects the most accurate model to project the future based upon that technique which has the least difference between actual and forecast for the set aside period (say, the past three months).

The **first example** is a company that imports a number of end items, primarily from China. It inspects and packages the goods for sale. Its customers are two large catalog companies (65% of sales), a retail chain (20% of sales), and various other retailers. The items sold are identical except that the packaging for the three largest customers is unique to each. A different (but the same) packaging is used for all other customers. The company designs the products and contracts with its overseas suppliers. Annual revenue is roughly $20,000,000. (The procedures following are equally applicable to larger and smaller companies.) Its executive team consists of the president, the financial vice president, the operations manager who is responsible for purchasing, packaging, inventory, shipping etc., and the sales manager who is charged with sales, customer service, and merchandising. Additionally, there are three managers who report to executive managers. Operational forecasting was previously the sales manager's responsibility. Sales estimates at that time were based upon those provided by the major customers plus a judgment call for all others. The catalog companies' forecasts were given as "courtesy copies". Orders to the company were placed on an as-needed basis. Company booking forecasts were derived from the courtesy copy forecast, and stock was maintained to satisfy the bookings forecast, with safety stock to meet bulk orders from the major customers. Then, the company waited for orders.

Although sales to consumers occur year around, catalog house sales are highly seasonal with peak months May and June for the summer catalogs and October through December for the winter catalogs. Retail store sales are also seasonal but to a lesser degree.

About two years ago the company recognized that there were several problems: the forecasts were inadequate for planning, requiring a large investment in inventory to insure on-time delivery to major customers, orders from the major customers were given with a short fuse and because products were bulk ordered demands were larger than forecast in some periods while in other periods there were zero orders, which were factors that contributed to the large buffer stock, and the real possibility that the major customers would buy product in total or in part from other suppliers. The company's products are not unique although they are different in some details from those of the competition. Customers expect service, especially on-time shipment of orders, indicating that large supplier inventories are expected. At that time, the catalog houses stocked the goods and shipped to their customers (consumers) from their distribution points.

Management realized that inventory affected cash flow, profit, and return on investment adversely, especially when goods had to be carried over to the next peak season. If forecasts could be more representative of actuality, it would significantly benefit the company. Management's first thought was to adopt a procedure for adjusting customer estimates by determining the "average" historical difference between the forecast and actual, thus requiring a smaller buffer. However, that idea did not work because actual sales were either less or more than the projections. A pattern could not be determined.

Next, the company toyed with the idea of making its own forecasts of consumer sales using one of the more common techniques. This notion was abandoned, as it seemed to be a procedure for outguessing the customer, a slippery slope. Another consideration was that no one in the company was really knowledgeable of forecasting methodology. The major customers had dedicated forecasting staffs that, obviously, were more knowledgeable. Sales levels were also affected by the state of the economy, which was another consideration for not forecasting on its own.

The lead-time from China contributed to the inventory problem. Normally, lead-time was sixty days: thirty days for manufacture and thirty days shipping time (rounded to two months). Large orders placed with suppliers, however, could take longer, and, under the current system, large orders are common because of the seasonality of the products. This condition also required that orders to the offshore supplier be placed well in advance of ship date. Additionally, shipping could take longer if the ports backlogged or there was a delay at Customs.

There was a real danger of losing a major customer's business. Another supplier might "buy the business," that is, sell initially at an unreasonably low price. The major customers could also shop the market for a lower price. Company management was continually stressing service to its customers and, in fact, had an outstanding order delivery record because of its large buffer stock. However, that factor alone might not be sufficient to prevent a customer from shopping the market. Of course, the company could lower its price in a competitive bidding war, but that would be destructive to profit.

Because the company was not in charge of its own destiny, the president decided that a new business approach was needed, one that would "lock in" its major customers and allow lesser inventory without affecting customer service. Each executive and manager was tasked with researching the literature for ideas. The management team met monthly to discuss each manager's findings. Initially, the meetings were in competitive mode, each manager touting his research. Also, the managers were not sure what systems might be applicable, thus a bit of confusion existed. With guidance from the president, meetings evolved into a cooperative effort where the objectives were defined and study directed specifically to solving the stated problems. Professional organizations were also helpful with information that directed the research to the inventory problems. Without knowing it, the company had taken the first step to sales and operations planning.

Finally, consensus was reached. Sales and operational planning and adoption of a supply chain approach would substantially reduce the problems. However, there were two concerns: the company management team is minimal (but adequate for company size) and the supply chain rationale would have to be sold to its major customers. As significant was the fact that each customer would have a different approach to supply chain management, resulting in several computer systems, rather than one, with a sizeable capital outlay.

Initially, the managers believed that they were already coordinating and cooperating sufficiently (no one wanted someone else looking over his shoulder). Discussion led to agreement that with one integrated reporting format there would be integrated management; that is, supply and demand plans coupled with financial plans could be readily appraised and appropriate actions taken. The adopted format is depicted in Figure 13-1. The planning report was not designed until after the supply chain system was implemented. It replaced some but not all of the other company reports.

The concept and implementation of supply chain management was a difficult sell, but the company had a scenario that was eventually agreed to by each major customer. The supply chain top level (tier-one) is the catalog houses and the retail chain. Each is the top level of a separate chain. Tier-two is the company, tier-three the overseas manufacturers, tier-four the suppliers to the manufacturers. Rather than developing common computer systems to be used throughout the chain, it was agreed that each would retain its own system (modified internally, if advantageous to that tier). The tier-one forecasts were the controlling documents. With the shift in inventory as discussed below there was actually an advantage at each of the first three tiers. This supply chain system is a substantial modification to the norm. The chain itself is relatively simple, thus, does not require a complex solution. A closer connection and better communication between tiers-one and -two and between tier-two and -three came about, which helped to cement relationships, a major benefit.

Forecasting was a difficult problem. The partnership role was first agreed upon before forecasting was discussed. In the end, tier-one catalog houses consented to participation by the company in the forecasting process for their products only, but in an advisory role. The company had decided to hire an additional manager knowledgeable of forecasting methodology and inventory management. Advantages accrued to the company: the manager had input (cautiously) to the major customers' forecasting processes and could gage their thinking, especially as regards changes to the level of the forecasts as occurs when the number of catalogs distributed increases, for example. Several monthly forecasts later, the new manager developed a model for measuring accuracy and tracking the effectiveness of the estimates (see Chapter 5). Then, a forecast range was calculated for each of the products. All these things together allowed the company to effectively track forecasts and aided in calculating realistic safety stock levels at tiers-two and -three. But the biggest gain in forecasting as it pertains to safety stock and inventory control resulted from the new inventory policy explained below.

The company's sales manager had always kept in contact with the catalog houses' buying executives. These contacts were the typical customer/supplier relationships. With the new agreement a subtle difference materialized, a more friendly association, individuals working together to achieve a common goal. Typical questions are: working together, how can we make the partnership better and what can we do to better meet requirements?

In the process of developing the partnership the company initiated a "new" inventory policy that eliminated the requirement for the tier-one catalog houses to maintain an inventory of the items that it purchased from the company. The company agreed that it would not only maintain an inventory of those items but would drop ship to all of the tier-one customers (individual consumers). The catalog houses agreed to a reasonable remuneration for providing this service, which covered the additional cost of handling and shipping. The catalog houses were relieved of the cost of maintaining inventory and shipping, a significant saving. At first blush this procedure appears to be expensive for the company because inventory would be transferred from the catalog houses to the company. But this is not the case.

Together, several factors contributed to inventory reduction. Accepting responsibility for shipping to the consumers puts control in the company's hands. Goods are ordered closer to the time that they are needed because one link in the chain is eliminated, which also reduces safety stock: the company knows when the goods need to be shipped and in what quantities based on the forecast. Previously, the company waited for bulk orders from the catalog houses. Although the company's stock was predicated on the forecast, a large buffer was required to insure availability when bulk orders arrived. Now, there is flexibility because there is a more constant flow of goods from the tier-three suppliers, thus smaller shipments arriving more frequently. The tier-one partner accepts the fact that there could be a reasonable delay in shipping to a small number of consumers if a forecast is significantly in error during a shipping period. This is a seldom occurrence because forecasts are reasonable as modified by the company, there is a two week shipping window, and goods arrive continually. Tier-three partners are also obligated to maintain a one-half month forward inventory in addition to producing goods to fulfill the shipping schedule provided by the company. The quantity in a forward inventory is based upon anticipated consumer sales in a period one and one-half months in the future, which is inventory plus in-transit time.

Because the company ships to the catalog houses' customers, the forecasts changed from bookings to demand by delivery date projections.

The company develops bookings and demand by delivery date forecasts for their retail customers. Bookings and delivery dates for the catalog houses are the same dates because orders received are for immediate shipment.

Catalog house consumer orders are transmitted computer to computer from the tier-one partners and shipping data is returned using the same program. The program also prints shipping labels. When shipments are scanned by the bar code on the labels, a shipping report that indicates the number and percentage of orders shipped within the two-week window and the number and percentage shipped late is printed as a running total for the month. The report also ages the few late orders.

The tier-three companies benefit because the relationship with the example company (tier-two) is solidified. The price of goods is set after mutual examination of cost of manufacturing and purchasing from the tier-four suppliers. It is a relationship of mutual trust that also applies to the tier-one houses.

Another outcome of the partnership is an agreement between the tier-one and tier-two companies to develop and market new products. The tier-three company is brought into the process when development of a new product is in the design stage.

For simplicity of explanation, the Sales and Operations Report following considers only the catalog houses. The report may be looked at as one product of several sold by the company. In practice, all customers would be included in the forecast section of the report, the major catalog and retail customers, each separately, and all other customers as one line

The time is December end. Calculations begin in January and continue through the following January. Forecasts are made for each of the next twelve months. They are revised each month for the next twelve months with the thirteenth month (in this case January) assumed to be the same as the first month, although the thirteenth month could be a continuation as predicted by the forecasting model with forecasts updated monthly. This is a running forecast.

Two entries are made manually: the forecasts and the purchase orders, as quantity ordered, see Figure 13-1a.

Remaining stock is beginning inventory. As orders are shipped, the system updates stock on-hand (remaining stock), thus it is a running total. The beginning inventory for purposes of calculation is the quantity available at the opening of business on the first of the month. Remaining stock = last month's remaining stock − this month's forecast + dues-in. For January: 350 - 120 + 0 = 230. For February: 230 − 125 + 0 = 105. These calculations are the on-hand quantities including safety stock.

Dues-in are the purchase quantities offset by lead-time. For example, a purchase placed the first working day of January will appear as a due-in in the March bucket because lead-time is two months, thus arrival is expected at the beginning of March. Orders are transmitted computer to computer on the first working day of the month.

Sales and Operations Report

Month	Forecast, Cust 1	Forecast, Cust 2	Total Forecast	Remaining Stock	Due-in	Order Quantity	Purchase Orders	Safety Tier-2	Safety Tier-3
Dec				350					
Jan	70	50	120	230	0	170.0	0	60.0	187.5
Feb	65	60	125	105	0	42.5	0	62.5	195.0
Mar	60	70	130	-25	0	-90.0	0	65.0	232.5
Apr	80	75	155	-180	0	-257.5	0	77.5	607.5
May	225	180	405	-585	0	-787.5	0	202.5	810.0
Jun	290	250	540	-1125	0	-1395.0	0	270.0	315.0
Jul	120	90	210	-1335	0	-1440.0	0	105.0	172.5
Aug	60	55	115	-1450	0	-1507.5	0	57.5	172.5
Sep	60	55	115	-1565	0	-1622.5	0	57.5	450.0
Oct	200	100	300	-1865	0	-2015.0	0	150.0	660.0
Nov	250	190	440	-2305	0	-2526.0	0	220.0	690.0
Dec	260	200	460	-2765	0	-2995.0	0	230.0	180.0
Jan			120	-2885	0	-2945.0	0	60.0	
Total	1740	1375	3235						

Figure 13-1a

Order quantity is the trigger for determining when to order and the quantity to order. It is (last month's remaining stock plus dues-in) minus (this month's forecast plus company safety stock). For January it is: (350 + 0) – (120+ 60) = 170. For February it is: (230 + 0) – (125 + 62.5) = 42.5. For the months of January and February the position is positive indicating that in-house inventory is sufficient to cover orders. March is a negative 90 meaning that there will not be enough goods to ship forecasted orders and retain the safety stock level. If orders equal forecast there is a shortage of twenty-five units in remaining stock. For March, the difference between –25 and –90 is the safety stock level. Note that the numbers in the columns show partial units, which is impossible. Normally, the system rounds to the nearest whole number. Here, it is retained to simplify the math for the reader.

The purchase order column specifies the amount on order and the time when ordered. In our example, orders are transmitted the first workday of the month.

Tier-two safety stock is the amount to be available that month to satisfy orders should they exceed the forecast or if a shipment from the tier-three supplier is late. In our example company, it is set at 0.5 months of forecast based upon historical data. For January it is: 120 x 0.5 = 60. Forecast accuracy is calculated monthly for each forecast to determine if (over time) modification should be made to the safety stock level.

The tier-three safety level is established at 1.5 months, which includes shipping time. The safety stock available January is the amount that can be shipped above the order quantity. It is safety for February available at the beginning of January. Thus, it is 125 x 1.5 = 187.5.

Note that the total estimate for the thirteen months is 3235 units. The shortage is 2885 units, which is 3235 minus the beginning inventory. The difference between 2945 and 2885 is safety stock.

The format is expandable and logically can incorporate purchase dollars and selling dollars by multiplying quantity by the unit cost of purchases and quantity by the unit price of sales. Sales dollars may be offset for aging, that is, the average time delay between invoice and receipt of payment from the customers. In like manner, purchases may be offset. Further expansion of the financial data is practical. Summary information is also a part of the report, for instance, data summed by customer, product family, and total for all products. Purchase order numbers are usefully included. An important addition is an orders received line for comparing forecast with orders. If the order quantities are different from forecast by a significant amount, the report can use the order amounts in lieu of forecast. Depending upon the situation, orders may be considered as orders booked by delivery date or alternately orders shipped.

Figure 13-1b illustrates the modifications that occur when purchases are made.

Sales and Operations Report

Month	Total Forecast	Stock	Due-in	Order Quantity	Purchase Orders	Stock	Due-in	Order Quantity	Purchase Orders
Dec		350				350			
Jan	120	230		170.0	90	230		170.0	90
Feb	125	105		42.5		105		42.5	170
Mar	130	65	90	0		65	90	0	530
Apr	155	-90		-167.5		80	170	2.5	610
May	405	-495		-697.5		205	530	2.5	
Jun	540	-1035		-1305.0		275	610	5.0	
Jul	210	-1245		-1350.0		65		-40.0	
Aug	115	-1360		-1417.5		-50		-107.5	
Sep	115	-1475		-1532.5		-165		-222.5	
Oct	300	-1775		-1925.0		-465		-615.0	
Nov	440	-2215		-2435.0		-905		-1125.0	
Dec	460	-2675		-2905.0		-1365		-1595.0	
Jan	120	-2795		-2855.0		-1485		-1545.0	

Figure 13-1b

Compare the numbers in Figure 13-1a with those in Figure 13-1b to see the affect that purchase orders have on the remaining stock and order quantity columns. The first shortage occurs in March. There is a net shortage of twenty-five units if the forecast is exactly on-track. With in-house safety stock, the shortage is ninety units (safety for March is 65). If ninety units are ordered in January (left side of Figure 13-1b), the March order quantity position is zero, that is, there is sufficient stock to deliver orders while maintaining the integrity of the safety stock. Note that the stock position equals safety stock in our example (when adjusted to whole units). In actuality, this will seldom occur. Remember that a positive number in the order quantity column indicates an excess amount. The next shortage is in April, as may be expected. The order shortage is 90 units and with safety 167.5 units.

It is still January. Referring to the right side of Figure 13-1b, four purchase orders are entered. Compare the stock positions with safety stock for April through June. Except for the slight differences in purchase order amounts, stock equals safety.

In January, four purchase orders are transmitted to the tier-three supplier to allow him to plan his production. In addition to the purchase order quantities, he is obligated to maintain the tier-three safety stock. By convention, four unfilled purchase orders are in the hands of the tier-three supplier at any one time. When one is filled, another is submitted. It is equally logical to stay three purchase orders ahead, if that is adequate. Under this procedure, the tier-three supplier ships monthly, which helps to control the inventory level. Probably, the least transportation cost (and least cost in comparison with inventory carrying cost) will be to ship in container lots, which with a number of different items being shipped each month should not be a problem.

Both the forecasted quantities and safety stock levels for the tier-three supplier fluctuate significantly month-to-month because of the seasonal nature of the item. The tier-three supplier may wish to smooth (level) his production to account for this condition.

Safety time can be added to the equation, either in place of or in addition to safety stock. Safety time allows for slippage when shipments are late, occasional transportation time increases, etc. It functions in much the same manner as safety stock. Another use for safety (lead) time is to guard against fluctuations in lead-time so that an order can be completed prior to its need date. It is especially applicable in manufacturing in conjunction with material requirements planning (MRP) and like systems. MRP is defined in the next example.

The company in adopting the S&OP and supply chain philosophies was able to realize important business advantages, not only to itself but also to all members of the partnership. Because of the company's relatively small size, its adaptation is a modified version. By adopting these approaches, however, the recognized need for change became a straight arrow line. Larger companies benefit equally by adopting these procedures.

The **second example** concerns an established supply chain: established with the proviso that a supply chain is always a work in progress. The partnership cooperates in finding better solutions not only to problems but also by examining methodologies that can be adopted across the chain. Partnership at its best is an evolutionary process. It should be noted that partnership implies cooperation, a collaborated effort. When that cooperation includes the internal workings of the suppliers -- the giving-up of sovereignty -- it becomes a difficult sell. However, that's when the partnership works best. Long time trust build-up is the key.

The tier-one manufacturer is a medium size company that produces a number of end items. Competitors sell similar products, most of which are interchangeable with the company's products. The key to success is customer service and cost control, major reasons for establishing a supply chain. But the partnership effort does not stop there. A task group consisting of members from each company studies various business methodologies that can be applied internally as well as across the chain, with the objectives of profit enhancement and increased productivity.

The chain consists of tier-two and tier-three suppliers and in a few cases tier-four vendors.Usually, those below tier-three are vendors whose parts are available on call. Tier-one is an assembly operation and tiers two and three supply major components and milled parts.

One of the early considerations of the tier-one company was the reliability of its primary suppliers, not only the tier-two suppliers but also reliability down the line. For instance, if a tier-three vendor failed to provide parts on time the whole chain could unravel. In initiating the supply chain, the predictability of the suppliers was an issue resolved by mutually examining problem areas and arriving at interim solutions such as creating inventories at each level sufficient to overcome delivery problems. This solution was recognized as unsatisfactory because inventories were too high. With the establishment of a cooperative forecasting system that included modules for measuring accuracy and tracking forecasts, safety levels (or safety time) were developed that minimized inventory at each level yet provided an almost perfect delivery performance.

Early in the process of establishing the supply chain, the partners decided that a **Just-in-Time** philosophy and system would enhance service, productivity, and profit and substantially lower inventory while producing product closer to the time of need. A team consisting of members from each partner was appointed. They were charged with developing procedures both internal to each partner and across the partnership spectrum. JIT encompasses all manufacturing processes required for producing a final product. The idea is to minimize inventory at each work center in each company by having the required product through the factory and ready at just the time needed with minimum through-put time in each production cell, to improve quality to zero defects, and to reduce lead times throughout the network. Reduction of set-up times and lot sizes (to the minimum possible) are integral to the practice. Kanban and other pull systems are examples of ways in which flow-through can be increased. Results properly implemented are dramatically reduced buffer stocks, lower cost because of more efficient operations, and greater service without manufacturing disruption. Items move between companies in small, frequently shipped lots. Overall, it is a process of network optimization. Of course, forecasts accurate to a high level are essential, but measuring forecast error and adjusting the short term as needed deal with the shortcomings in the estimates. If demand is substantially different than estimate, JIT allows for that contingency. Short production runs lend themselves to quick adjustment. JIT is practiced as one integrated entity in the supply chain; sovereignty is shared. This can be a problem, of course. Companies are reluctant – reasonably so – to share information concerning their internal processes and procedures. If the companies function as a supply chain for some items but compete in others a further dilemma exists. In this case, trust prevailed and sharing to a rational level was experienced. Brainstorming and then trying a well-formed idea on an experimental basis helped to cement the relationship.

The participants realized that there were two phases in the process: in each company internally bringing about JIT and integrating it throughout the supply chain. But because of trust the two phases were combined. It was also understood, that JIT was a continuing process that would never be finished.

Initially, independent research was undertaken so that each team member would gain an understanding of the fundamentals. At meetings each briefed the others on his/her findings and understanding of the ways in which JIT could benefit each in the chain. Although there was redundancy (as expected), the presentations increased perspective. (It would also be feasible to bring in an outside consultant.)

The team recognized the following requirements:

❖ Manufacture to meet customer (next higher level) demand, produce no more or no less than demand, and deliver neither early nor late in the exact quantities required. The forecasts are basic instruments in that they are the demands unless there is a real difference between actual demand and projection. Forecasts also set manufacturing capacity within the forecast range.

❖ Although the short-term forecasts provide the primary production planning instruments, the companies need the ability to quickly shift production to fulfill unexpected demands, and to do so without undue disruption.

❖ Develop flexible manufacturing through small lot sizes and the ability for quick changeover, all within a framework of balanced workflow. This capability entails a probable reorganization of work center and assembly operations.

❖ Shorten lead times throughout the chain, which radically reduces buffer inventory (queue). Back-up inventory at workstations, for example, lengthens lead-time because all that work is in need of production. When work can be handed off to the next station without cumbersome inventory pile-up it exposes problems, which then can be solved. It causes quick flow-through of the right items.

Because each partner had the will and the ability to succeed, partnership was defined as a state in which all partners participated in near equality. (Of course, the tier-one company was a bit more equal than the others.) This definition applies to both the supply chain and JIT endeavors.

Early on, a statement of purpose was formulated: provide quality products at a fair and equitable price while emphasizing customer service and on-time delivery. Work together to improve efficiency throughout the network, solve mutual problems, and improve profitability at each level.

Initially, purchasing and financial transactions were automated to include purchase orders, invoices, payments, shipping intentions and actual shipments, and the like. These actions alone saved considerable time and money and resulted in more accurate data. Later, purchase orders were discontinued except for first raw material purchases when forecasts became the driving force.

With the forecasts as the first component, the next step was to develop an integrated master production scheduling (MPS) and material requirements planning (MRP) system to time phase manufacture at each tier level. The end item forecast team provides input to the process and consists of representatives from each partner. Collaborated forecasting allows each level to bring its expertise to the table, which includes marketing and customer intelligence and the impact that promotions or other marketing strategies have upon the forecasts. The final demand forecasts, however, are the responsibility of the tier-one company. These projections synchronize the production and inventory planning of each partner. Each operates from a single set of estimates that constitutes the anticipated levels of demand for the end items. With the addition of MRP, there is one master plan for the chain. Deviations from the estimates are covered by safety stock, which is established based upon measures of accuracy and reliability. If errors exceed the established parameter, the partners address the problem. With the initiation of JIT, safety stock is minimized.

One objective is to develop automated data architecture that allows management by exception. Soon after initiating the first step in supply chain management it was recognized that data accuracy would be a problem. Partners believed that their data were accurate. Reluctantly, they examined their records and found that improvements were necessary. A lack of accuracy at one level affects all levels. A 95% accuracy rate was recognized as the minimum acceptable, with 98% the target. Some examples of critical data areas are bills of material, inventory balances of both end items and materials and parts, unfilled purchase orders and open shop orders, lead times, routings, and engineering change orders.

Benefits from the supply chain system are many: fewer errors (data integrity improved), reduction in the cost of data entry (time spent on data entry and the management of data), inventory reduction (everyone operating from the same demand forecasts and master plan), and improved customer service at each level (actions are integrated). Overall, there is a reduction in cost and an increase in profit at each tier, and each company reaps the benefits of close collaboration.

The tier-one master production schedule kicks off the process (but see below). It is the anticipated build schedule developed by the master scheduler. It is the plan of manufacture time phased specifically by item and quantity. It drives MRP. Per se, the master schedule is not the forecast. Although the forecast is integral to the MPS, capacity, backlog, inventory, raw material availability and other factors must be considered. Master scheduling is normally considered an internal function of individual companies, however, in our example supply chain, this is modified.

Before embarking on our example a few definitions are helpful. Closed loop MRP consists of a series of planning and execution functions with feedback from execution to the planning modules. In sequence, the accepted parts are sales and operations planning (production planning), master production scheduling, capacity requirements planning (including input-output control), and supplier scheduling. The production plan (S&OP) is the level of manufacture in aggregate planned. It is in agreement with the business plan. The production plan is converted into the detailed MPS. Explanation of this total planning function is beyond the scope of this book, therefore, we will concentrate on forecasting, MPS and MRP.

In the beginning the tier-one company prepares an S&OP and a business plan. Forecasts are the drivers in the process. At the S&OP level forecasts are aggregated by product family. Once the S&OP is approved, the individual end item forecasts become the raw material for developing the MPS. It would be good if the end item forecasts could be used directly as the MPS. However, an MPS must take into account the availability of capacity and materials and the flow of work through the factory. A major objective is to schedule lots to flow at a level rate or a rate as level as possible with minimum change over-time, but simultaneously to adopt JIT to the process; that is to optimize production cost as it pertains to scheduling. These two parts of the objective appear to be in conflict, but that will be resolved as the process is implemented. The tier-one master scheduler arranges to fulfill the forecasts by effectively using factory resources to manufacture the right products so that they will be available for sale when needed. There cannot be past due items because this will create past due material requirements and generally foul-up the factory. One objective of the MPS is to eliminate shortage lists and expediting as the scheduling method. If plant production cannot be leveled in a way that produces goods on time, the master schedule is revised. If that is not possible, the company must reevaluate its forecasts: reality beckons. To work with back pocket scheduling will adversely affect profit, customer service (taking orders that cannot be made by the delivery date or delivering late), and will increase materials inventory (bringing in parts per MRP although the end items cannot be produced until later). The forecasts are continuously monitored to insure that the master schedules remain real, that sales are happening as forecasted. If not, the forecasts are revised, thus requiring revised master schedules. If a part turns out to be scrap and there is not another available, the master schedule is revised unless the materials manager can find a replacement for the scraped item. With the implementation of JIT, many of the potential problems will be nullified. At the tier-two and tier-three levels, MRP indicates what is needed and when it is needed. The master scheduler follows MRP as if it were an MPS, modified only to account for special conditions in the factories.

Sales are compared to forecast. Any substantial deviations are a matter to be resolved. If, for instance, end item sales exceed forecast in a period, does this require a forecast change? Perhaps it does if this is considered a new sales level. Perhaps not if sales can be expected to return to the forecast level. If a booking cannot be filled by the requested delivery date, a new promise date is given to (or negotiated with) the customer. An alternative is to prioritize production in the short term to fulfill a specific order. If, however, prioritizing or expediting becomes the norm or a common practice, something is basically wrong, and that shortcoming may point all the way back to the forecasts. The companies are careful not to disrupt the JIT process in any short-term scheduling alterations.

Forecasts are generated for a twelve-month period. When one month is completed, a new month is added to the forecasts. The MPS is expressed in weekly time buckets with the first four weeks firm. The master scheduler can make changes beyond this time fence. Within the time fence, the vice presidents of marketing and manufacturing must approve the changes. Investigation is accomplished through the S&OP team. The factors of customer service and disruption to the production facility are considered and the additional cost – calculated in approximation by formula – is estimated. Equally important is the affect that the change will have on tier-two and tier-three companies. With manufacturing and marketing marching to different drummers, it was a major effort to get them to see the situation from each other's perspective, but it happened. Changes within the time fence are rare because of the cooperation between marketing and manufacturing. Without going into detail, the initiation of MPS/MRP in the supply chain caused many problems to surface where they could be examined and solved.

The MPS at the tier-one company is a control document. It is the schedule of the end items to be produced and is the primary input to MRP. One question in the mind of the master scheduler is: does the MPS support the forecast for that item? Another question is: is the MPS realistic and doable? The MPS for each end item is exploded through the appropriate bill of material to produce the material requirements plan. MRP time phases the parts, materials, and components needed after subtracting inventory. For our example supply chain, the MRP includes the items to be provided by the lower level tiers. The relationship is illustrated below.

At the lower levels, the MRP from the tier-one company is the master schedule (almost). It states what is needed and when it is needed by the next higher level and is net of inventory. The master scheduler at these levels may not produce exactly to the MRP. Efficiency in manufacture – the JIT process in its beginning phase -- is considered, but on-time delivery is paramount. In forming the supply chain, the capacities and capabilities of each tier level were considered. Where it was determined that there could be capacity shortfalls, capacity changes were made.   Note that in a supply chain all companies are interdependent, somewhat as if they are one company, a binding relationship.

Safety stock or time is part of the system, which is established based upon the historical comparison between actual sales and forecasted sales (see Chapter 5).

Figures 13-2a, b, and c are an illustration of the master production schedule with the additions of forecast, inventory, demand, and available to sell. The schedule is in abbreviated form for illustration. Normally, schedules cover several months. Analysis of these charts allows the master scheduler to evaluate the situation for the purpose of revising the master schedule to fulfill demand and forecast needs and to guide the sales department regarding shipping promise dates. Not always will the scheduler be able to revise the master schedule to meet all estimated needs. However, the charts indicate if there is a need for action or change.

The master schedule is the weekly plan of manufacture. A separate schedule is prepared for each end item. Because forecasts are generated by month, the scheduler subdivided the forecast into weekly time buckets.

Master Production Schedule

End Item 100

Week	0	1	2	3	4	5	6	7	8
Forecast		300	300	300	300	350	350	350	350
Master Schedule		250	250	180	260	280	400	400	400
Demand				400	1000				
Ending Inventory	250	500	750	530	-210	70	470	870	1270

Unsold inventory = 350 units; safety stock = 100 units

Figure 13-2a

In Figure 13-2a, the forecast is entered because of its importance. The overall objective is to produce the number of end items demanded by the forecast or by sales if sales are larger than forecast. An eyeball comparison between forecast, demand, and the production schedule is thus available to the master scheduler.

The master schedule (MPS) is the plan of manufacture – the production schedule – prepared by the master scheduler.

Demand is actual sales entered by required ship date. The demand for the first month is 1400 units and the forecast is 1200 units.

Ending inventory is the quantity of that item in stock at the end of the week, less safety. The ending inventory becomes the beginning inventory for the following week. Week 0 shows an inventory of 250.

This is the total inventory of 350 less the safety stock of 100. It is also the beginning inventory for week 1.

The calculation for determining ending inventory is: beginning inventory plus production minus demand. For week 1 it is 250 + 250 – 0 = 500; for week 3 it is 750 + 180 – 400 = 530.

What do the entries portray?

The master schedule calls for production slightly less than that required by the forecast for the first month (the first four weeks): forecast is 1200 units and production plus beginning inventory is 1190. On its face this looks reasonable, but actual demand also enters the picture. Sales are 1400 units for the month, 200 units more than forecast. All 1400 units are due by month end, however, 110 units will be one week late (210 less safety if used). Had the scheduler increased production in the first four weeks, on-time delivery could have been met. Orders for other items that use the same capacity are also in the system and this compromise was determined to be the best solution. One week past due was cleared with the customer who would be affected. Was there a better solution? By looking at the available to promise report, Sales can see when a manufacturing time bucket is filled and with customer cooperation space orders so that there is no over-commitment in a given time period.

In this case, the scheduler increased the production level for this item in week 6. At the end of week 8 the unsold inventory will be 1270 units, however, orders constantly flow-in. Safety stock of 100 is also replenished. Note that the forecast for the second month is 1400 units (350 x 4). The unsold inventory of 1270 units (to be manufactured) is 130 units short if the forecast is correct (1270 – 1400). What options are available to the scheduler? Possibly, the master schedule could be increased. The feasibility of doing so depends upon the other items that share the capacity: is there open capacity or can Sales change the delivery dates for other items? Orders could be promised for a later date if capacity cannot be altered. The best solution, however, is not to take orders for periods in which there is not adequate open capacity available. Abiding by the available to promise (open dates) solves the problem before it begins.

The forecast was not changed to reflect that sales for the month are 200 units above forecast. Variation from forecast is not an unusual occurrence even in the short run. Note the inventory build-up in the first few weeks, necessary to be able to deliver on time. Perhaps, some customers will allow their orders to be shipped a week or two early. Perhaps some orders could have been booked for earlier delivery at the time that the orders were taken, thus reducing inventory. If overbooking is a common practice and expediting is the adopted solution, manufacturing is disrupted, efficiency slides, and JIT is seriously affected.

Forecast vs. Schedule

Week	0	1	2	3	4	5	6	7	8
Forecast		300	600	900	1200	1550	1900	2250	2600
Schedule	250	500	750	930	1190	1470	1870	2270	2670
Net Position		200	150	30	-10	-80	-30	20	70

Safety = 100 units

Figure 13-2b

Figure 13-2b compares the master schedule with the forecast. Note that both the forecast and master schedule are cumulative. The scheduler intends to produce 2670 units (includes 250 beginning inventory) against a forecast of 2600 units. The production requirement equals forecast plus safety (remember safety was used), which is 2700 units. Additionally, during the negative periods the factory will be under producing the amounts needed to meet the forecast. The scheduler will examine the plan and actual sales to date for the second month with the objective of adding production during weeks 5 and 6, if needed. From experience and in consultation with the sales department, the scheduler concludes that the forecast for the first eight weeks is correct even considering that demand was higher than forecast the first four weeks. Whatever actions appear to be appropriate for this item, the requirements for all items using this capacity are evaluated. The capacity plan (not shown) identifies the total amount of capacity available each week for each manufacturing cell or work center and cumulatively at the MPS level, likely expressed in standard hours. Production units would therefore be translated into standard hours in the capacity plan and shortcomings in the MPS would be recognized.

The above explanation assumes that there is a high degree of reliability in manufacturing to adhere to the schedule and that orders generally average forecast. If conditions were different, if there was factory slippage, for example, the master scheduler would consider that situation.

A demand vs. schedule chart in cumulative form can be prepared. The available balance line would be the same as in the MPS.

Figure 13-2c illustrates the time buckets and quantities in which planned production has not been sold. The master schedule is cumulative. The available to sell (promise) equation is: master schedule for the period minus total orders, thus week 1 is 500 – 1400 = -900 and week 3 is 930 – 1400 = -470. Only the positive numbers indicate unsold production. Available to sell (promise) is cumulative. In week 8, for instance, open capacity is listed as 1270 units, but that is total open capacity through week 8, not for that week only. The available to sell line is identical to the ending inventory line in the master schedule once both demands have been satisfied. The demands are entered at different places in the two reports because each serves a different purpose.

Available to Promise

Week	0	1	2	3	4	5	6	7	8
Master Schedule	250	500	750	930	1190	1470	1870	2270	2670
Demand	1400								
Available to Sell		-900	-650	-470	-210	70	470	870	1270

Safety = 100 units; on hand = 0

Figure 13-2c

Time offset for manufacture may be different than depicted. If so that would change the time periods in which data is entered. When programmed into the computer, safety stock offset, for instance, would be automatically accounted for and once the basic data were entered, the charts would be automatically generated. What-if is practical because the scheduler can manipulate the base data.

Note that safety stock is set at 100 units. In an established JIT system the safety level could be lower, percentage-wise. Perhaps it should be, but total capacity within a work center or assembly line in comparison to the numbers and quantities of all items being produced therein is considered. As reliability increases and lot sizes decrease, a lower safety stock is probable.

Material Requirements Plan

Week	1	2	3	4	5	6	7	8
Gross Requirements	250	250	180	260	280	400	400	400
Scheduled Receipts			400	400				
Available Balance	250	0	220	360	80	-320	-720	-1120
Planned Releases			400					

Lead time = 1 week plus 1 week safety time
Lot size = 400
Beginning inventory = 500 parts
1 part per end item, highest level part/component in BOM

Figure 13-3

Figure 13-3 shows the material requirements plan for one part. Because this part is the highest level in the bill-of-material, the master schedule (MPS) is the source for the projected gross requirement. It is processed through the bill of material and projects the need and the time when each part or component is needed in order to produce the end items at the time specified by the schedule. Scheduled receipts are orders in production (work-in-process) or releases to suppliers. The available balance is the sum of the on-hand quantity (ending available balance the past week) plus the scheduled receipt minus the gross requirement. It is the expected inventory balance, which can be negative in weeks in which scheduled receipts plus inventory do not equal or exceed the gross requirement. Planned order releases are planned releases to the factory or to vendors, backed off for lead-time and converted to lot sizes, but not yet released.

The available balance for week 1 is $500 + 0 - 250 = 250$; for week 4 it is $220 + 400 - 260 = 360$. The scheduled receipts are either lots in production or firm vendor orders. The planned release will be released at the beginning of week 3, the time at which the scheduler changes it to a scheduled release. With two weeks lead-time, the receipt is due week 5 (convention dictates how the lead time offset is calculated). A planned order release at an upper level becomes the gross requirement at the next lower level in the bill-of-materials. This is applicable to every level in the BOM except for the highest-level part; its gross requirements are taken from the master schedule. Generally, MRP systems include a pegged requirement feature. This feature traces where the requirement originated (the higher level from which it came) and may trace it all the way to the end item.

Assume that this part requires another part that is supplied by the tier-two partner in our example. The planned release at tier-one becomes the gross requirement at tier-two. The gross requirement tells the tier-two supplier the amount required and when it is needed, and the available balance indicates the quantity and timing of shortages to be filled. By convention, time fences are established and requirements within a fence are firm. There is a shortage of 1120 parts, however, the only order for this part at this time is the planned release of 400.

This discussion of MPS/MRP is fundamental only. In practice, it will be a bit more complex. There are several conditions that can cause the system to fail, such as inaccurate BOM's and routings. One of the most important failures is maintaining a backlog of work at a production line or work center. Flow means go.

At this stage of its development the partnership has incorporated a plain vanilla MRP system. As the partnership matures, Manufacturing Resource Planning (MRP II), Enterprise Resources Planning (ERP), and Advanced Planning and Scheduling (APS) will be examined, of which there are many software versions. These practices extend MRP. Fundamentally, MRP II addresses the financial functions in dollars, adds a what-if capability, and incorporates sales and operations planning and capacity planning. ERP adds sophistication to the process and has the capability of linking multiple manufacturing facilities. APS techniques analyze and plan logistics and manufacturing from the short-term through the long-term. Using advanced mathematical algorithms the system performs optimization in the areas of finite capacity scheduling, resource planning, demand management, and other functions. Simultaneously, it considers a range of constraints to provide real time planning and scheduling. Determining the vital interlocking functions in a supply chain and the complexity of the chain itself dictates the level of sophistication needed. One consideration, almost inviolate, is: schedule to finite capacity only, even a basic system needs this capability. Business is complex, but the rule of as simple as possible to profitably run the business (chain) is still a good rule. An excellent source for learning about manufacturing systems is APICS (see References).

Since the introduction of MRP, it and the later scheduling and planning suites described above have had critics. Basically, that the least complex are not adaptable to many manufacturing environments and that the more complicated are difficult to understand and apply. There is a mixed bag regarding the success of the suites. Because of the expense of software packages, it is vital to have a good understanding before committing.

In this example the lot size is 400 units with three weeks lead-time. In a JIT (or lean manufacturing) environment an objective is to minimize lot size, idealistically to one-unit lots. Producing closer to the needed date and in smaller quantities substantially reduces inventory and cost. It also allows a greater mix of products to be scheduled in a given time bucket. An important consideration, however, is the cost of production changeover (set-up and tear-down times). Our supply chain has reduced changeover time by careful examination of the manufacturing process, new methods, and engineering and tooling adjustments, thus it is in position to reduce lot size.

Assume that the company found in its JIT voyage that it could in an economically feasible way reduce lead-time to one week, eliminate safety time, and decrease lot size to 100 units. Much good came from these changes. Planned releases are scheduled closer to the time of need. If short run changes just beyond the time fence are necessary there is less disruption throughout the manufacturing chain. Inventory spirals downward as illustrated in Figure 13-4.

JIT Material Requirements Plan

Week	1	2	3	4	5	6	7	8
Gross Requirements	0	250	180	260	280	400	400	400
Scheduled Receipts		100	100	200	300	400	400	400
Available Balance	300	150	70	10	30	30	30	30
Planned Releases								

Figure 13-4

For purposes of illustration there are no planned releases. In actuality, it is doubtful the scheduler would release lots this far in advance. With the short lead-time, it is unnecessary. Note how the inventory level is minimized by producing in 100 unit lots (400 units of scheduled receipts is four individual lots, for instance).

Suppliers below the tier-one level may have customers that use the same items but are not part of the supply chain. This complicates master production scheduling. With the inclusion of where used and the quantity and timing each customer requires, the scheduler has the knowledge needed for effective MRP scheduling.

A number of feed back reports are necessary for effective operations. They include customer service rate (orders shipped on time), order change report, open to sell, percent MPS attained, measurement of sales compared with forecast, and production compared to plan.

The example supply chain is somewhat idealized. What collaboration is possible, what internal territory a company is willing to open to others, and what equality is probable are limiting factors. It may also occur that, say, a tier-one and tier-two company are part of a supply chain for some products but are direct competitors for other products. Openness becomes a serious problem: what can and what cannot be revealed?

Our **last example** is a company that makes an assembled product that because of the many options that can be ordered by a customer is a complex assembly operation. Trying to forecast the quantity and timing of each option proved to be a frustrating and impossible task. Some options were frequently ordered by customers and some were purchased less frequently, but all needed to be available. Consider that this company has fifteen options that can be used alone or in combination with each other. That means that there are a staggering multitude of possibilities. The product less options is manufactured and a final assembly schedule is generated when customer orders are received (assemble to order). The master schedule is derived from the forecast for the base product only. The base product is the item to be scheduled. The forecast for each individual option is the percentage that that option historically has been needed; for example, if 1000 base products are forecast and historically 20% of the base products included that option, the option forecast is 200.

At this point, the process becomes complicated. The engineering bill of material is translated into a modular bill of material, that is a planning bill that is arranged in product modules or options. From the modular bill a master schedule incorporating the option percentages can be developed for each option to trigger the MRP simulation. The form is dependent upon such factors as whether the options are purchased or produced in-house and the timing of production in relation to the manufacture of the base item. There are many considerations beyond the scope of this book. As regards forecasting, the base products are master scheduled from the forecasts and then the options are scheduled based upon customer orders.

Postscript

A few final words about forecasting:

* Although forecasts are not decision-making and planning tools per se, they are the essential forerunner to those activities, thus, they are critical to the success of a business. Forecasts and the analyses that follow influence marketing, financial, production and purchasing, and capacity planning, for instance. In fact, about all activities within a company whether that company is a manufacturer, importer, distributor, retailer or service provider require the forecasting tool. Generally, both the long-term and short-term is essential in the forecasting equation. As simple as possible is a good rule, but developing forecasts that have a high degree of accuracy and reliability is more important.

* Forecasting responsibility and accountability is formally assigned. Although it is a cooperative endeavor, there should be one responsible party. Sales and operations planning as discussed previously is an excellent vehicle for planning. Forecasts are an integral part of the process. It is important to understand the nature of the decisions that will emanate from the forecasts and to coordinate with the decision-making parties.

* Consider your customers' forecasts when developing your own. To what extent do they influence your final forecasts? It depends upon their willingness, their forecasting ability historically, and how important their business is to your profit line. All works best in a partnership (supply chain) environment. Customer demand forecasts and order forecasts may be different. A demand forecast is how much the customer expects to sell and an order forecast is how much he expects to order from you. In a simple example, if a major customer has too much inventory he will buy less than he sells.

* Historically, the sales force has been a forecasting resource, but how trustworthy are their estimates? The sales force by the nature of their jobs has to be optimistic, thus a tendency to overestimate. Conversely, they may receive bonuses dependent upon the amount that their sales exceed budget, thus a tendency to underestimate. Estimates may not be all inclusive, that is

sales are projected only for the larger customers, thus precluding the ability to accurately predict demand patterns. Unbiased forecasting methodology is critical, which suggests quantitative methods as described in this book, perhaps supplemented by or incorporating qualitative elements. The final forecast is an objective appraisal of the future. But this does not preclude participation by the sales force. It takes back and forth communication to determine the validity of judgmental estimates and their place in the final forecasts. The sales force can best be of help in determining the impact of the significant factors listed at the end of Chapter 1. Manager input may be important in the overall forecasting scene. Know how projections are to be used and what marketing factors influence sales. Forecasters know your place: managers are the decision-makers, but remember that forecasts are unbiased estimates.

❖ Good forecasts depend upon an accurate database and records kept at the appropriate level of detail for forecasting. Routine reports are sometimes obsolete because of the timing of the reports. The data in different reports produced for different purposes may not be compatible, for example, financial data versus sales data. Obviously, forecasts – regardless of their unbiased nature – must proceed from an accurate and appropriate database.

❖ Objectivity is key to forecasting. The practitioner remains above the pressure that often raises its corporate head as when a sunny projection is expected, but he is also flexible when necessity dictates, as when the model no longer adequately describes the situation.

❖ Forecast presentation to management avoids complexity. It is done in the terms that management understands. Although the model may be complex, presentation is reduced to basics, such as a comparison of last year with this year or last quarter with this quarter or the trend or the anticipated increase because of a new marketing program. Change as a percent as well as number differences may be fitting. If this level of simplicity is inadequate, obey the rule of keeping it as uninvolved as possible. Talk in terms your audience understands. The source of the forecasting data may also be pertinent. In the same vane, the selling of a forecasting methodology avoids serious mathematical explanations unless management is relatively knowledgeable of statistics. I remember (in ancient times) a new employee telling me that in his former company he tried to sell exponential smoothing as the forecasting method (rather than judgment). When he said alpha factor, every brain (audibly) clicked off. That was the end of that.

❖ Throughout this book we have stressed the importance of forecasting as it pertains to planning and decision-making; thus, to the welfare and orderly conduct of a business. In manufacturing it interplays with the master schedule (MPS), a hand-in-hand relationship. Therefore, one last thought: the master schedule (MPS) is the production schedule that guides manufacture. It is derived from a forecast or a forecast modified by orders when orders differ from the forecast. It seems obvious that the factory therefore would follow the schedule (perhaps some shop floor changes that do not change the schedule overall). Is this always so? Off the top, my memory recalls three instances where the manufacturing manager not only failed to follow the production schedule, but also manufactured an item not on the schedule. Here is one example: for years a large retail chain purchased an item unique to them at a specified time and for a specified quantity. They stopped buying that item so the item did not appear in the production schedule. The plant manager, however, made the item anyway. When asked about it, he said that the retailer always bought the item and he did not want to be late in delivering it. Seems strange? All three instances were in billion dollar corporations. That considered, perhaps the last words should be: communication that leads to understanding is the key to success.

Selected References

Books: the following is a very selective list of books that relate to forecasting or practices that are described in this book.

Chaman L. Jain (editor), 2001, *Practical Guide to Business Forecasting*, Graceway Publishing Company, Inc, Flushing, NY (see Institute of Business Forecasting below).

George J. Kress and John Snyder, 1994, *Forecasting and Market Analysis Techniques*, Quorum Books, Westport CT.

John T. Mentzer and Carol C. Bienstock, 1998, *Sales Forecasting Management*, SAGE Publications, Inc., Thousand Oaks, California.

John V. Crosby, 1997, *Cycles, Trends, and Turning Points: Practical Marketing & Sales Forecasting Techniques*, NTC Business Books, Lincolnwood, Illinois (American Marketing Association).

J. Scott Armstrong, 1985, *Long-Range Forecasting, from Crystal Ball to Computer*, John Wiley & Sons, New York (available from Campus Copy).

Richard C. Ling and Walter E. Goddard, 1988, *Orchestrating Success: Improve Control of Business with Sales and Operations Planning*, Oliver Wight Limited Publications, Inc., Essex Junction, VT.

Bernard T. Smith, 1997, *Focus Forecasting, Computer Techniques for Inventory Control*, BookCrafters, Fredericksburg, VA.

Oliver W. Wight, 1981, *Manufacturing Resource Planning: MRP II: Unlocking America's Productivity Potential*, Oliver Wight Limited Publications, Inc., Essex Junction, VT.

Walter E. Goddard, 1986, *Just-in-Time: Surviving by Breaking Tradition*, Oliver Wight Limited Publications, Inc., Essex Junction, VT.

Resource for books regarding supply chain management, Just-in-Time, Sales & Operations Planning, production & planning systems, etc.: APICS The Association for Operations Management.

Additional resources are professional organizations and services and government web sites, for example:

Conference Board
www.globalindicators.org and www.conference-board.org/

APICS The Association for Operations Management
www.apics.org

American Management Association
www.amanet.org

American Marketing Association
www.marketingpower.com

Institute of Business Forecasting
www.ibf.org

Micrometrics
www.micrometrics-inc.com

Index

ABC categorization...274
Acceleration principle 234-236
Accuracy ....See Measures of Accuracy
Adaptive filters 82-88
Annual growth rate 206, 213
ARIMA 112
Bayesian Method 7.....................................See Probability Trees
Box-Jenkins 9, 14, 112-114
Business Cycle 17, 24, 26, 49, 153, 176, 177
    Cyclical indicators 35-37, 40, 177
    Turning points 4, 39-41, 177, 179-181, 197-205, 215
Business plan 261, 268, 270
Coefficient of correlation ....See Correlation Analysis
Coefficient of determination ....See Correlation Analysis
Combined forecasting 207-210
Conference Board 137, 153, 198, 201, 242
Confidence coefficients...129
Correlation analysis...
    Coefficient of correlation, r 132, 142, 144, 147
    Coefficient of determination, r^2.......130-132, 135, 136, 141, 142, 144
    Durbin-Watson 134-135, 141, 144, 150, 151
    f test 132-134, 135, 151
    t distribution and t test.......................129-130, 134-136, 168
    z values 129
Correlation matrix 144
Data...
    Sources...18
Data Transforms...See Transformations
Decision trees 229
Decomposition...8, 20, 23-25
    Components...25-27
    Cyclical...35-37

Forecasting..38-42
Random..37-38
Seasonal..28-31
Trend..32-35
Delphi method 7, 229, 240
Dependent variable 9, 112-113, 122, 123, 126, 134-146
Differencing..113
Diffusion index 180, 181-184
Dummy variables 146, 234, 238
Durbin-Watson..................................See Correlation Analysis
Econometrics..173-175
Economic Structure..175-176
Erratic demand..109-112, 238, 264
Excel..139-143, 145
Executive judgment..7, 239
Exponential Curve ....See Non-Linear Trend
Exponential smoothing..................................8, 9, 67-82,208, 209
First order smoothing..68-70
Second Order Smoothing..70-74
Third order smoothing..74-78
Winters Model 78-82
f test...See Correlation Analysis
Forecast error ....See Measures of Accuracy
Forecast range ....See Standard Deviation
Forecast reliability 2, 50-52, 65
Gompertz Curve ....See Non-Linear Trend
Gross Domestic Product 122, 139, 143, 173, 176, 179-180, 197, 205-206, 210-217
Growth Curve 76, 121, 250-253
Growth Rate ....See Rate of Change
Heteroskedasticity..138
Homoskedasticity..138
Independent variable 9, 112-113, 122, 123, 126, 134-146
Just-in-Time..284-286
Lag..100
Leading indicators...................10, 40-41, 122, 177-179, 181-183
Least Squares Trend..104-106
Logarithms..116-119

Logistic curve..250
Long-range plan.......................3-5, 213, 217-218, 254-257, 262
Macroeconomics 173
MAPE ....See Measures of Accuracy
Market research 241-42
Master plan..268, 270, 273
Master schedule..287-294, 296
Material requirements planning................283, 286-289, 294-297
Measures of accuracy...42-52, 90-92
    Mean absolute deviation.......................42-43, 48, 50, 52, 91
    Mean absolute percent error.................42, 45-46, 50, 51, 91
    Mean squared error....................................42, 45, 48, 50, 91
    Standard deviation...........................42, 43-45, 46, 50, 91-94
Microeconomics...173
Mission statement..254, 259
Moving Averages...8, 53-55
    Basic double moving average.......................................57-58
    Double moving average difference.............................58-59
    Moving average difference...55-56
    Percent of Change...56-57
    Simple moving average...55
    Weighted moving average...66-67
MPD ....See Measures of Accuracy
Multicollinearity..138, 140
National Bureau of Economic Research.........177, 179, 180, 197
National Income and Product Accounts................................175
Non-linear trend analysis..
    Exponential Curve...119-120
    Gompertz Curve...116-119
    Parabola..114-116
Normal distribution..43, 44, 47
                     See Also Standard Deviation
Operational forecasting..263-266
Panel consensus...7, 239-240
Parabola..See Non-Linear Trend
Percent of Sales Model..106-109
Price Elasticity of Demand...219-226
Price equilibrium...225-226

Probability Trees...242-249
R and R^2 ....See Correlation Analysis
Random fluctuation ....See Decomposition
Rate of change......40, 80, 182, 184-192, 193-196, 198, 212, 213
Relational analysis...157
    Control group...161-162
    Direct Sales Comparison.............................159-161
    Time as Control..162-163
    Trade Show Approach...............................158, 161
Ripple effect...233-234
S-curve..104
Sales and Operations Planning...............267-270, 298
Seasonal variation.............................18, 24, 26, 28-31
Significance.......................................132-136, 150, 151
Standard deviation.............................See Measures of Accuracy
Standard Deviation of Regression,....................127-128
Standard Error of the Estimate 127, 148
Standard Error of the Forecast........................128-129
Strategic goals...255, 260
Structural break...139
Supply chain.......................270-274, 283-289, 295, 298
SWOT analysis...254
t Test analysis......................................See Correlation Analysis
Technological forecasting.................................249-250
Tracking.......................................12, 42, 95-103
Transformation 138, 145-146
Trend 17, 24, 25, 32-35
Turning Points...197-205
Vision statement...255, 259
Z values 129